MW01145882

DARIUS THE MEDE
AND THE
FOUR WORLD EMPIRES
IN THE
BOOK OF DANIEL

DARIUS THE MEDE

AND THE

FOUR WORLD EMPIRES

IN THE

BOOK OF DANIEL

*A Historical Study
of Contemporary Theories*

BY

H. H. ROWLEY

Ὀδηγήσει ὑμᾶς εἰς πᾶσαν τὴν ἀλήθειαν.

Wipf & Stock
PUBLISHERS
Eugene, Oregon

Wipf and Stock Publishers
199 W 8th Ave, Suite 3
Eugene, OR 97401

Darius the Mede and the Four World Empires in the Book of Daniel
A Historical Study of Contemporary Theories
By Rowley, H. H.
Copyright©1964 University of Wales Press
ISBN: 1-59752-896-X
Publication date 8/24/2006
Previously published by University of Wales Press Board, 1964

This edition of Darius the Mede and the Four World Empires in the
Book of Daniel is published by arrangement with University of Wales Press.

Licensed for sale in North America only; not for export.

TO THE UNKNOWN AUTHOR
OF THE
BOOK OF DANIEL
WHOSE FAITH AND VISION
YIELD
UNDYING INSPIRATION

PREFACE

FEW books have occasioned more discussion than the book of Daniel, and few have given rise to keener disagreements. On the one side are those who are no longer able to hold the traditional views of its date and authorship, and on the other those who feel that the surrender of such views involves the surrender of the very foundation of their faith. Yet on neither side is there any agreement on the two inter-related questions which form the subject of the present study. Amongst the 'orthodox' the widest variety of views has been found, as the student soon learns, while among the 'critics' there is less uniformity than he may have supposed. Moreover, while those who belong to the 'orthodox' school are fond of supposing that they hold the monopoly of faith, there may be some who suppose that the 'critics' hold the monopoly of learning. Neither supposition is warranted. Every 'critic' is not a Porphyry, nor are his opponents all unlettered babblers, and all such prejudices may be laid aside.

The present work does not seek to set forth any new and revolutionary interpretations, though it may be found that at many points it has original contributions to make. Its primary purpose is to provide a critical analysis of the arguments that have been advanced in favour of the various current views, though I have not hesitated to indicate the conclusions to which I am forced. In a literature so vast as that which has gathered in two millennia around these questions, I cannot hope to have read more than a fragment of the material, though I trust I have missed nothing of outstanding importance, at any rate on the side of the views I have rejected. I have tried to acquaint myself with the positions of every school, and my occasional references to works which can by no stretch of the imagination be called scholarly will show that even they have not been ignored, though I have naturally given my chief attention to abler and more scholarly advocates of the various interpretations.

The references will be found to be full, and perhaps, to the general reader, wearisome. To the student who wishes to pursue any point further they may save many hours of patient toil. My obligations to friends and to libraries, both at home and abroad, for access to works which are not easily to be seen, are too numerous to be detailed here, but I would record the gratitude I feel for the ready help I have received on every side.

To the University of Wales Press Board my warmest thanks are given for making it possible for my study to appear, and to the Oxford University Press for all the care they have given to its printing.

H. H. ROWLEY.

CARDIFF,
November 1934.

NOTE

THE reprinting of this book has given me the opportunity to make one or two slight corrections, and in particular on pp. 167 f., where I had not quite correctly represented the view of Harenberg, to whose work I was able to obtain access only after the publication of my book.

CONTENTS

PRINCIPAL ABBREVIATIONS EMPLOYED . . xi

LIST OF WORKS CONSULTED xiii

INTRODUCTION 1

DARIUS THE MEDE

I. DARIUS THE MEDE IS NOT CAMBYSES . 12

II. DARIUS THE MEDE IS NOT GOBRYAS . . 19

III. DARIUS THE MEDE IS NOT ASTYAGES . 30

IV. DARIUS THE MEDE IS NOT CYAXARES . 37

V. THERE IS NO RELIABLE EVIDENCE FOR ANY DARIUS THE MEDE 44

VI. DARIUS THE MEDE IS A CONFLATION OF CONFUSED TRADITIONS . . . 54

THE FOUR WORLD EMPIRES

I. THE FIRST KINGDOM IS THE NEO-BABYLONIAN 67

II. THE FOURTH KINGDOM IS THE GREEK . 70

III. THE SECOND AND THIRD KINGDOMS ARE THE MEDIAN AND THE PERSIAN RESPECTIVELY 138

IV. THE INTERPRETATIONS THAT FIND FOUR KINGS, INSTEAD OF KINGDOMS, ARE UN-SATISFACTORY 161

CONCLUSION 175

TABLE OF VARIETIES OF INTERPRETATION OF THE FOUR KINGDOMS 184

INDEXES 187

PRINCIPAL ABBREVIATIONS EMPLOYED

AHNE = Hall's *Ancient History of the Near East*.

AJSL = *American Journal of Semitic Languages and Literatures*.

CAH = *Cambridge Ancient History*.

CIG = Boeckh's *Corpus Inscriptionum Graecarum*.

CIS = *Corpus Inscriptionum Semiticarum*.

DB = Hastings's *Dictionary of the Bible*.

DCB = Smith and Wace's *Dictionary of Christian Biography*.

DLZ = *Deutsche Literaturzeitung*.

EB = Cheyne and Black's *Encyclopaedia Biblica*.

EBrit = *Encyclopaedia Britannica*.

EJ = *Encyclopaedia Judaica*.

ET = *Expository Times*. (Also = English translation, the context indicating which meaning is intended.)

FHG = Müller's *Fragmenta Historicorum Graecorum*.

GGA = *Göttingische gelehrte Anzeigen*.

GJV = Schürer's *Geschichte des jüdischen Volkes*.

HJP = Schürer's *History of the Jewish People*, ET of foregoing.

HS = Bevan's *House of Seleucus*.

HSAT = Kautzsch's *Die Heilige Schrift des Alten Testaments*.

JAOS = *Journal of the American Oriental Society*.

JBL = *Journal of Biblical Literature*.

JE = *Jewish Encyclopaedia*.

JHS = *Journal of Hellenic Studies*.

JTS = *Journal of Theological Studies*.

JTVI = *Journal of the Transactions of the Victoria Institute*.

KAT = Schrader's *Die Keilinschriften und das Alte Testament*.

KB = Schrader's *Keilinschriftliche Bibliothek*.

LOT = Driver's *Introduction to the Literature of the Old Testament*.

MGWJ = *Monatsschrift für Geschichte und Wissenschaft des Judenthums*.

MVAG = *Mitteilungen der Vorderasiatischen Gesellschaft*.

NKZ = *Neue kirchliche Zeitschrift*.

NTT = *Nieuw Theologisch Tijdschrift*.

PG = Migne's *Patrologia*, Series Graeca.

PL = Migne's *Patrologia*, Series Latina.

PRE = Herzog's *Real-Encyclopädie für protestantische Theologie und Kirche*.

PS = Graffin's *Patrologia Syriaca*.

PW = Pauly-Wissowa's *Real-Encyclopädie der klassischen Altertumswissenschaft*.

RArch = *Revue archéologique*.

RAss = *Revue d'assyriologie et d'archéologie orientale*.

RB = *Revue biblique*.

RGG = *Die Religion in Geschichte und Gegenwart*.

RHPR = *Revue d'histoire et de philosophie religieuses.*
RS = *Revue sémitique.*
TCA = *Transactions of the Connecticut Academy of Arts and Sciences.*
TSBA = *Transactions of the Society of Biblical Archaeology.*
TSK = *Theologische Studien und Kritiken.*
ZA = *Zeitschrift für Assyriologie.*
ZAW = *Zeitschrift für die alttestamentliche Wissenschaft.*
ZNW = *Zeitschrift für die neutestamentliche Wissenschaft.*

LIST OF WORKS CONSULTED

In the foot-notes throughout the present work, the titles of the following works are abbreviated, as far as possible, and editions and dates are normally omitted. In all cases of uncertainty, reference to the following list will show which edition has been used.

Abbot, R. (Abbatt on title-page): *Antichristi demonstratio, contra fabulas Pontificias, et ineptam Roberti Bellarmine de Antichristo disputationem*, 1603.

Albertus Magnus: *Commentarius in librum Danielis prophetae*, in *Opera*, 1651 ed., vol. viii.

Alcazar, L. ab: *In eas Veteris Testamenti partes quas respicit Apocalypsis*, 1631.

Alexandre, C.: ΧΡΗΣΜΟΙ ΣΙΒΥΛΛΙΑΚΟΙ, 2 vols., 1841–56; 2nd ed., without Excursus, 1869.

Alfrink, B.: *Die Gaddsche Chronik und die Heilige Schrift*, in *Biblica*, viii, 1927, pp. 385–417.

Der letzte König von Babylon, ibid. ix, 1928, pp. 187–205.

Darius Medus, ibid. ix, 1928, pp. 316–40.

Amner, R.: *An Essay towards an Interpretation of the Prophecies of Daniel*, 1776.

Andrews, H. T.: *Daniel*, in A. S. Peake's *Commentary on the Bible*, 1920, pp. 522–33.

Aphraates: *Homilies*. For Syriac text, see Wright, W., and Parisot, D. J.; for German translation, see Bert, G.; for English translation, see Gwynn, J.

Appian: *Historia Romana*, ed. L. Mendelssohn, 2 vols., 1878; text and ET by H. White, in Loeb ed., 4 vols., 1912–13.

pseudo-Aquinas: *In Danielem Prophetam Expositio*, in Aquinas' *Opera omnia*, Parma ed. (25 vols., 1852–73), xxiii, 1869, pp. 134–94.

Expositio I super Apocalypsim, ibid., pp. 325–511.

Cf. *Dissertationes criticae in S. Thomam Aquinatem*, in Aquinas' *Opera omnia*, Leonine ed. (12 vols., 1882–1906), i, 1882, pp. lv–cccxlvi.

Arrian: *Anabasis et Indica*, ed. Fr. Dübner, 1877.

Assembly's Annotations = Annotations upon all the Books of the Old and New Testament, by the labours of certain learned Divines thereunto appointed, and therein employed, 2nd ed., 2 vols., 1651. (Daniel stands in vol. ii; the pages are not numbered.)

Athenaeus: *Deipnosophistae*, ed. G. Kaibel, 3 vols., 1887–90.

Auberlen, C. A.: *The Prophecies of Daniel and the Revelations of St. John, viewed in their mutual relation, with an exposition of the principal passages*, ET by A. Saphir, 1856.

Auchincloss, W. S.: *The Book of Daniel Unlocked*, 1905. (Introduction by A. H. Sayce.)

Darius the Median, in *Bibliotheca Sacra*, lxvi, 1909, pp. 536–8.

Augusti, J. C. W.: *Grundriss einer historisch-kritischen Einleitung in's Alte Testament*, 2nd ed., 1827.

Augustine: *De Civitate Dei*, ed. Migne, PL xli, 1844; ET by M. Dods, in 2 vols., 1871, being vols. i and ii of his ed. in 15 vols. of Augustine's *Works*, in English, 1871–6.

Ausonius: *Opuscula*, ed. R. Peiper, 1886, in *Bibliotheca Teubneriana*; text and ET by H. G. E. White, in Loeb ed., 2 vols., 1919–21.

Babelon, E.: *Nouvelles remarques sur l'histoire de Cyrus*, in *Annales de philosophie chrétienne*, New Series, iv, 1881, pp. 674–83.

Les Perses achéménides, 1893, in *Catalogue des monnaies grecques de la Bibliothèque Nationale*.

Bade, J.: *Christologie des Alten Testamentes*, 3 vols. in 4, 1850–1.

Barhebraeus: *see* Freimann, J.

Barnes, W. E.: *The Development of the Religion of Israel from the Return to the death of Simon the Maccabee*, in *The People and the Book*, ed. by A. S. Peake, 1925, pp. 289–322.

Barton, G. A.: *The Composition of the Book of Daniel*, in JBL xvii, 1898, pp. 62–86.

Bate, H. N.: *The Sibylline Books, Books III–V*, 1918, in *Translations of Early Documents* (S.P.C.K.).

Batten, L. W.: *A Critical and Exegetical Commentary on the Books of Ezra and Nehemiah*, 1913, in *The International Critical Commentary*.

Baumgartner, W.: *Das Buch Daniel*, 1926, in *Aus der Welt der Religion*, Alttestamentliche Reihe, Heft 1.

Neues keilschriftliches Material zum Buche Daniel?, in ZAW, New Series, iii, 1926, pp. 38–56.

Das Aramäische im Buche Daniel, ibid. iv, 1927, pp. 81–133.

de Beausobre, I.: *Remarques historiques, critiques et philologiques sur le Nouveau Testament*, 1742.

Becmann, J. C.: *Dissertatio de quarta Monarchia*, 4th ed., 1684.

Behrmann, G.: *Das Buch Daniel übersetzt und erklärt*, 1894, in Nowack's *Handkommentar zum Alten Testament*.

Bellarmine, R.: *De Romano Pontifice*, 1698 ed., in *Bibliotheca Maxima Pontifica*, xviii.

Bengel, J. A.: *Ordo temporum a principio per periodas oeconomiae diviniae historicas atque propheticas ad finem usque*, 1770.

Bensly, R. L.: *The Fourth Book of Maccabees and kindred Documents in Syriac*, ed. W. E. Barnes, 1895.

Benzel, H.: *Problema historicum de quatuor orbis monarchiis*, in *Syntagma Dissertationum*, 1745, i, pp. 1–50.

Bernstein, G. H.: *Chrestomathia Syriaca*, 2 vols., 1832–6.

Bert, G.: *Aphrahat's des persischen Weisen Homilien aus dem Syrischen übersetzt und erläutert*, 1888, in Gebhardt and Harnack's *Texte und Untersuchungen zur Geschichte der altchristlichen Literatur*, iii, Heft 3 and 4.

Bertholdt, L.: *Daniel neu übersetzt und erklärt*, 1806–8.

Bertholet, A.: *Die Bücher Esra und Nehemia erklärt*, 1902, in Marti's *Kurzer Hand-commentar zum Alten Testament*.

Daniel und die griechische Gefahr, 1907, in *Religionsgeschichtliche Volksbücher*, 2 Reihe, xvii.

Bevan, A. A.: *A Short Commentary on the Book of Daniel for the use of Students*, 1892.

Bevan, E. R.: *The House of Seleucus*, 2 vols., 1902.

Jerusalem under the High Priests, 4th impression, 1920.

A History of Egypt under the Ptolemaic Dynasty, 1927.

Bewer, J. A.: *The Literature of the Old Testament in its Historical Development*, 1922, in *Records of Civilization: Sources and Studies*.

Biblia Rabbinica: The second *Biblia Rabbinica*, ed. D. Bomberg, 4 vols., Venice, 1524–5, contains the commentaries of Ibn Ezra and pseudo-Saadia on Daniel; the sixth *Biblia Rabbinica*, ed. J. Buxtorf, the Elder, 4 vols., Basle, 1618–19, contains the commentaries of Ibn Ezra, pseudo-Saadia, and Rashi on Daniel; the seventh *Biblia Rabbinica*, published under the title ספר קהלות משה, 4 vols., Amsterdam, 1724–7, contains, *inter alia*, the commentaries of Rashi, Ibn Ezra, pseudo-Saadia, and Ibn Yahya on Daniel; the most recent *Biblia Rabbinica*, ed. Levensohn, published under the title מקראות גדולות, 12 vols., Warsaw, 1860–6, contains the commentaries of Ibn Ezra, Rashi, and pseudo-Saadia on Daniel.

Birks, T. R.: *The Four Prophetic Empires and the Kingdom of Messiah*, 1844.

The Two Later Visions of Daniel historically explained, 1846.

Bleek, F.: *Über Verfasser und Zweck des Buches Daniel: Revision der in neuerer Zeit darüber geführten Untersuchungen*, in Schleiermacher, de Wette, and Lücke's *Theologische Zeitschrift*, Heft iii, 1822, pp. 171–294.

Die messianische Weissagungen im Buche Daniel, in *Jahrbücher für deutsche Theologie*, v, 1860, pp. 45–101.

Bludau, A.: *Die alexandrinische Übersetzung des Buches Daniel und ihr Verhältniss zum massorethischen Text*, 1897, in O. Bardenhewer's *Biblische Studien*, ii. ii and iii.

Boeckh, A.: *Corpus Inscriptionum Graecarum*, 4 vols., 1828–77.

Boehmer, J.: *Reich Gottes und Menschensohn im Buche Daniel*, 1899.

Bonwetsch, G. N.: see Hippolytus.

Bosanquet, J. W.: *Messiah the Prince, or the Inspiration of the Prophecies of Daniel*, 1866.

Bouché-Leclercq, A.: *Les oracles sibyllins*, in *Revue de l'histoire des religions*, vii, 1883, pp. 236–48; viii, 1883, pp. 619–34; ix, 1884, pp. 220–33.

Histoire des Lagides, 4 vols., 1903–7.

Histoire des Séleucides, 2 vols., 1913–14.

b

xvi LIST OF WORKS CONSULTED

Bousset, W.: *Neueste Forschungen auf dem Gebiet der religiösen Litteratur des Spätjudentums*, in Theologische Rundschau, iii, 1900, pp. 287–302, 327–35, 369–81.

Die Beziehungen der ältesten jüdischen Sibylle zur chaldäischen Sibylle und einige weitere Beobachtungen über den synkretistischen Character der spätjüdischen Literatur, in ZNW iii, 1902, pp. 23–49.

Die Religion des Judentums im späthellenistischen Zeitalter, 3rd ed., edited by H. Gressmann, 1926.

Boutflower, C.: *The Historical Value of Daniel v and vi*, in JTS xvii, 1915–16, pp. 43–60.

In and Around the Book of Daniel, 1923.

Dadda-'Idri, or the Aramaic of the Book of Daniel, 1931.

Box, G. H.: *The Ezra-Apocalypse*, 1912.

Judaism in the Greek Period, from the rise of Alexander the Great to the Intervention of Rome, 1932, in The Clarendon Bible, Old Testament, vol. v.

Breithaupt, J. F.: *R. Salomonis Jarchi commentarius hebraicus in prophetas majores et minores ut et Hiobum et Psalmos latine versus*, 2 vols., 1713.

Briggs, C. A.: *Messianic Prophecy: the prediction of the fulfilment of redemption through the Messiah*, 1886.

Broughton, H.: *Works*, 1662 ed.

Browne, H.: *Ordo Saeclorum: A Treatise on the Chronology of the Holy Scriptures*, 1844.

Browne, L. E.: *Early Judaism*, 1920 (2nd ed., 1929).

Buber, S.: *Midrasch Tanchuma: ein agadischer Commentar zum Pentateuch von Rabbi Tanchuma ben Rabbi Abba*, 1885.

Bullinger, H.: *Daniel sapientissimus Dei propheta expositus homiliis LXVI*, 1565.

Bunsen, C. C. J.: *Gott in der Geschichte, oder der Fortschritt des Glaubens an eine sittliche Weltordnung*, Part i, 1857.

Buzy, D.: *Les Symboles de Daniel*, in RB, New Series, xv, 1918, pp. 403–31.

Les Symboles de l'Ancien Testament, 1923.

Calmet, A.: *Commentaire littéral sur Daniel*, 1730, in Commentaire littéral sur tous les livres de l'Ancien et du Nouveau Testament, vol.xvi.

Calovius, A.: *Biblia Testam. Veteris illustrata*, 2 vols., 1672. (*Annotata ad Danielem* in vol. ii.)

Calvin, J.: *Praelectiones in librum prophetiarum Danielis*, 1561; ET by T. Myers, as *Commentaries on the Book of the Prophet Daniel*, 2 vols., 1852–3, pub. by the Calvin Translation Society.

Calwer Bibel-lexikon = Biblisches Handwörterbuch illustriert, ed. by P. Zeller, 1885 ed.

Cambridge Ancient History, ed. by J. B. Bury, S. A. Cook, F. E. Adcock, and M. P. Charlesworth, vols. i–ix, 1924–32 (in progress).

Cary, M.: *A History of the Greek World from 323 to 146 B.C.*, 1932, in Methuen's *History of the Greek and Roman World*, vol. iii.

Caspari, C. P.: *Widerlegung zweier neuern Ansichten über die vier Weltmonarchieen des Buches Daniel, als negativer Beweis, das die vierte Monarchie die Römische sei*, in *Zeitschrift für die gesammte lutherische Theologie und Kirche*, ii, 1841, 4th Quartalheft, pp. 121–53.

Zur Einführung in das Buch Daniel, 1869.

Ceriani, A. M.: *Translatio Syra Pescitto Veteris Testamenti ex codice Ambrosiano sec. fere vi. photolithographice edita*, 2 vols., 1876–83.

Charles, R. H.: *The Book of Daniel*, in *The Century Bible*, 1913.

A Critical and Exegetical Commentary on the Book of Daniel, with Introduction, Indexes and a new English Translation, 1929.

Charles, R. H., ed. by: *The Apocrypha and Pseudepigrapha of the Old Testament in English, with Introductions and critical and explanatory Notes to the several Books*, 2 vols., 1913.

Cheyne, T. K.: *Bible Problems and the new material for their solution*, 1904, in *The Crown Theological Library*.

von Christ, W.: *Geschichte der griechischen Literatur*, 5th and 6th ed., 2 vols. in 3, 1912–20, in Iwan Müller's *Handbuch der klassischen Altertums-wissenschaft*, vol. vii.

Chrysostom, St. John: *In Danielem prophetam interpretatio*, in *Opera omnia quae exstant*, ed. B. de Montfaucon (13 vols., 1718–38), vi, 1724, pp. 200–53, or ed. Migne, PG lvi, 1859, cols 193–246.

Cicero: *De divinatione*, Text and ET by W. A. Falconer, in Loeb ed., 1922.

Letters to his Friends, Text and ET by W. G. Williams, in Loeb ed., 3 vols., 1927–9.

Clay, A. T.: *The Babylonian Expedition of the University of Pennsylvania*, Series A, vol. viii, Part i: *Legal and Commercial Transactions*, 1908.

Aramaic Indorsements on the Documents of the Muraŝû Sons, in *Old Testament and Semitic Studies in Memory of William Rainey Harper* (2 vols., 1908), i, pp. 287–321.

Gobryas, Governor of Babylonia, in JAOS xli, 1921, p. 466 f.

Cocceius, J: *Observationes ad Danielem*, in *Opera omnia* (10 vols.), 3rd ed., 1701, iii, pp. 319–66.

Conring, H.: *De Germanorum imperio Romano (1643)*, in *Opera* (7 vols., 1730), i, pp. 26–107.

Discursus ad Lampadium posterior ex manuscripto editus Tractatus de republica Romano-Germanica, ibid. ii, pp. 238–461.

Cook, S. A.: *A Lydian-Aramaic Bilingual*, in JHS xxxvii, 1917, pp. 77–87.

Cooke, G. A.: *A Text-book of North Semitic Inscriptions*, 1903.

Cornill, C.: *The Prophets of Israel*, ET by S. F. Corkran, 1901.

Corpus Inscriptionum Semiticarum, Pars secunda, inscriptiones aramaicas continens, 1889–1926 (in progress).

Cosmas Indicopleustes: *Topographia Christiana*, ed. Migne, PG lxxxviii, 1860; ET by J. W. McCrindle, as *The Christian Topo-*

graphy of Cosmas, an Egyptian Monk, 1897, printed for the Hakluyt Society.

Cowles, H.: Ezekiel and Daniel, with Notes, critical, explanatory and practical, 1867.

Cowley, A. E.: Aramaic Papyri of the Fifth Century B.C., 1923.

Ctesias: see Müller, C.

Cyril of Jerusalem: Catecheses, ed. Migne, PG xxxiii, 1857, cols. 331–1128; ET by Church in Pusey's Library of the Fathers, 1838, or by E. H. Gifford in Wace and Schaff's Select Library of Nicene and Post-Nicene Fathers of the Christian Church, 2nd series, vii, 1894.

Dalman, G.: Die Worte Jesu, 2nd ed., 1930; ET of 1st ed., as The Words of Jesus, by D. M. Kay, 1902.

Dathe, J. A.: Prophetae Majores ex recensione textus hebraici et versionum antiquarum latine versi notisque philologicis et criticis illustrati, 1779.

Davidson, S.: Introduction to the Old Testament, 3 vols., 1862–3.

Deane, H.: Daniel: His Life and Times, 1888, in Men of the Bible.

Delitzsch, Friedrich: Nachträgliches zu O. E. Hagens Cyrus-Texten, in Delitzsch and Haupt's Beiträge zur Assyriologie, ii, 1894, pp. 248–57.

Dereser, T. A.: Die Propheten Ezechiel und Daniel, 2nd ed., revised by J. M. A. Scholz, 1835, in Dereser's Die heilige Schrift des alten Testaments.

Desprez, P. S.: Daniel, or the Apocalypse of the Old Testament, 1865.

Des-Vignoles, A.: Chronologie de l'histoire sainte et des histoires étrangères qui la concernent depuis la sortie d'Égypte jusqu'à la captivité de Babylone, 2 vols., 1738.

Dinon: Fragments, in Müller's FHG, q.v.

Diogenes Laertius: De clarorum philosophorum vitis, dogmatibus et apophthegmatibus libri decem, ed. by C. G. Cobet, 1850.

Dougherty, R. P.: Nabonidus and Belshazzar: a study of the closing events of the Neo-Babylonian Empire, 1929, in Yale Oriental Series, Researches, vol. xv.

Driver, G. R.: The Aramaic of the Book of Daniel, in JBL xlv, 1926, pp. 110–19.

The Aramaic Language, ibid., pp. 323–5.

Driver, S. R.: The Book of Daniel, with Introduction and Notes, 1900, in The Cambridge Bible for Schools and Colleges. (The reprint of 1922 has been used.)

An Introduction to the Literature of the Old Testament, 9th ed., 1913, in International Theological Library.

Drummond, J.: The Jewish Messiah: a critical history of the Messianic idea among the Jews from the rise of the Maccabees to the close of the Talmud, 1877.

Dübner, Fr., ed. by: Scholia Graeca in Aristophanem, 1883 ed.

Düsterwald, Fr.: Die Weltreiche und das Gottesreich nach den Weissagungen des Propheten Daniel, 1890.

Ebrard, A.: Die Offenbarung Johannes erklärt, 1853, in Olshausen's

Biblischer Commentar über sämmtliche Schriften des Neuen Testaments.
Review of J. F. Füller's *Der Profet Daniel erklärt*, in *Allgemeiner literarischer Anzeiger für das evangelische Deutschland*, ii, 1868, pp. 265–8.

Eerdmans, B. D.: *De Godsdienst van Israël*, 1930, 2 vols.
Origin and Meaning of the Aramaic Part of Daniel, in *Actes du xviiie congrès international des orientalistes*, 1932, pp. 198–202.

Eichhorn, J. G.: *Einleitung in das Alte Testament*, 2nd ed., 3 vols., 1787; 3rd ed., 3 vols., 1803; 4th ed., 5 vols., 1823–4.
Die hebräischen Propheten, 3 vols., 1816–19. (Daniel in vol. iii.)

Eisenmenger, J. A.: *Entdecktes Judenthum*, 2 vols. in 1, 1711.

Eissfeldt, O.: *Einleitung in das Alte Testament, unter Einschluss der Apokryphen und Pseudepigraphen*, 1934.

l'Empereur, C.: *Paraphrasis Iosephi Iachiadae in Danielem, cum versione et annotationibus*, 1633.

Encyclopaedia Biblica, ed. by T. K. Cheyne and J. S. Black, 4 vols., 1899–1907.

Encyclopaedia Britannica, 14th ed., 24 vols., 1929.

Encyclopaedia Judaica: das Judentum in Geschichte und Gegenwart, ed. by J. Klatzkin and I. Elbogen, 1928 (in progress).

d'Envieu, F.: *Le Livre du prophète Daniel*, 2 vols., 1888–91.

Ephraem Syrus: *Opera omnia quae exstant, Graece, Syriace, Latine, in sex tomos distributa*, Syriac and Latin in 3 vols., ed. Peter Benedict and S. Assemani, 1737–43. (Vol. ii, containing comments on Daniel, 1740.)

Eusebius: *Chronicon*, ed. A. Mai, 1818; ed. Migne, PG xix, 1857; ed. A. Schoene, 2 vols., 1875, 1866 [*sic*].
Demonstratio Evangelica, ed. Migne, PG xxii, 1857; ET by W. J. Ferrar, as *The Proof of the Gospel*, 2 vols., 1920, in *Translations of Christian Literature* (S.P.C.K.).
Ecclesiastical History, in Syriac—*see under* Wright, W.

Ewald, H.: *Abhandlungen über Entstehung, Inhalt, und Werth der Sibyllinischen Bücher*, 1858.
Die Propheten des Alten Bundes, 2 vols., 1840–1; 2nd ed., 1868; ET by J. F. Smith, as *The Prophets of the Old Testament*, 5 vols., 1875–81.

Farrar, F. W.: *The Book of Daniel*, 1895, in *The Expositor's Bible*.

Fischer, B.: *Daniel und seine drei Gefährten in Talmud und Midrasch*, 1906.

Freimann, J., ed. by: *Das Gregorius Abulfarag, gen. Bar-Hebräus, Scholien zum Buche Daniel*, 1892, in *Beiträge zur Geschichte der Bibelexegese*, Heft 1.

Fruin, R.: *De 'historische Achtergrond' van het Boek Daniël*, in NTT xvi, 1927, pp. 85–105.
De Voorstelling, die de Joodsche en Israelietischen Schrijvers uit het Hellenistische Tijdperk sich hebben gevormd van de Periode der Ballingschap, ibid. xvii, 1928, pp. 225–41.

Füller, J. L.: *Der Profet Daniel erklärt*, 1868.

Fuller, J. M.: *Daniel*, in *The Speaker's Bible*, ed. by F. C. Cook, vi, 1876, pp. 210–397.

Gadd, C. J.: *The Fall of Nineveh: the newly discovered Babylonian Chronicle, No. 21,901, in the British Museum*, 1923.

Gaebelein, A. C.: *The Prophet Daniel: a key to the visions and prophecies of the Book of Daniel*, 1911.

von Gall, A. F.: *Die Einheitlichkeit des Buches Daniel*, 1895.

ΒΑΣΙΛΕΙΑ ΤΟΥ ΘΕΟΥ, *eine religionsgeschichtliche Studie zur vor-kirchlichen Eschatologie*, 1926, in *Religionswissenschaftliche Bibliothek*, vol. vii.

Gallé, A.-F.: *Daniel avec commentaires de R. Saadia, Aben-Ezra, Raschi, etc., et variantes des versions arabe et syriaque*, 1900.

Gardner, P.: *A History of Ancient Coinage*, 1918.

Gärtner, J. M.: *Erklärung des Propheten Daniel und der Offenbarung Johannis*, 1863.

Geffcken, J.: *Die Oracula Sibyllina*, 1902, in *Die griechischen Christlichen Schriftsteller der ersten drei Jahrhunderte*.

Komposition und Entstehungszeit der Oracula Sibyllina, 1902, in *Texte und Untersuchungen zur Geschichte der altchristliche Literatur*, New Series, viii, Heft 1.

Geier, M.: *Praelectiones academicae in Danielem prophetam*, in *Opera omnia*, vol. ii, 1696.

Goettsberger, J.: *Das Buch Daniel übersetzt und erklärt*, 1928, in Feldmann and Herkenne's *Die Heilige Schrift des alten Testamentes*.

Graserus, C.: *Historia Antichristi illius magni*, 1608.

Gressmann, H.: *Der Ursprung der israelitisch-jüdischen Eschatologie*, 1905.

Der Messias, 1929, in *Forschungen zur Religion und Literatur des Alten und Neuen Testaments*, New Series, Heft 26.

Grotius, H.: *Opera omnia theologica in quatuor tomos divisa*, 1732 ed. (The commentary on Daniel stands in vol. i, pp. 453–85.)

Gunkel, H.: *Schöpfung und Chaos in Urzeit und Endzeit*, 1895.

von Gutschmid, A.: *Der zehnte Griechenkönig im Buche Daniel*, in *Rheinisches Museum für Philologie*, New Series, xv, 1860, pp. 316–18, reprinted in *Kleine Schriften*, ii, 1890, pp. 175–9.

Kleine Schriften, 5 vols., 1889–94.

Gwynn, J.: *Selections translated into English from the Hymns and Homilies of Ephraim the Syrian and from the Demonstrations of Aphrahat the Persian Sage*, 1898, in *A Select Library of Nicene and Post-Nicene Fathers of the Christian Church*, 2nd series, vol. xiii.

Hagen, O. E.: *Keilschrifturkunden zur Geschichte des Königs Cyrus*, in Delitzsch and Haupt's *Beiträge zur Assyriologie*, ii, 1894, pp. 205–48.

Halévy, J.: *Balthasar et Darius le Mède*, in *RS* ii, 1894, pp. 186–91.

Hall, H. R.: *The Ancient History of the Near East*, 7th ed., 1927.

Haller, M.: *Das Alter von Daniel 7*, in *TSK* xciii, 1921, pp. 83–7.

Das Judentum: Geschichtschreibung, Prophetie und Gesetzgebung nach dem Exil, übersetzt, erklärt, und mit Einleitungen versehen, 2nd ed., 1925, in *Die Schriften des Alten Testaments in Auswahl.*

von der Hardt, H.: *De quatuor monarchiis Babyloniae pro antiquae historiae Judaicae luce ad illustrandum Colossum in insomnio Nebucadnezaris Dan. ii, 1708.*

Danielis quatuor animalia, non quatuor monarchiarum fabula, sed quatuor regum Babylonis Nebucadnezaris, Evilmerodachi, Belsazaris et Cyri, historia, 1710 (?).

Harpocration: *Lexicon in decem oratores Atticos,* ed. W. Dindorf, 2 vols., 1853.

Hastings, J., ed. by: *A Dictionary of the Bible,* 5 vols., 1898–1904.

Hävernick, H. A. C.: *Commentar über das Buch Daniel,* 1832.

Neue kritische Untersuchungen über das Buch Daniel, 1838.

Havet, E.: *Le Christianisme et ses origines,* 4 vols., 1871–84.

Études d'histoire religieuse: la modernité des Prophètes, in *Revue des deux mondes,* xciv, 1889, pp. 516–65, 799–830.

Hawkins, J.: *A Treatise on the Second Chapter of the Prophet Daniel,* 1814.

Head, B. V.: *The Coinage of Lydia and Persia from the earliest times to the fall of the Achaemenids,* 1877.

Historia Numorum, 2nd ed., 1911.

Hengstenberg, E. W.: *Die Authentie des Daniel und die Integrität des Sacharjah,* 1831, in *Beiträge zur Einleitung ins Alte Testament,* vol. i; ET by B. P. Pratten, as *Dissertations on the Genuineness of Daniel and the Integrity of Zechariah,* 1848.

Henry, A. B.: *Les difficultés critiques et historiques du livre de Daniel,* 1898.

Herntrich, V.: *Ezechielprobleme,* 1932, in *Beihefte zur ZAW,* No. 61.

Herodotus: *Historiarum libri ix,* ed. W. Dindorf, 1845; ET by G. Rawlinson, 4 vols., 1858–60, reprinted in *Everyman's Library,* 2 vols., 1910; Text and ET by A. D. Godley, in Loeb ed., 4 vols., 1920–4.

Hertlein, E.: *Der Daniel der Römerzeit,* 1908.

Herzfeld, L.: *Geschichte des Volkes Israel von Vollendung des zweiten Tempels bis zur Einsetzung des Mackabäers Schimon zum hohen Priester und Fürsten,* 2 vols., 1855–7.

Herzog, J. J., ed. by: *Real-Encyclopädie für protestantische Theologie und Kirche,* 2nd ed., edited by G. L. Plitt, 18 vols, 1877–88; 3rd ed., edited by A. Hauck, 24 vols., 1896–1913.

Hezel, W. F.: *Die Bibel mit vollständig-erklärenden Anmerkungen,* 1780–91. (Daniel is in vol. vi, 1785.)

Hilgenfeld, A.: *Die jüdische Apokalyptik in ihrer geschichtlichen Entwickelung,* 1857.

Die jüdische Apokalyptik und die neuesten Forschungen, in *Zeitschrift für wissenschaftliche Theologie,* iii, 1860, pp. 301–62.

Die Propheten Esra und Daniel und ihre neuesten Bearbeitungen, 1863.

Die jüdischen Sibyllen und der Essenismus, in *Zeitschrift für wissenschaftliche Theologie,* xiv, 1871, pp. 30–59.

Hill, G. F.: *Historical Greek Coins,* 1906.

Hilprecht, H. V., dedicated to: *Hilprecht Anniversary Volume*, 1909.

Hippolytus: *Hippolyt's Kommentar zum Buche Daniel*, ed. by G. N. Bonwetsch, 1897, in *Die griechischen christlichen Schriftsteller der ersten drei Jahrhunderte* (Hippolytus Werke, vol. i); or ed. Migne, PG x, 1857, cols. 633–88; ET in *Extant Works and Fragments*, by S. D. F. Salmond, 1869, in *Ante-Nicene Christian Library*, vols. vi and ix.

Hitzig, F.: Review of Hengstenberg's *Die Authentie des Daniel und die Integrität des Sacharjah*, in *Heidelberger Jahrbücher der Literatur*, xxv, 1832, pp. 113–46.

Das Buch Daniel erklärt, 1850, in *Kurzgefasstes exegetisches Handbuch zum Alten Testament*.

Hoffmann, G.: *Namen und Sachen*, in ZA ii, 1887, pp. 45–57.

Hoffmann, J. F.: *Antiochus IV Epiphanes König von Syrien*, 1873.

Hoffmann, J. G. E.: *Julianos der Abtrünnige: Syrische Erzählungen*, 1880.

Hofmann, J. C. K.: *Weissagung und Erfüllung im alten und im neuen Testamente*, 2 vols., 1841–4.

Hölscher, G.: *Die Entstehung des Buches Daniel*, in TSK xcii, 1919, pp. 113–38.

Komposition und Ursprung des Deuteronomiums, in ZAW xl, 1922, pp. 161–255.

Geschichte der israelitischen und jüdischen Religion, 1922, in *Sammlung Töpelmann*, I. vii.

Hesekiel: der Dichter und das Buch, 1924, *Beihefte zur ZAW*, No. 39.

Problèmes de la littérature apocalyptique juive, in RHPR ix, 1929, pp. 101–14.

Holtzinger, H.: *Zur Menschensohnfrage*, in *Beiträge zur alttestamentliche Wissenschaft*, ed. K. Marti, 1920 (*Beihefte zur ZAW*, No. 34), pp. 102–6.

Holtzmann, H. J.: *Die Jüngern Propheten und die Schriften*, 1870, in Bunsen's *Vollständiges Bibelwerk für die Gemeinde*, vol. vi.

Hommel, Fr.: *Geschichte Babyloniens und Assyriens*, 1885, in W. Oncken's *Allgemeine Geschichte in Einzeldarstellungen*.

The Apocalyptic Origin of the Expression 'Son of Man', in ET xi, 1899–1900, pp. 341–5.

Die Abfassungszeit des Buches Daniel und der Wahnsinn Nabonids, in *Theologisches Literaturblatt*, xxiii, 1902, No. 13, cols. 145–50.

Hoonacker, A. Van: *Néhémie et Esdras, une nouvelle hypothèse sur la chronologie de l'époque de la restauration*, 1890, (reprinted from *Le Muséon*, ix, 1890, pp. 151–84, 317–51, 389–401).

Néhémie en l'an 20 d'Artaxerxès I; Esdras en l'an 7 d'Artaxerxès II, 1892.

The Four Empires of the Book of Daniel, in ET xiii, 1901–2, pp. 420–3.

La succession chronologique Néhémie-Esdras, in RB xxxii, 1923, pp. 481–94, and xxxiii, 1924, pp. 33–64.

L'Historiographie du livre de Daniel, in *Le Muséon*, xliv, 1931, pp. 169–76.

Huet, P. D.: *Demonstratio Evangelica*, 1679.

Hugo of St. Chère: *Liber Danielis*, in *Opera omnia in universum Vetus et Novum Testamentum* (8 vols., 1754), vol. v, pp. 146–66.

Huit, E.: *The Whole Prophecie of Daniel explained*, 1644.

Hulsius, A.: ריב יהוה עם יהודה, *sive Theologiae Judaicae, pars prima, de Messia*, 1653.

Ibn Yaḥya: *see* l'Empereur, and *Biblia Rabbinica*.

Irenaeus: *Contra Haereses*, ed Massuet, in Migne, PG vii, 1857, or ed. W. W. Harvey, *Sancti Irenaei libros quinque adversus Haereses*, 2 vols., 1857; ET by J. Keble in *The Five Books of Irenaeus*, 1872, in Pusey's *Library of the Fathers*, or by A. Roberts and W. H. Rambaut, 1869, in *Ante-Nicene Christian Library*, vols. v and ix.

Isidore of Pelusium: *Epistolarum libri quinque*, ed. Possinus, in Migne, PG lxxviii, 1860.

Jackson, S. M., ed. by: *The New Schaff-Herzog Encyclopedia of Religious Knowledge*, 13 vols., 1908–14.

Jahn, G.: *Das Buch Daniel nach der Septuaginta hergestellt, übersetzt und kritisch erklärt*, 1904.

Jahn, J.: *Einleitung in die göttlichen Bücher des Alten Bundes*, 4 vols., 1802–3. (Cf. *An Introduction to the Old Testament*, 1827, translated by S. H. Turner and W. R. Whittingham from the Latin work of Jahn, *Introductio in libros sacros Veteris Foederis*, 1814, with some supplementation from the earlier German work.)

Jan, J. W.: *Dissertatio historico-politica de quatuor monarchiis*, 1712.

Antiquae et pervulgatae de quatuor monarchiis sententiae contra recentiorum quorundam objectiones plenior et uberior assertio, 1728.

Jelf, W. E.: *A Grammar of the Greek Language*, 5th ed., 2 vols., 1881.

Jephet Ibn 'Ali: *see* Margoliouth, D. S.

Jerome: *Commentaria in Danielem*, ed. Migne, PL xxv, 1845, cols. 491–584.

Jewish Encyclopaedia ed. by I. Singer, 12 vols. (Volumes undated.)

Josephus, Flavius: *Opera, graece et latine*, ed. W. Dindorf, 2 vols., 1845–7; or *Opera*, ed. B. Niese, 6 vols., 1885–94; *Antiquitatum Judaicarum epitoma*, ed. B. Niese, 1896; ET by W. Whiston, in many editions (that of 1825, in 2 vols., has been used); Text and ET by H. St. J. Thackeray, in Loeb ed., in 8 vols. (of which four have been issued, 1926–30, including one volume of the *Antiquities*, containing Books i–iv). (In all references to Josephus in the present work, the commonly employed system, by Book, chapter, and section, is adopted, and the reference by Niese's system, by Book and section, is added in brackets.)

Joye, G.: *The Exposicion of Daniel the Prophet gathered oute of Philip Melanchton/ Johan Ecolampadius/ Chonrade Pellicane & out of Johan Draconite*, 1545.

Junius, F.: *Expositio Prophetae Danielis*, in *Opera omnia theologica*, 1613, i, cols. 1155-1326.

Junker, H.: *Untersuchungen über literarische und exegetische Probleme des Buches Daniel*, 1932.

Justin: *Historiae Philippicae*, ed. A. Gronovius, 2 vols., 1822.

Kahrstedt, U.: *Syrische Territorien in hellenistischer Zeit*, 1926, in *Abhandlungen der Gesellschaft der Wissenschaften zu Göttingen*, philologisch-historische Klasse, New Series, xix, 2.

Kamphausen, A.: *Daniel*, 1867, in Bunsen's *Vollständiges Bibelwerk für die Gemeinde*, iii, pp. 638-87.

Das Buch Daniel und die neuere Geschichtsforschung, 1893.

The Book of Daniel, in *The Sacred Books of the Old Testament*, 1896.

Kautzsch, E., ed. by: *Die Heilige Schrift des Alten Testaments*, 2 vols., 3rd ed., 1910; 4th ed., by A. Bertholet, 1923.

Keil, C. F.: *Biblischer Commentar über den Propheten Daniel*, 1869, in Keil and Delitzsch's *Biblischer Commentar über das Alte Testament*; ET by M. G. Easton, as *The Book of the Prophet Daniel*, 1877.

Das Buch Esra, 1870, in Keil and Delitzsch's *Biblischer Commentar*; ET by S. Taylor, 1879.

Kelly, W.: *Notes on the Book of Daniel*, 1865.

Kennett, R. H.: *The Origin of the Aaronite Priesthood*, in JTS vi, 1904-5, pp. 161-86, and vii, 1905-6, pp. 620-4 (cf. A. H. McNeile, ibid., pp. 1-9).

The Date of Deuteronomy, in JTS vii, 1905-6, pp. 481-500.

History of the Jewish Church from Nebuchadnezzar to Alexander the Great, in *Cambridge Biblical Essays*, 1909, pp. 99-135.

Deuteronomy and the Decalogue, 1920.

The Church of Israel: studies and essays, ed. by S. A. Cook, 1933.

King, L. W.: *A History of Babylon*, 1919.

King, L. W., and Thompson, R. C.: *The Sculptures and Inscription of Darius the Great on the Rock of Behistun in Persia*, 1907.

Kittel, R.: *The Religion of the People of Israel*, ET by R. C. Micklem, 1925.

Kliefoth, Th.: *Das Buch Daniels übersetzt und erklärt*, 1868.

Knabenbauer, J.: *Commentarius in Danielem prophetam*, 1891, in Cornely's *Cursus Scripturae Sacrae*. (2nd ed., 1907, I have not seen.)

Köhler, H. O.: *Die Schriftwidrigkeit des Chiliasmus*, in *Zeitschrift für die gesammte lutherische Theologie und Kirche*, xxii, 1861, pp. 412-74.

König, E.: *Der Menschensohn im Danielbuche*, in NKZ xvi, 1905, pp. 904-28.

Geschichte der alttestamentliche Religion, 1912.

Kranichfeld, R.: *Das Buch Daniel erklärt*, 1868.

Kuenen, A.: *The Prophets and Prophecy in Israel: an historical and critical enquiry*, ET by A. Milroy, 1877.

Kühner, R.: *Ausführliche Grammatik der griechischen Sprache*, 4 vols., 1890-4.

Küper, —: *Das Prophetenthum des Alten Bundes*, 1870.

Lactantius: *Divinae Institutiones*, ed. Migne, PL vi, 1844; ET by W. Fletcher, in *Ante-Nicene Christian Library*, xxi, 1877; German translation by S. Brandt in *Corpus scriptorum ecclesiasticorum latinorum*, xix, 1890.

Lacunza, M. (Julian Josaphat Ben Ezra): *The Coming of Messiah in Glory and Majesty*, ET from the Spanish, by E. Irving, 2 vols., 1827.

Lagarde, P. de: *Prophetae Chaldaice*, 1872.

Review of Havet's *Études d'histoire religieuse: la modernité des prophètes*, in GGA, 1891, pp. 497–520.

Lagrange, M.-J.: *Les Prophéties messianiques de Daniel*, in RB, New Series, i, 1904, pp. 494–520.

Le Judaïsme avant Jésus-Christ, 1931.

Lanchester, H. C. O.: *The Sibylline Oracles*, in Charles's *Apocrypha and Pseudepigrapha*, 1913, ii, pp. 368–406.

Langdon, S.: *Die Neubabylonischen Königsinschriften*, translated into German by R. Zehnpfund, 1912, in *Vorderasiatische Bibliothek*.

Babylon and the Land beyond the River, in ET xxx, 1918–19, pp. 461–3.

Lange, J. P.: *Theologisch-homiletische Einleitung in das Alte Testament*, prefixed to *Genesis* in his *Bibelwerk*, 1864; ET by T. Lewis, 1868.

a Lapide, Cornelius: *Commentaria in quatuor Prophetas majores*, 1728 ed. (The Commentary on Daniel bears the date 1727, and is found on pp. 1255–1414; it is also reprinted in A. Crampon's *Commentaria in Scripturam Sacram R. P. Cornelii a Lapide*, xiii, 1860, ed. J. M. Péronne. The work was first published in 1622.)

Larocque, J.: *Sur la date du troisième livre des oracles sibyllins*, in RArch, New Series, xx, 1869, pp. 261–70.

Lee, S., ed. by: *Vetus Testamentum Syriace*, 1823.

Lee, S.: *An Inquiry into the Nature, Progress and End of Prophecy*, 1849. *The Events and Times of the Visions of Daniel and St. John investigated, identified and determined*, 1851.

Lehmann-Haupt, C. F.: *Gobryas und Belsazar bei Xenophon*, in *Klio*, ii, 1902, pp. 341–5.

Lengerke, C. von: *Das Buch Daniel verdeutscht und ausgelegt*, 1835.

Lenormant, F.: *La divination et la science des présages chez les Chaldéens*, 1875.

Lidzbarski, M.: *Ephemeris für semitische Epigraphik*, 3 vols., 1900–15.

Lightfoot, J.: *A Chronicle of the Times and the Order of the Texts of the Old Testament*, in *Works* (2 vols., 1684), i, pp. 1–147.

Lightfoot, J. B.: *The Apostolic Fathers: revised texts, with short Introductions and English translations*, ed. by J. R. Harmer, 1891.

Littmann, E.: *Lydian Inscriptions*, in *Sardis* (Publications of the American Society for the Excavation of Sardis), VI. i, 1916.

Lofthouse, W. F.: *Israel after the Exile, sixth and fifth centuries B.C.*, 1928, in *The Clarendon Bible, Old Testament*, vol. iv.

Löhr, M.: *Daniel*, in Kittel's *Biblia Hebraica*, 2nd ed., 1913.

Lowth, W.: *Commentary upon the Prophets*, 1727.

Luther, M.: *Der Prophet Daniel Deudsch,* 1530.

Kurtze Erclerung uber dē Propheten Danielem, 1544. (The copy in the British Museum, which has been consulted, is incomplete.) *Auslegung des Propheten Daniels*, in *Sämtliche Schriften*, ed. by J. G. Walch (24 vols., 1740-50), vi, 1741.

de Lyra, Nicolaus (Lyranus): *Biblia Sacra cum glossa interlineari, ordinaria, Nicolai Lyrani expositionibus, Burgensis additionibus et Thoringi replicis*, 7 vols., 1588. (Daniel is in vol. iv.)

Madden, F. W.: *Coins of the Jews*, 1881.

Mahaffy, J. P.: *The Empire of the Ptolemies*, 1895.

Mai, A.: *Scriptorum veterum nova collectio, e Vaticanis codicibus edita*, 10 vols., 1825-38. (Vol. i contains *Polychronius in Danielem*, and *Commentarii Variorum in Danielem*. The volume is not continuously paged, the several sections being independently numbered. In the edition of vol. i which bears the date *1825*, Polychronius is numbered 105-60, and *Commentarii Variorum* 161-221, and a Latin translation accompanies the texts. But in the edition which bears the date *1825 et 1831* (which has been chiefly used in the present study) Polychronius is paged 1-27, and *Commentarii Variorum* 27-56, and the Latin translation is wanting.)

Maitland, Captain C.: *A Brief and Connected View of Prophecy*, 1814.

Maitland, S. R.: *An Attempt to elucidate the Prophecies concerning Antichrist*, 1830.

Maldonatus, J.: *Commentarius in Danielem*, in *Commentarii in praecipuos Sacrae Scripturae libros Veteris Testamenti*, 1643 ed., pp. 681-778.

Malter, H.: *Saadia Gaon: his life and works*, 1921, in *The Morris Loeb Series*.

Manchester, George, Duke of: *The Times of Daniel*, 1845.

Margoliouth, D. S., ed. by: *Jephet Ibn 'Ali the Karaite: A Commentary on the Book of Daniel*, 1889, in *Anecdota Oxoniensia*, Semitic Series, vol. i, part iii.

Margoliouth, J. P.: *Supplement to the Thesaurus Syriacus of R. Payne Smith*, 1927.

Marti, K.: *Das Buch Daniel erklärt*, 1901, in Marti's *Kurzer Handcommentar zum Alten Testament*.

Das Buch Daniel, in HSAT, q.v. (*sub* Kautzsch).

Mathews, H. J., ed by: *Commentary on Ezra and Nehemiah by Rabbi Saadiah*, 1882, in *Anecdota Oxoniensia,* Semitic Series, vol. i, part i.

Maurer, F. J. V. D.: *Commentarius grammaticus criticus in Vetus Testamentum*, 3 vols., 1835-47. (Daniel in vol. ii, 1838.)

Mede, J.: *Revelatio Antichristi, sive de numeris Danielis MCCXC, MCCCXXXV*, in *Works*, 1672 ed., pp. 717-24.

Meinhold, J.: *Die Composition des Buches Daniel*, 1884.

Beiträge zur Erklärung des Buches Daniel, 1888.

Das Buch Daniel ausgelegt, 1889, in Strack-Zöckler's *Kurzgefasster Kommentar*.

Einführung in das Alte Testament, 3rd ed., 1932, in *Sammlung Töpelmann*.

Mencken, G.: *Das Monarchienbild*, in *Schriften* (7 vols., 1858), vii, pp. 105–66. (Preface dated 1809.)

Merx, E. O. A.: *Cur in libro Danielis juxta Hebraeam Aramaea adhibita sit dialectus explicatur*, 1865.

Meyer, E.: *Ursprung und Anfänge des Christentums*, 3 vols., 1921–3.

Michaelis, C. B.: *Uberiores Adnotationes in Danielem*, in *Adnotationes phil.-exeg. in Hagiographos*, iii, 1720.

Midrash Rabba—Warsaw ed., 5 vols., 1877.

M(igne), J. P.: *Scripturae Sacrae cursus completus*, vol. xx, 1841— contains a valuable catena of comments on Daniel in cols. 9–444.

Mikraoth Gedoloth (מקראות גדולות)—see *Biblia Rabbinica*.

Montgomery, J. A.: *A Critical and Exegetical Commentary on the Book of Daniel*, 1927, in *The International Critical Commentary*.

Moore, G. F.: *Judaism in the First Centuries of the Christian Era*, 3 vols., 1927–30.

More, H.: *A Plain and Continued Exposition of the Several Prophecies or Divine Visions of the Prophet Daniel*, 1681.

Müller, C.: *Fragmenta Historicorum Graecorum*, 5 vols., 1878–85 ed. *Ctesiae Cnidii Fragmenta*, 1887.

Newton, Sir Isaac: *Observations upon the Prophecies of Daniel and the Apocalypse of St. John*, 1733; new ed., entitled *Daniel and the Apocalypse*, ed. by W. Whitla, 1922.

Niebuhr, M. von: *Geschichte Assur's und Babel's seit Phul*, 1857.

Niese, B.: *Geschichte der griechischen und makedonischen Staaten seit der Schlacht bei Chäronea*, 3 vols., 1893–1903, in *Handbücher der alten Geschichte*, Series II, Div. ii.

Nikel, J.: *Grundriss der Einleitung in das Alte Testament*, 1924.

Nöldeke, Th.: *Aufsätze zur persischen Geschichte*, 1887.

Noth, M.: *Zur Komposition des Buches Daniel*, in *TSK* xcviii–xcix, 1926, pp. 143–63.

Obbink, H. W.: *Daniël*, 1932, in *Tekst en Uitleg: Praktische Bijbelverklarung*.

Oecolampadius, J.: *Commentarii omnes in libros prophetarum*, 2 vols., 1558. (The Commentary on Daniel is entitled *Commentariorum in Danielem libri duo*, and is found in vol. ii, and dated 1553.)

Oehler, G. F.: Review of Hävernick's *Untersuchungen* in *Literarischer Anzeiger für christliche Theologie und Wissenschaft*, 1842, Nos. 50, 51, cols. 393–400, 405–8.

Oesterley, W. O. E.: *II Esdras*, 1933, in *Westminster Commentaries*.

Oesterley, W. O. E., and Robinson, T. H.: *A History of Israel*, 2 vols., 1932.

Oestreicher, Th.: *Das Deuteronomische Grundgesetz*, 1923.

Orelli, C. von: *The Old Testament Prophecy of the Consummation of*

God's Kingdom, traced in its historical development, ET by J. S. Banks, 1885.

Origen: *Selecta in Genesim*, in *Opera omnia*, ed. Delarue, vol. ii (in Migne, PG xii), 1857, cols. 91–146.

Osiander, A.: *Biblia Sacra*, 1600.

Parisot, D. J., ed. by: *Aphraatis Demonstrationes*, 1894, in R. Graffin's *Patrologia Syriaca*, Pars prima, vol. i.

Parker, T.: *The Visions and Prophecies of Daniel expounded*, 1646.

Paton, L. B.: *A Critical and Exegetical Commentary on the Book of Esther*, 1908, in *The International Critical Commentary*.

Pauly-Wissowa: *Real-Encyclopädie der klassischen Altertumswissenschaft*, 1894 (in progress).

Payne Smith, R.: *see* Smith, R. Payne.

Peake, A. S.: *The Servant of Yahweh and other lectures*, 1931.

Peiser, F. E.: *Texte juristischen und geschäftlichen Inhalts*, 1896, in Schrader's KB iv.

Studien zur orientalischen Altertumsurkunde, in MVAG, 1897, Heft 4.

Pererius, B.: *Commentariorum in Danielem libri sexdecim*, 1591.

Petrus Archidiaconus: *Quaestiones in Danielem*, ed. Migne, PL xcvi, 1851, cols. 1347–62.

Petrus Comestor: *Historia Libri Danielis*, ed. Migne, PL cxcviii, 1855, cols. 1447–76.

Pinches, T. G.: *On a Cuneiform Inscription relating to the Capture of Babylon by Cyrus, and the Events which preceded and led to it*, in TSBA vii, 1880, pp. 139–76.

The Last Days of Babylon's Independence, in ET xxviii, 1916–17, pp. 183 f.

Pintus, H.: *In divinum vatem Danielem commentarii*, 1579.

Piscator, J.: *In prophetam Danielem commentarius*, 1614.

Plato: *Opera*, ed. Schneider, 3 vols., 1846–73, or ed. Burnet, 5 vols., 1901–6; ET by B. Jowett, as *The Dialogues of Plato*, 5 vols., 1892; Text and ET of *Laws*, by R. G. Bury, in Loeb ed., 2 vols., 1926.

Polanus à Polansdorf, A.: *In Danielem prophetam visionum amplitudine difficillimum, vaticiniorum majestate augustissimum commentarius*, 1599.

Polyaenus: *Strategemata*, ed. Wölfflin-Melber, 1887, in *Bibliotheca Teubneriana*.

Polybius: *Histories*, ed. F. Hultsch, 4 vols., 1867–72; Text and ET by W. R. Paton, in Loeb ed., 6 vols., 1922–7.

Polychronius: *see* Mai, A.

Poole, M.: *Synopsis criticorum aliorumque commentatorum in Danielem*, in *Synopsis criticorum aliorumque S. Scripturae interpretum* (1669–76), iii, 1673, cols. 1389–1612.

Annotations upon the Holy Bible, 2 vols., 1688. (The pages are not numbered; Daniel is in vol. ii.)

Porges, N.: *Saadia's Commentar zu Daniel*, in MGJW xxxiv, 1885, pp. 63–73.

Prášek, J. V.: *Geschichte der Meder und Perser bis zur Makedonischen Eroberung*, 2 vols., 1906–10, in *Handbücher der alten Geschichte*, I. v, vols. 1 and 2.

Preiswerk, H.: *Der Sprachenwechsel im Buche Daniel*, 1903.

Prideaux, H.: *The Old and New Testament connected, in the history of the Jews and neighbouring nations, from the declension of the kingdoms of Israel and Judah to the time of Christ*, 1845 ed., in 2 vols. (The work was originally published in 1715.)

Prince, J. D.: *Mene Mene Tekel Upharsin: an historical study of the fifth chapter of Daniel*, 1893.

A Critical Commentary on the Book of Daniel, designed especially for readers of the English Bible, 1899.

Pusey, E. B.: *Daniel the Prophet: Nine lectures delivered in the Divinity School of the University of Oxford*, 8th ed., 1886. (The work was originally published in 1864.)

Rapoport, S. J.: בכורי העתים in ,תולדות רבינו סעדי׳ גאון וקורות ספריו (*Bicure Haitim*), ix, 1828, pp. 20–37.

Rashi: see *Biblia Rabbinica*, Breithaupt, J. F., and Gallé, A.-F.

Redepenning, E. R.: Review of Hengstenberg's *Die Authentie des Daniels* and Rosenmüller's *Scholia in Danielem*, in TSK vi, 1833, pp. 831–75.

Reichel, H. L.: *Die vier Weltreiche des Propheten Daniel, in* TSK xxi, 1848, pp. 943–62.

Die Religion in Geschichte und Gegenwart, 5 vols., 1st ed., 1909–13, edited by F. M. Schiele and L. Zscharnack; 2nd ed., 1927–31, edited by H. Gunkel and L. Zscharnack.

Reuss, E.: *Littérature politique et polémique*, 1879, in *La Bible: traduction nouvelle avec introductions et commentaires*, vol. vii.

Die Geschichte der Heiligen Schriften Alten Testaments, 1890.

Révillout, E.: *Note sur les plus anciennes monnaies hébraïques*, in *Annuaire de la société française de numismatique et d'archéologie*, viii, 1884, pp. 113–37.

Riehm, E.: *Messianic Prophecy: its origin, historical growth and relation to New Testament fulfilment*, ET by L. A. Muirhead, new ed., 1900.

Riessler, P.: *Das Buch Daniel erklärt*, 1902, in *Kurzgefasster wissenschaftlicher Commentar*.

Rigaux, Béda: *L'Antéchrist et l'opposition au royaume messianique dans l'Ancien et le Nouveau Testament*, 1932.

Rogers, R. W.: *Cuneiform Parallels to the Old Testament*, 1912.

A History of Ancient Persia from its earliest beginnings to the death of Alexander the Great, 1929.

Rohling, A.: *Das Buch des Propheten Daniel, übersetzt und erklärt*, 1876.

Rollock, R.: *In librum Danielis prophetae*, 1591.

Rosenmüller, E. F. C.: *Scholia in Vetus Testamentum*, Part x, *Danielem continens*, 1832.

Rowley, H. H.: *The Belshazzar of Daniel and of History*, in *Expositor*, 9th series, ii, 1924, pp. 182–95, 255–72.

The Interpretation and Date of Sibylline Oracles III. 388-400, in ZAW, New Series, iii, 1926, pp. 324-7.

The Aramaic of the Old Testament: a grammatical and lexical study of its relations with other Early Aramaic dialects, 1929.

The Historicity of the Fifth Chapter of Daniel, in JTS xxxii, 1930-1, pp. 12-31.

Rule, W. H.: *An Historical Exposition of the Book of Daniel the Prophet*, 1869.

Rupert of Deutz: *In Danielem prophetam commentarii*, in *Opera omnia* (2 vols., 1602), i, pp. 613-27, or ed. Migne, PL clxvii, 1854, cols. 1499-1536.

De victoria Verbi Dei, Op. omn. ii, pp. 487-604, or ed. Migne, PL clxix, 1854, cols. 1217-1502.

Ryle, H. E.: *The Books of Ezra and Nehemiah, with Introduction, Notes and Maps*, 1893, in *Cambridge Bible for Schools and Colleges*. (The reprint of 1923 has been used.)

Rzach, A.: *Oracula Sibyllina*, 1891.

pseudo-Saadia: see *Biblia Rabbinica*, and Gallé, A.-F.

Scaliger, J.: *Opus de emendatione temporum: hac postrema editione ex auctoris ipsius manuscripto, emendatius, magnaque accessione auctius*, 1629 ed. (Earlier editions were issued in 1583 and 1598.)

Schaeder, H. H.: *Esra der Schreiber*, 1930, in *Beiträge zur historischen Theologie*, v.

Schaff-Herzog: *see* Jackson, S. M.

Scharfenberg, J. G.: *Specimen animadversionum quibus loci nonnulli Danielis et interpretum ejus veterum praesertim Graecorum illustrantur emendantur*, 1774.

Scheil, V.: *Prise de Babylon par Cyrus*, in RB ii, 1892, pp. 250-6.

Le Gobryas de la Cyropédie et les textes cunéiformes, in RAss xi, 1914, pp. 165-74.

Schenkel, D., ed. by: *Bibel-lexikon*, 5 vols., 1869-75.

Schmidt, N.: *The 'Son of Man' in the Book of Daniel*, in JBL xix, 1900, pp. 22-8.

Schrader, Eb., ed. by: *Keilinschriftliche Bibliothek*, 6 vols., 1889-1915.

Schrader, Eb.: *Die Nabonid-Cyrus-Chronik*, in KB III. ii, 1890, pp. 128-37.

Die Keilinschriften und das Alte Testament, 3rd ed., 1903, ed. by H. Zimmern and H. Winckler.

Schürer, E.: *Geschichte des jüdischen Volkes im Zeitalter Jesu Christi*, 4th ed., 3 vols. and Index, 1901-11; ET of 2nd ed., as *A History of the Jewish People in the time of Jesus Christ*, by J. Macpherson, S. Taylor, and P. Christie, in 5 vols. and Index, 1890.

Schwenzner, W.: *Gobryas*, in *Klio*, xviii, 1922-3, pp. 41-58, 226-52.

Sellin, E.: *Einleitung in das Alte Testament*, 6th ed., 1933; ET of 3rd ed., as *Introduction to the Old Testament*, by W. Montgomery, 1923.

Geschichte des israelitisch-jüdischen Volkes, 2 vols., 1924-32.

Smith, J.: *The Book of the Prophet Ezekiel: a new interpretation*, 1931.

Smith, R. Payne, ed. by: *Thesaurus Syriacus*, 2 vols., 1879–1901.

Smith, S.: *Babylonian Historical Texts relating to the capture and downfall of Babylon*, 1924.

Smith, W., ed. by: *A Dictionary of the Bible*, 1st ed., 3 vols., 1860; 2nd ed., edited by Sir W. Smith and J. M. Fuller, vol. i only, in two parts, 1893.

Smith, W., and Wace, H., ed. by: *A Dictionary of Christian Biography, Literature, Sects and Doctrines during the first eight centuries*, 4 vols., 1877–87.

Spiegel, H.: *Saadia al-Fajjûmi's arabische Danielversion*, 1906.

Spinoza: *Tractatus theologico-politicus*, 1670 ed.; ET (by R. Willis), 1862.

Staerk, W.: *Das Problem des Deuteronomiums: ein Beitrag zur neuesten Pentateuchkritik*, 1924, in *Beiträge zur Förderung christlicher Theologie*, xxix, Heft 2.

Steuernagel, C.: *Lehrbuch der Einleitung in das Alte Testament*, 1912, in *Sammlung theologischer Lehrbücher*.

Stevens, W. C.: *The Book of Daniel: a composite revelation of the last days of Israel's subjugation to Gentile powers*, 2nd ed., 1918.

Stokmann, G.: *Die Erlebnisse und Gesichte des Propheten Daniel*, 1922.

Strack, H. L.: *Einleitung in das Alte Testament*, 4th ed., 1895.

Stuart, M.: *A Commentary on the Book of Daniel*, 1850.

Suidas: *Lexicon*, ed. G. Bernhardy, 2 vols., 1853.

Sulpicius Severus: *Libri qui supersunt*, ed. C. Halm, 1866, in *Corpus scriptorum ecclesiasticorum latinorum*, vol. i; ed. Migne, PL xx, 1845; ET by A. Roberts in *A Select Library of Nicene and Post-Nicene Fathers of the Christian Church*, 2nd series, xi, 1894.

Swete, H. B., ed. by: *The Old Testament in Greek according to the Septuagint*, 3 vols., 1887–94.

Swete, H. B.: *An Introduction to the Old Testament in Greek*, 2nd ed., revised by R. R. Ottley, 1914.

Syncellus, George: *Georgius Syncellus et Nicephorus CP*, ed. by W. Dindorf, 1829, in *Corpus scriptorum historiae Byzantiae*, Part VII, vols. i and ii.

Talmud Babilonski (Babylonian Talmud), Warsaw ed., 20 vols., 1859–64.

Tattam, H.: *Prophetae majores in dialecto linguae aegyptiacae memphitica seu coptica*, 2 vols., 1852.

Theodoret: *Commentarius in visiones Danielis prophetae*, in Migne's PG lxxxi, 1859, being vol. ii of J. L. Schulze's ed. of *Opera omnia*, 5 vols. (PG lxxx–lxxxiv, 1859–60).

Historia Ecclesiastica, in PG lxxxii, 1859, being vol. iii of Schulze's Theodoret; ET by B. Jackson, in *A Select Library of Nicene and Post-Nicene Fathers*, 2nd series, iii, 1892.

Thilo, M.: *Die Chronologie des Danielbuches*, 1926.

Thompson, R. C.: *see under* King, L. W.

Tiele, C. P.: *Babylonisch-assyrische Geschichte*, 2 vols., 1886–8, in *Handbücher der alten Geschichte*, i. iv.

Tillmann, F.: *Der Menschensohn, Jesu Selbstzeugnis für seine Messianische Würde*, 1907, in Bardenhewer's *Biblische Studien*, vol. xii, Parts i and ii.

Tisdall, W. St. Clair: *The Book of Daniel: some linguistic evidence regarding its date*, in JTVI liii, 1921, pp. 206–45.

Todd, J. H.: *Discourses on the Prophecies relating to Antichrist in the writings of Daniel and St. Paul*, 1840.

Torrey, C. C.: *Notes on the Aramaic Part of Daniel*, in TCA xv, 1909, pp. 241–82.

Ezra Studies, 1910.

The Bilingual Inscription from Sardis, in AJSL xxxiv, 1917–18, pp. 185–98.

Pseudo-Ezekiel and the Original Prophecy, 1930, in *Yale Oriental Series*, Researches, vol. xviii.

Tregelles, S. P.: *Remarks on the Prophetic Visions in the Book of Daniel*, 5th ed., 1864.

Turmel, J.: *Étude sur le livre de Daniel*, in *Annales de philosophie chrétienne*, 3rd series, i, 1902–3, pp. 5–37.

Tyso, J.: *An Elucidation of the Prophecies, being an exposition of the Books of Daniel and the Revelation*, 1838.

Unger, G. F.: *Kyaxares und Astyages*, in *Abhandlungen der philosophisch-philologischen Classe der königlich-bayerischen Akademie der Wissenschaften*, xvi, 1882, Abteilung iii, pp. 235–319.

Vatke, W.: *Historisch-kritische Einleitung in das Alte Testament*, ed. H. G. S. Preiss, 1886.

Venema, H.: *Dissertationes ad vaticinia Danielis emblematica*, 2nd ed., 1768. (The work was originally published in 1745.)

Vigouroux, F.: *La Sainte Bible polyglotte*, 8 vols., 1900–9. (Daniel is in vol. vi, 1906.)

Vigouroux, F., ed. by: *Dictionnaire de la Bible*, 5 vols., 1895–1912.

Violet, B.: *Die Esra-Apokalypse (IV Esra)*, erster Teil, 1910, in *Die griechischen christlichen Schriftsteller der ersten drei Jahrhunderte*.

de Vogüé, M.: *Inscription araméenne trouvée en Égypte*, in *Comptes rendus de l'Académie des Inscriptions et Belles Lettres*, 1903, pp. 269–76.

Volck, W.: *Vindiciae Danielicae*, 1866.

Völter, D.: *Die Menschensohnfrage neu untersucht*, 1916.

Volz, P.: *Jüdische Eschatologie von Daniel bis Akiba*, 1903.

Walton, B.: *Biblia Sacra Polyglotta*, 6 vols., 1653–7.

Watson, C. F.: *Darius the Median identified, or the true chronology of the ancient monuments recovered*, 1885.

Weissbach, F. H.: *Die Keilschriften der Achämeniden*, 1911, in *Vorderasiatische Bibliothek*.

Welch, A. C.: *Visions of the End: a study in Daniel and Revelation*, 1922.

The Code of Deuteronomy: a new theory of its origin, 1924.

Deuteronomy: the Framework to the Code, 1932.

Westminster Assembly: see *Assembly's Annotations*.

de Wette, W. M. L.: *Lehrbuch der historisch-kritischen Einleitung in die Bibel Alten und Neuen Testaments*, 2 vols., 1817–26; 6th ed. of vol. i (AT only), 1845; ET of vol. i only, made from the 5th German ed., by T. Parker, 2 vols., 1843.

Willet, A.: *Hexapla in Danielem: that is, A sixfold Commentarie*, 1610— in two books, continuously paged.

Willet, H. L.: *Daniel*, in *The Abingdon Commentary*, ed. by F. C. Eiselen, E. Lewis, and D. G. Downey, 1929.

Wilson, J. D.: *Did Daniel write Daniel?* 1906.

Wilson, R. D.: *The Aramaic of Daniel*, in *Biblical and Theological Studies by the Members of the Faculty of Princeton Theological Seminary*, 1912, pp. 263–306.

Studies in the Book of Daniel, 1917.

Darius the Mede, in *Princeton Theological Review*, xx, 1922, pp. 177–211.

The Prophecies of Daniel, ibid. xxii, 1924, pp. 377–401.

Winckler, H.: *Untersuchungen zur altorientalische Geschichte*, 1889.

Die Zeit der Herstellung Judas, in *Altorientalische Forschungen*, 2 Reihe, ii, 1899, pp. 210–27.

Daniel als Geschichtsquelle, in *Altorientalische Forschungen*, 2 Reihe, iii, 1901, pp. 433–57.

Winer, G. B.: *Biblisches Realwörterbuch zum Handgebrauch*, 2 vols., 2nd ed., 1833–8; 3rd ed., 1847–8.

Wintle, T.: *Daniel: an improved version attempted*, 1792.

Wright, C. H. H.: *Daniel and his Prophecies*, 1906.

Daniel and its Critics, 1906.

Wright, W.: *The Homilies of Aphraates, the Persian Sage*, vol. i, the Syriac text, 1869.

Wright, W. and McLean, N.: *The Ecclesiastical History of Eusebius in Syriac*, 1898.

Wyngarden, M. J.: *The Syriac Version of the Book of Daniel*, 1923.

Xenophon: *Opera omnia*, ed. E. C. Marchant, 5 vols., 1900–20; ET by H. G. Dakyns, in *The Works of Xenophon*, 4 vols., 1890–7 (does not include *Cyropaedia*), and *The Education of Cyrus*, 1914 (in *Everyman's Library*); Text and ET of *Anabasis* by C. L. Brownson, in Loeb ed., 2 vols., 1921–2, and of *Cyropaedia*, by W. Miller, in Loeb ed., 2 vols., 1914.

Zimmern, H.: see Schrader, Eb.

Zöckler, O.: *Der Prophet Daniel theologisch-homiletisch bearbeitet*, 1870, in J. P. Lange's *Bibelwerk*; ET by J. Strong, as *The Book of the Prophet Daniel*, 1876.

Zöckler, O., ed. by: *Handbuch der theologischen Wissenschaften in encyclopädischer Darstellung*, 2nd ed., 5 vols., 1885–6.

Zündel, D.: *Kritische Untersuchungen über die Abfassungszeit des Buches Daniel*, 1861.

SUPPLEMENTARY LIST

Albright, W. F.: *The Date and Personality of the Chronicler*, in JBL xl, 1921, pp. 104–24.

The Archaeology of Palestine and the Bible, 1933.

The History of Palestine and Syria, in JQR, New Series, xxiv, 1933–4, pp. 363–76.

Bertholet, A.: Review of Hertlein's *Der Daniel der Römerzeit*, in DLZ xxxi, 1910, cols. 2062–4, 2523–5 (reply by Hertlein, cols. 2520–23).

Cedrenus, G.: *Compendium historiarum a mundo condito usque ad Isaacium Comnenum Imperatorem*, in Migne, PG cxxi, cxxii, 1864.

Hoonacker, A. Van: *Notes sur l'histoire de la restauration juive après l'exil de Babylone*, in RB x, 1901, pp. 5–26, 175–99.

Horner, J.: *Daniel, Darius the Median, Cyrus the Great: a chronologico-historical study*, 1901.

Ibn Ezra: see *Biblia Rabbinica*, and Gallé, A.–F.

Imbert, J.: *Le Temple reconstruit par Zorobabel*, in *Le Muséon*, vii, 1888, pp. 77–87, 221–35, 302–14, 584–92; viii, 1889, pp. 51–64.

Jeremias, A.: *The Old Testament in the Light of the Ancient East*, ET by C. L. Beaumont, 2 vols., 1911.

Kittel, R.: *Geschichte des Volkes Israel*, vol. iii, 1927–9.

Kolbe, W.: *Beiträge zur syrischen und jüdischen Geschichte*, 1926.

Kosters, W. H.: *Het Herstel van Israël in het perzische Tijdvak*, 1893; German translation by Basedow, as *Die Wiederherstellung Israels in der persische Period*, 1895.

Kraeling, E. G. H.: *Some Babylonian and Iranian Mythology in the Seventh Chapter of Daniel*, in *Oriental Studies in honour of Cursetji Erachji Pavry*, 1933, pp. 228–31.

Marsham, J.: *Canon chronicus aegyptiacus, ebraicus, graecus, et disquisitiones*, 1676 ed.

Meillet, A.: *Grammaire du vieux perse*, 1915; 2nd. ed., revised by E. Benveniste, 1931.

Möller, W.: *Einleitung in das Alte Testament*, 1934.

de Moor, Fl.: *Les Juifs captifs dans l'empire chaldéen depuis l'avènement de Nabuchodonosor jusqu'après la mort de Darius le Mède*, in *Le Muséon*, xv, 1896, pp. 19–26, 153–74, 233–47, 321–41.

Nestle, Eb.: *Marginalien und Materialen*, 1893.

Oesterley, W. O. E., and Robinson, T. H.: *An Introduction to the Books of the Old Testament*, 1934.

Paris Polyglott = *Biblia, 1. Hebraica, 2. Samaritana, 3. Chaldaica, 4. Graeca, 5. Syriaca, 6. Latina, 7. Arabica*, Paris, 1629–45.

Quatremère, E. M.: *Mélanges d'histoire et de philologie orientale*, 1861.

Ricciotti, G.: *Storia d'Israele*, 2 vols., 1933–4.

Scott, R. B. Y.: *1 Daniel, The original Apocalypse*, in AJSL xlvii, 1930–1, pp. 289–96.

Stier, F.: *Gott und sein Engel im Alten Testament*, 1934, in *Alttestamentliche Abhandlungen*, xii. 2.

Trochon, C.: *La Sainte Bible avec commentaires: Les Prophètes—Daniel*, 1882.

Vernes, M.: *Précis d'histoire juive depuis les origines jusqu'à l'époque persane*, 1889.

Winter, J., and Wünsche, A.: *Geschichte der rabbinischen Litteratur während des Mittelalters und ihrer Nachblüthe in der neueren Zeit*, 2 vols., 1891–4.

INTRODUCTION

DURING the last generation there has been anything but stagnation in the field of Old Testament criticism. Positions which were regarded as established have been challenged again and again, and on a variety of questions what were once regarded as 'the assured results of criticism' can scarcely be accepted without examination as 'assured' to-day. Even the date of the publication of the Deuteronomic Code, the very sheet-anchor of the whole critical position, has been challenged within the critical school, Oestreicher[1] and Welch[2] arguing for it an origin much earlier than has been commonly allowed, and Kennett[3] and Hölscher[4] seeking to carry it down to post-Exilic days. More recently the book of Ezekiel has attracted considerable attention, and fresh views have been advanced by Hölscher,[5] Torrey,[6] James Smith,[7] and Herntrich,[8] making it quite impossible to begin the study of that book with the assumption that it is from a single hand, as was so generally done but a few years ago.

Nor has the book of Daniel escaped without feeling the effects of this re-inquiry into what were accepted positions. A generation ago there was a critical orthodoxy over against an anti-critical orthodoxy. The one regarded the whole book as the product of an author of the Maccabean age, and

[1] *Das deut. Grundgesetz.* Cf. also Staerk, *Das Problem des Deuteronomiums.*

[2] *The Code of Deut.,* and *Deut.: The Framework to the Code.*

[3] *Deut. and the Decalogue,* or *The Origin of the Bk. of Deut.,* in *The Church of Israel,* pp. 73–98. Cf. id., *The Origin of the Aaronite Priesthood,* in JTS vi, 1904–5, pp. 161–86, and vii, 1905–6, pp. 620–4 (cf. McNeile, ibid., pp. 1–9), and *The Date of Deut.,* ibid., pp. 481–500; also his Essay on *The Hist. of the Jewish Ch. from Neb. to Alex. the Great,* in *Camb. Bib. Essays,* pp. 99–135.

[4] *Komp. u. Ursprung des Deut.,* in ZAW xl, 1922, pp. 161–255. Cf. also his *Gesch. der israel. u. jüd. Relig.,* pp. 130–4.

[5] *Hesekiel: Der Dichter u. d. Buch.*

[6] *Pseudo-Ezek. and the Orig. Proph.*

[7] *The Bk. of the Proph. Ezek.*

[8] *Ezechielprobleme.*

the other held it to be from the pen of Daniel himself, a courtier of Babylon in the Exilic age[1]. The anti-critical orthodoxy still flourishes, indeed, and since the beginning of the present century it has been represented in the works of Wright[2], J. D. Wilson[3], R. D. Wilson[4], Boutflower[5], and Stokmann[6], while Dougherty has recently devoted a whole volume[7] to the rehabilitation of Daniel v as a respectable historical document, and Alfrink has published some important studies[8] of special questions. But here again critical orthodoxy has also been challenged from the critical side. The unity of the book has been denied by a long and growing list of scholars, until it is fast becoming the newer orthodoxy to hold the dual origin of the work. At the beginning of the century the views of Barton and Meinhold were rare exceptions to the prevailing critical view. The former had then but lately assigned[9] the book to a number of authors, somewhat after the fashion of Bertholdt[10] a

[1] Amongst the defenders of the traditional date of the book there had been some who disputed its integrity. Thus, Lenormant (*La Divination . . . chez les Chald.*) held that there were many later glosses in the first half of the book, while the second half was a later work, and several writers held that much in the second half of the book consisted of Maccabean interpolations. So Lange (*Einl. in d. AT*, prefixed to Genesis in his *Bibelwerk*, p. xxxv, ET, p. 38), Zöckler (*Bk. of Dan.*, ET, pp. 5, 17, 257), Bosanquet (*Messiah the Prince*, pp. 110 f.), Küper (*Das Prophetenthums d. A. Bundes*, p. 395).

[2] *Dan. and his Proph.* and *Dan. and its Critics.* Wright follows the view noted above, that the text has been interpolated, holding chap. xi to be overlaid with Maccabean glosses. See *Dan. and his Proph.*, pp. 317 ff.

[3] *Did Dan. write Dan.?* and the article on Daniel in Jackson's *New Schaff-Herzog Encyc.* iii, pp. 350 f.

[4] *Studies in the Bk. of Dan.*, and a long series of articles in the *Princeton Theological Review*. Cf. also his Essay on *The Aramaic of the Bk. of Dan.*, in *Bib. and Theol. Stud.*, pp. 263–306 (on which cf. my *Aram. of OT*).

[5] *In and Around the Bk. of Dan.*, and *Dadda-'Idri.* Cf. also his article on *The Hist. Value of Dan. v and vi*, in JTS xvii, 1915–16, pp. 43–60. Boutflower finds Maccabean glosses in Daniel xi. See *In and Around the Bk. of Dan.*, pp. 4 ff.   [6] *Die Erleb. u. Ges. des Proph. Dan.*

[7] *Nab. and Belsh.* (Cf. my reply in JTS xxxii, 1930–1, pp. 12–31.)

[8] *Die Gaddsche Chron. u. d. HS*, in *Biblica*, viii, 1927, pp. 385–417; *Der letzte Kön. von Bab.*, ibid., ix, 1928, pp. 187–205; *Darius Medus*, ibid., pp. 316–40.

[9] *The Comp. of the Bk. of Dan.*, in JBL xvii, 1898, pp. 62–86.

[10] *Dan. neu übers. u. erkl.*, pp. 49 ff. Cf. too Augusti, *Grundriss einer hist.-krit. Einl. in's AT*, pp. 319 ff.

century earlier, while the latter had for some years argued[1] that the Aramaic part of the book was older than the Maccabean age, his division of the sources being almost the same as that of Eichhorn[2] in an earlier day[3]. But scarcely had the present century begun, when Preiswerk proposed[4] to divide the narratives of chapters i–vi from the visions of chapters vii–xii, and more recently Dalman[5], Torrey[6], Montgomery[7] and Eissfeldt[8] have all reached the same conclusion. Here again there were forerunners of this group in the division of the book; for Newton[9] and Beausobre[10] had long ago proposed the same division. But whereas these older writers held the latter half of the book to be the genuine work of Daniel and the former half to be of later origin, the moderns hold the latter half to be Maccabean and the former half to be somewhat older, and Torrey believes[11] he can even date the former half with precision in the middle of the third century B.C. Nor is this the only variety of recent division-hypothesis. For Hölscher proposed, now fifteen years ago[12],

---

[1] *Die Comp. des B. Dan.*, p. 38; *Beitr. zur Erkl. des B. Dan.*, pp. 68 ff.; *Das B. Dan.*, p. 262. Strack also held a similar view. Cf. PRE, 2nd ed., vii, p. 419; Zöckler's *Handb. der theol. Wiss.*, 2nd ed., i, p. 173; *Einl. in das AT*, 4th ed., pp. 145 f.

[2] *Einl. in das AT*, 4th ed., iv, pp. 515 ff. Eichhorn held ii. 4b–vi to come from one hand, and i. 1–ii. 4a, vii–xii to come from another. (Cf. 2nd ed., iii, pp. 361 ff., and 3rd ed., iii, pp. 421 ff.) Meinhold held ii. 4b–vi to date from c. 300 B.C., and vii to be a later appendix, while i. 1–ii. 4a, viii–xii he held to be Maccabean.

[3] Lagarde (GGA, 1891, pp. 497–520) had also held the composite authorship of the book, maintaining that chaps. vii and ix–xii were unknown to Josephus as parts of the book of Dan., and that they were written in the first century A.D. Havet (*Le Christ. et ses Orig.* iii, pp. 304 ff.) had earlier argued for the composite authorship of the book of Dan., holding the second half to date from Herodian times, and Antiochus Epiphanes to be but a lay figure for the depicting of Herod. Cf. also id., *Revue des Deux Mondes*, xciv, 1889, pp. 825–8.　　[4] *Der Sprachenwechsel im B. Dan.*, pp. 115 f.

[5] *Words of Jesus*, ET, p. 13 (or *Die Worte Jesu*, 2nd. ed., p. 11).

[6] *Notes on Aram. Part of Dan.*, in TCA xv, 1909, pp. 241–51. Cf. also E. Brit., 14th ed., vii, pp. 28 ff.

[7] *Comm. on Dan.*, pp. 90 f.　　[8] *Einl. in das AT*, pp. 580 f.

[9] *Obs. upon Dan. and Apoc.*, 1733, p. 10 (Whitla's ed., p. 145).

[10] *Remarques . . . sur le NT*, p. 70.

[11] TCA, loc. cit., p. 250.

[12] *Die Entst. des B. Dan.*, in TSK xcii, 1919, pp. 113–38.

to divide the book at the end of chapter vii. Once more it
was a division that had been more anciently proposed. For
Spinoza[1] had long since held this view. But whereas
Spinoza believed the closing chapters to be from the pen of
Daniel and the rest to be later, Hölscher holds the closing
chapters to be Maccabean and the first seven chapters to
date from the third century B.C., the seventh chapter being
an appendix to the first six of slightly later date and different
authorship. Moreover, he finds it necessary to remove from
the sections he regards as pre-Maccabean a number of
passages, which he declares to be Maccabean glosses[2].
Sellin[3] is in substantial agreement with Hölscher, and
Meinhold now says[4] that their views are an improvement
on his earlier view. Haller[5], though following Hölscher in
the main, holds chapter vii to be older than chapters i–vi,
and to date from the fourth century B.C., while Baumgartner[6]
goes farther and holds chapters i–vi to be based on a source
belonging to the Persian period, and chapter vii to belong
in its earliest form to the time of Alexander. Similarly
Welch[7] holds that chapters i–vi, and probably also chapter
vii, had a Babylonian origin, and had already taken literary
shape before they were taken over by the author of our
present book, and Eerdmans[8], while believing that the
Aramaic story-book is not older than the fourth century B.C.,

---

[1] *Tract. theol.-pol.*, p. 130 (ET, p. 209).

[2] More recently, however, Hölscher refers (RHPR ix, 1929, p. 108) to 'Le
premier livre des Maccabées, connu et utilisé par Daniel', from which it
would appear that he had radically revised his earlier view, and now located
a part, at any rate, of the book of Dan. much later than the reign of Ant. IV.

[3] *Einl. in das AT*, 6th ed., pp. 153 f. (ET of 3rd ed., p. 234).

[4] *Einf. in das AT*, 3rd ed., p. 355.

[5] *Das Alter von Dan.* 7, in TSK xciii, 1921, pp. 83–7; cf. *Das Judentum*,
2nd ed., p. 273.

[6] *Das B. Dan.*, p. 9; ZAW, New Series iii, 1926, p. 39; RGG, 2nd ed., i,
cols. 1781 f. Lenormant earlier adopted a view in some respects similar to
this, attributing the first part of the book to the time of the Great Synagogue,
and holding that the author of the second part was acquainted with the first.
He found it necessary to remove from the text a number of supposed glosses,
however. Cf. *La Divination . . . chez les Chald.*, pp. 171 f., 221.

[7] *Visions of the End*, p. 54.

[8] *Actes du xviii° cong. des orient.*, p. 202.

dates chapters i–vii earlier than the Maccabean chapters viii–xii. Hertlein[1], on the other hand, while making the same division of the book, regards chapters i–vii as younger than the closing chapters, and places them in the first century A.D. It is clearly impossible to take for granted as established the positions which once seemed so secure, and even those who still hold that they are secure must present a defence against these varied assaults.

The present study is limited to the related questions of Darius the Mede and the Four World Empires of Nebuchadnezzar's dream and of Daniel's first vision. So far as Darius the Mede is concerned, it is still generally agreed within the critical school that he has no place in history, and that he is a fictitious creation out of confused traditions[2]. But anti-critical orthodoxy has not given up the attempt to find a place in history for him. For centuries it was customary to identify him with the Cyaxares II of Xenophon's *Cyropaedia*, but in recent years this view has fallen into the background. Its advocacy has been carried into the present century, however, by Knabenbauer[3] and Auchincloss[4]. The modern defenders of the traditional view of the origin of the book of Daniel have rather sought to find fresh strength in the Babylonian texts which the Assyriologists have opened up, and have identified Darius the Mede with Gobryas, or with Cambyses. Within the present century Wright[5] and R. D. Wilson[6] have maintained the former identification, and Boutflower[7] the latter. A further view,

---

[1] *Der Dan. der Römerzeit.*

[2] This does not necessarily mean that the author of Daniel created him. Cf. Bousset, *Theol. Rundschau*, iii, 1900, p. 333, 'Die meisten geschichtlichen Irrtümer hat eben das Danielbuch nicht geschaffen sondern nur übernommen'.

[3] In the second ed. of his *Comm. in Dan.*, 1907. To this ed., however, I have not had access.

[4] *Darius the Median*, in *Bibliotheca Sacra*, lxvi, 1909, pp. 536–8. Cf. id., *The Bk. of Dan. Unlocked*, pp. 48, 95 ff. [5] *Dan. and his Proph.*, pp. 135 ff.

[6] *Darius the Mede*, in *Princeton Theol. Rev.* xx, 1922, pp. 177–211, and *Studies in Bk. of Dan.*, chaps. vii–xii.

[7] *In and Around the Bk. of Dan.*, chaps. xiv, xv. Cf. id., *The Hist. Value of Dan. v and vi*, in JTS xvii, 1915–16, pp. 43–60.

itself a revival of an older view, has been recently advanced by Alfrink[1], who holds that Darius the Mede is to be identified with Astyages.

So far as the Four World Empires are concerned, the issue is not between critical orthodoxy and anti-critical orthodoxy. For here almost every solution which is proposed, either in the critical or in the anti-critical school, goes back far beyond the foundation of the critical school. For more than a millennium and a half three principal views have been held. One, found anciently in Ephraem Syrus[2], identified the four kingdoms as (1) Babylonian, (2) Median, (3) Persian, and (4) Greek. Another, found already in Porphyry[3] and Polychronius[4], identified them as (1) Babylonian, (2) Medo-Persian, (3) the Greek kingdom of Alexander, and (4) Alexander's successors. The third, found in Jerome[5] and many other Fathers, identified them as (1) Babylonian, (2) Medo-Persian, (3) Greek, and (4) Roman. The centuries of discussion have brought little agreement, and all three views have been held by defenders of the traditional view of the origin of the book of Daniel. The first view has now been abandoned by all such defenders, however, and it had become the critical orthodoxy of a generation ago. The second view has been held by a long succession of writers, of whom none but Bertholdt and Maurer can be placed in the critical school, and it has been carried to our own day by Lagrange[6] and Buzy[7]. The third

---

[1] See *Biblica*, ix, 1928, pp. 328 ff.

[2] *Op. omn.*, Syr. and Lat. ii, pp. 205 f., 214.

[3] Apud Jerome, on Dn vii. 7 (ed. Migne, col. 530).

[4] In Mai's *Script. vet. nov. coll.* i, 1825 et 1831, p. 4. (Note that the pagination in this edition is quite different from that in the edition which bears only the date 1825. See Bibliographical list in the present work.) Polychronius was the brother of Theodore of Mopsuestia, according to Theodoret, *Hist. Eccl.* v. xxxix (ed. Schulze in Migne, PG lxxxii, col. 1277; ET by Jackson, p. 159). Cf. Swete in DCB iv, pp. 434 ff.

[5] On Dn ii. 40 and vii. 7 (ed. Migne, cols. 504, 530).

[6] RB, New Series, i, 1904, p. 503.

[7] *Les Symboles de l'AT*, pp. 267, 282; and RB, New Series, xv, 1918, pp. 413 ff.

view has been by far the most popular traditional view, and it is still the one generally held in the anti-critical school. Wide differences of interpretation have appeared amongst its holders, however, and many Protestants have given an anti-Papal turn to the interpretation that is not shared by Roman Catholic writers. Moreover, Hertlein[1] has presented a fresh variety of this third view, from a standpoint quite alien to that of anti-critical orthodoxy. For he dates the relevant parts of the book of Daniel in the Christian era. Nor are these three the only contemporary varieties of identification of the four empires. For Van Hoonacker[2] and Goettsberger[3] have argued that they are to be identified as (1) Nebuchadnezzar, (2) Belshazzar, (3) the Medo-Persian empire, and (4) the Greek empire. This view is by no means new, for it was proposed already by Conring[4] nearly three centuries ago, and again by Hitzig[5] and Redepenning[6] a hundred years ago. Again Eerdmans[7] has suggested that the four empires of chapter ii are all to be equated with individual reigns, which he finds in those of (1) Nebuchadnezzar, (2) Evil-merodach, (3) Neriglissar, and (4) Nabonidus. Once more there is nothing essentially new in this view, for with but very slight variations it was found a century and a half ago in the works of Harenberg[8], Dathe[9] and Hezel[10], whose view was itself but a modification of that found yet earlier in von der Hardt[11]. Finally, we have to note the view of Riessler[12], who similarly identified the empires with individual

---

[1] *Der Dan. der Römerzeit.* Hertlein's interpretation owes much to that of Lagarde, in GGA, 1891, pp. 497–520.

[2] ET xiii, 1901–2, pp. 420 ff., and *Le Muséon*, xliv, 1931, pp. 169 ff.

[3] *Das B. Dan. übers. u. erk.*, pp. 25, 54.

[4] *Disc. ad Lamp. post.* (in *Opera*, ii), p. 363.

[5] *Heidelberger Jahrb. der Lit.* xxv, 1832, pp. 131 f., and *Das B. Dan. erk.*, 1850, p. 37.   [6] TSK vi, 1833, p. 863.

[7] *Orig. and Meaning of the Aram. Part of Dan.*, in *Actes du xviii^e congr. des orient.*, pp. 198–202.

[8] *Aufklärung des Buchs Daniel*, 1773, ii, p. 304.

[9] *Proph. Maj.*, pp. 608 f.

[10] *Die Bib. mit vollst.-erk. Anm.* vi, pp. 733 ff.

[11] *De Quat. mon. bab.*, pp. 15 ff., and *Dan. quat. anim.*, pp. 15 ff.

[12] *Das B. Dan. erk.*, pp. 17 f., 68 ff.

reigns, but found them in (1) Nebuchadnezzar (= Nabonidus), (2) Belshazzar, (3) Cyrus, and (4) Cambyses (= Darius the Mede).

Two things will immediately appear from this brief summary. The first is that there is room for a fresh examination of the whole subject—not, indeed, in the effort to find some wholly new solution, but in the effort to find which of these many views is the most probable. Where there has been so much discussion, spread over so long a period, and where such great variety of view has been found, it is unlikely that the real solution has been missed by all. But where so many views are found in contemporary writers, it is impossible to treat the question as finally closed.

The second is that, apart from Riessler's view, every theory advanced in our own day is of much older origin, and while recent writers may have contributed much that is new in the details of their views, or in the arguments by which they are supported, the views themselves are fundamentally not new. Hence it is necessary, in discussing the views, to take note not merely of their contemporary advocates, but to consider too the advocacy they have commanded in earlier days.

The present study will therefore be limited to the consideration of theories on Darius the Mede and the Four World Empires which have appeared in writings published within the present century, but will take into account the advocacy of those theories both before and during this century. It will aim to determine which of these theories may be accepted, and to show why those rejected are untenable. It will also aim to strengthen the defences of the positions adopted against the many challenges which surround them, and to advance fresh considerations for their support.

DARIUS THE MEDE

THE references to Darius the Mede in the book of Daniel have long been recognized as providing the most serious historical problem in the book. For here we read that after the death of Belshazzar, Darius the Mede received the kingdom[1]. We are told that he was sixty-two years of age at the time[2], and that he was the son of Ahasuerus[3]. Moreover, he organized the kingdom into a hundred and twenty satrapies[4]. He appears to have been succeeded by Cyrus the Persian[5]. All of this would cause the simple reader to suppose that Darius the Mede occupied the throne of Babylon between the death of Belshazzar and the reign of Cyrus. Yet our extra-Biblical sources of information leave no room for such a reign. For it is known with certainty that the overthrower of the Neo-Babylonian empire was Cyrus, and that he succeeded Nabonidus in the control of the Babylonian dominions.

Even before the decipherment of the cuneiform records, the difficulty of reconciling the statements of the book of Daniel with those of the Greek writers was felt to be a real one, and various identifications with persons known from extra-Biblical sources were proposed. The commonest identification was with the fictitious Cyaxares II, but other proposals were also known. Syncellus[6] identified Darius with Astyages and both with Nabonidus. The identification of Darius with Nabonidus has appeared in more than one writer, indeed, including Grotius[7], Scaliger[8], and Ebrard[9], but no longer

---

[1] Dn vi. 1 (EV v. 31).   [2] Ibid.   [3] Dn ix. 1.   [4] Dn vi. 2 (EV vi. 1).
[5] Dn vi. 29 (EV vi. 28). The LXX states that he died and Cyrus took the kingdom, showing clearly that the translators understood Cyrus to be the successor of Darius.
[6] *Chronographia*, p. 209 (ed. Dindorf, 1829, p. 393).
[7] *Op. omn. theol.* i, p. 463.
[8] *De emend. temp.*, 1629 ed., pp. xxxiv, 580 ff.
[9] *Die Off. Joh. erk.*, p. 44 n., and *Allg. lit. Anzeiger*, ii, 1868, p. 267.

survives. That with Astyages, however, has not only found
a few succeeding writers to adopt it, but in our own day has^
secured reasoned presentation. Harenberg[1] believed that
Darius was none other than Neriglissar, and in this view
d'Envieu[2] concurred. These varying views in part depended
on the views held concerning Belshazzar, who was equally
unknown from secular sources, and who was variously held
to be Evil-merodach[3], Labashi-marduk[4], and Nabonidus[5].
But Belshazzar is now securely known to us as the son of
Nabonidus, in whose hands lay the actual administration of
the state for much of his father's reign. This alone makes
the equation of Darius the Mede with Neriglissar or with
Nabonidus impossible, and since neither of these views has
found an advocate since the beginning of the present century,

[1] *Aufkl. des B. Dan.* ii, pp. 172 f., 244 f., 354 ff.
[2] *Le Livre du Proph. Dan.* i, pp. 368, 426. Cf. von Gutschmid, *Neue Jahrb.
für Phil.* lxxxi, 1860, pp. 442 f.
[3] So, e.g., Cornelius a Lapide (*Comm. in quat. Proph. Maj.*, 1727 ed.,
p. 1307), Harenberg (pp. 172, 237 f., 348 f.), Hävernick (*Neue krit. Unters.*,
p. 73—cf. his earlier view, noted below), Oehler (*Litt. Anzeiger für christ.
Theol. u. Wiss.*, 1842, No. 50, cols. 398 f.), Niebuhr (*Gesch. Ass. u. Bab.*,
pp. 42, 91), Zündel (*Krit. Unters. über die Abf. des B. Dan.*, p. 33), Kliefoth
(*Das B. Dan. übers. u. erk.*, p. 154), Kranichfeld (*Das B. Dan. erk.*, pp. 37 ff.),
Füller (*Der Prof. Dan. erk.*, p. 124), Keil (*The Bk. of the Proph. Dan.*, ET,
pp. 174 ff.), Zöckler (*The Bk. of Dan.*, ET, pp. 30 f.), d'Envieu (*Le Livre du
Proph. Dan.* i, p. 367), Winckler (*Altor. Forsch.*, 2 Reihe, ii, p. 213), Stokmann (*Die Erleb. u. Ges. des Proph. Dan.*, p. 14). Ibn Yahya thought rather
of a son of Evil-merodach (*Paraph. Ios. Iach. in Dan.*, ed. l'Empereur, p. 89),
and so Pintus (*In div. vat. Dan. comm.*, p. 112 cd), Rollock (*In lib. Dan.
proph.*, p. 122), Willet (*Hexapla in Dan.*, p. 148), the Annotators of the Westminster Assembly (*Assembly's Ann.*, 2nd ed., on v. 31), and Quatremère
(*Mél. d'hist. et de phil. orient.*, pp. 388 ff.). This view is based on *a priori*
grounds, and rests on the assumption that Jer. xxvii. 7 must have been fulfilled. Willet identified the son of Evil-merodach with Nabonidus, and the
same idea seems to be implied by others who followed this view.
[4] So, e.g., Scaliger (*De emend. temp.*, 1629 ed., Appendix, p. 15), Grotius
(*Op. omn. theol.* i, p. 462), Venema (*Diss. ad vat. Dan. emb.*, pp. 76 ff.), Rosenmüller (*Schol. in Vet. Test.*, part x, p. 179), Ebrard (*Die Off. Joh. erk.*, p. 45 n,
and *Allg. lit. Anzeiger*, ii, 1868, p. 267).
[5] So, e.g., Josephus (*Ant.* x. xi. 2 (x. 231, ed. Niese, ii, p. 381)), Willet (see
note 3 above), Lowth (*Comm. upon the Proph.*, p. 364a), Dathe (*Proph. Maj.*,
p. 609), Hezel (*Die Bib. mit vollst.-erk. Anm.* vi, p. 736), Hengstenberg (*On
Gen. of Dan.*, ET, p. 39), Hävernick (*Comm. über das B. Dan.*, p. 172; cf.
his later view, noted above), Dereser (*Die Proph. Ezech. u. Dan.*, 2nd ed.,
p. 341).

they do not fall to be considered here. The equations with Astyages and Cyaxares, however, since they have found recent advocates, both require to be examined, and will be considered below.

It is not merely Greek writers who provide our extra-Biblical data to-day, but archaeology has unearthed much material from Babylon itself, which Assyriology has opened up to us. These new texts have determined the identification of Belshazzar, as has been said; and beyond that, they have brought to light material which is relevant for the discussion of the question of Darius, and in view of the unimpeachable reliability of the sources now open to us, the reconciliation of the book of Daniel with history in this matter is quite impossible. That is not to say the task has been abandoned, however. Lost causes are always sure of defenders, and the defenders of the historicity of the book of Daniel have but changed their ground to base their case on the identification of Darius with Gobryas or Cambyses.

Four views, therefore, fall to be examined, since they have all found advocates in the twentieth century—the identifications with Astyages, Cyaxares, Gobryas, and Cambyses.[1] Boutflower claims[2] that the cuneiform evidence definitely relegates all save Cambyses and Gobryas to the limbo of the past, while Alfrink[3] subjects both of these identifications to damaging criticism in his effort to revive the claim of Astyages. In fact, we shall find ample reason to conclude that all of these theories labour under insuperable difficulties.

---

[1] The curious extravagances of Horner, who sought to identify Darius the Mede, Gobryas, Cyaxares, and the Ahasuerus of Ezra iv. 6 (*Dan., Dar., Cyr.*, p. 107) may be noted, but do not call for refutation. It will be shown that Darius cannot be equated with Gobryas, or with Cyaxares, and the mere combination of impossibilities is not less impossible.

[2] *In and Around the Bk. of Dan.*, p. 144.

[3] *Darius Medus*, in *Biblica*, ix, 1928, pp. 316 ff.

I. DARIUS THE MEDE IS NOT CAMBYSES

THE identification of Darius with Cambyses was proposed by Winckler[1], and has been adopted by Riessler[2] and Boutflower[3]. The last named has presented the fullest argument for the theory, which is, indeed, in my judgement, the only effort to harmonize the book of Daniel here with known history that can claim the slightest plausibility. For a number of contract tablets have survived, dated in the first year after Cyrus' conquest of Babylon, but bearing the names of both Cambyses, king of Babylon, and Cyrus, king of lands[4]. From these it is clear that Cyrus associated his son Cambyses with himself on the throne, establishing him as subordinate king of Babylon, much as Asshurbanipal had earlier installed Shamash-shum-ukin. It is also clear that, for some unknown reason, ere a year had passed, the arrangement came to an end, and Cyrus himself became king of Babylon, his son's name no longer appearing, therefore, beside his on contracts[5].

Here, then, we have an intermediate king of Babylon, between the régime of Nabonidus and Belshazzar and that of Cyrus, attested beyond doubt. His occupation of the throne was a brief one, but long enough, it is claimed, to satisfy the conditions of the book of Daniel, which nowhere makes mention of more than the first year of Darius the Mede[6]. It is to be noted, however, that we find a reference

[1] *Altor. Forsch.*, 2 Reihe, ii, p. 214, and KAT, 3rd ed., p. 287 f.

[2] *Das B. Dan. erk.*, pp. xiv, 53.

[3] JTS xvii, 1915–16, pp. 48 ff., and *In and Around the Bk. of Dan.*, chaps. xiv, xv.

[4] Collected references to these tablets may be found in Boutflower, ibid., p. 148, and in Alfrink, loc. cit., p. 319. Cf. also Wright, *Dan. and its Critics*, pp. 223 ff. For the evidence that these texts belong to the beginning of Cyrus' control of the Bab. empire, and not to a later period, see Alfrink, loc. cit., p. 319 n., and Peiser, *Stud. zur orient. Altertumsk.*, in MVAG, 1897, Heft iv, pp. 1–12 (pp. 296–307 of volume).

[5] Cf. CAH iv, 1926, p. 14, and Boutflower, op. cit., p. 150.

[6] Cf. Rashi, who says that Darius the Mede reigned for one year (*Miḳ.*

in retrospect to the first year of Darius in Dn xi. 1, in a speech purporting to have been made in the reign of Cyrus. This would seem to imply that his reign had lasted for more than a year. Boutflower suggests[1] that it is the incident recorded in Dn vi which accounts for his removal from the throne. His ministers first made him their tool, after which he turned on them and cast them all to the lions, arousing such resentment in Babylon that Cyrus was forced to take personal control of the situation.

When we come to examine the Biblical material and our extra-Biblical sources in detail, however, we find many difficulties in the way of the harmonization this theory requires, and on several grounds we are compelled to pronounce it untenable.

(a) *Cambyses was certainly not sixty-two years of age at this time*

Boutflower does not, indeed, claim that he was, but prefers to emend his Biblical source to bring it into accord with probability. He therefore proposes to read 'twelve' years instead of 'sixty-two'. He argues[2] that if the numerals were expressed by letters, as we know they were in later times, the corruption would have been a simple one in the old characters. But he is able to adduce no evidence that numerals were expressed by letters in the old characters. He admits that the oldest known example of the usage amongst the Greeks dates from the reign of Ptolemy II, and amongst the Jews from an uncertain and much-disputed date. But he claims that the fact that on weights from Assyria the symbol ב is held to stand, most probably, for 'double' proves that letters were used for numerals in ancient Semitic circles[3]. It is unfortunate for his argument that in the very Assyrian

Ged. xii, p. 67b, or Latin tr. of Breithaupt, p. 760, or Gallé, *Dan. avec comm.*, p. 70).   [1] *Op. cit.*, p. 165.

[2] *Ibid.*, pp. 157 ff., 165 ff. Cf. JTS xvii, 1915–16, p. 54 and *Dadda-'Idri*, pp. 46 f.

[3] *In and Around the Bk. of Dan.*, p. 157, and JTS, loc. cit., p. 55.

Aramaic texts to which he appeals[1], the numerals are expressed by wholly different symbols, and the method there employed is the one that continued to be used in Phoenician inscriptions, and in all our known old Aramaic texts, whether from Babylonia, Egypt, Asia Minor, or Nabataea, until a relatively late date.

Other writers, indeed, have found peculiar significance in the number sixty-two. Thus pseudo-Saadia[2] and Rashi thought it was intended to signify that the future destroyer of the Neo-Babylonian empire was born at the very moment when Nebuchadnezzar was despoiling Jerusalem[3]. Similarly Jephet Ibn 'Ali[4], who notes that this is the only occasion on which we have the age of a Gentile king at his accession recorded in Scripture. The same explanation appears in the Annotations of the Westminster Assembly, where it is observed that Daniel tells the king's age 'to shew how God provided a remedy when he stroke'[5]. Winckler[6] thought the number bore some relation to the sixty-two weeks of Dn ix. 26, while Torrey[7] thought it was

---

[1] CIS ii. 1, 2, 3, 4, 5.

[2] The Commentary which stands in Rabbinical Bibles as Saadia's on Dan. is not really his. This was first established by Rapoport (*Bicure Haitim*, ix, 1828, pp. 34 f.). Mathews (*Comm. on Ezra and Neh. by Rabbi Saadiah*, pp. vii ff., esp. xx) dates it not later than the twelfth century, and possibly as early as Rashi. Similarly Porges (*Saadia's Comm. zu Dan.*, in MGWJ xxxiv, 1885, pp. 63–73), and Spiegel (*Saadia al-Fajjûmi's arab. Danielvers.*, pp. 13 f.), the latter of whom places it at latest A.D. 1187. Cf. too Malter, *Saadia Gaon*, pp. 325 f. (Saadia lived A.D. 892–942.)

[3] See Gallé, *Dan. avec comm.*, p. 61, Breithaupt, *Jarchi comm. in proph. maj.*, p. 757. The equation is made, indeed, by suppositions quite out of accord with history. It is assumed that Evil-merodach reigned twenty-three years, and Belshazzar two years, which, together with the thirty-seven remaining to Nebuchadnezzar after his eighth year, in which the attack on Jehoiakim took place, make up the required sixty-two.

[4] See Margoliouth, *Jephet Ibn 'Ali's Comm. on Dan.*, pp. 28 f.

[5] *Assembly's Ann.*, 2nd ed., on v. 31.

[6] *Altor. Forsch.*, 2 Reihe, iii, pp. 439 f. Elsewhere he suggests that the purpose of the number was to make the birth of Darius synchronize with the taking of Daniel captive—in agreement with the view of pseudo-Saadia and Rashi. See op. cit., 2 Reihe, ii, pp. 214 ff.

[7] TCA xv, p. 280, and *Ezra Studies*, p. 38. In the latter passage he argues that since Darius came to the throne at the age of sixty-two, his reign cannot have lasted much more than twenty years. By supposing it to have been

connected somehow with the seventy years of the Babylonian captivity prophesied by Jeremiah. There is as little
basis for any of these suggestions as for Boutflower's
emendation, which rests, as has been said, on no evidence
whatever, and is merely dictated by the theory it is intended
to accommodate.

(b) *The name of Cambyses was not Darius*

This consideration is more positively damaging to the
theory. Montgomery remarks[1] that Boutflower offers no
explanation of the equation of Darius the Mede with
Cambyses the Persian. That is not quite fair to Boutflower,
who certainly does offer an explanation[2], albeit an inade-
quate one. For he quotes Josephus[3] for the assertion that
Darius the Mede had another name amongst the Greeks,
and assumes this other name to have been Cambyses. To
this passage, indeed, all harmonizers appeal, and fill in the
alternative name according to their own theory. Most of
them make the further claim, which Boutflower also
presents[4], that Darius, Xerxes, and Artaxerxes were appellatives, rather than proper names. But whether or no they
were appellatives, they were the throne-names of various
Persian kings, whereas the throne-name of Cambyses was
certainly not Darius. But in the book of Daniel we are

twenty-one years, and adding to this the forty-nine years from the destruction of the Temple to the fall of Babylon, he secures the required seventy
years before the first year of Cyrus. On p. 136 n. he asks 'Is it not likely that
this statement (Dn vi. 1) was first made and adopted with the express purpose of providing *definitely* for the seventy years?' How it does so is the
reverse of clear. For the crucial figure 21, which Torrey is forced to assume,
can hardly be said to be *definitely* provided for in a statement that Darius was
sixty-two when he ascended the throne. We are offered no evidence to show
that one who ascended the throne at the age of sixty-two *must* die at the age
of eighty-three.   [1] *Comm. on Dan.*, p. 64.
   [2] JTS xvii, 1915–16, pp. 52 f., and *In and Around the Bk. of Dan.*,
pp. 152 ff.
   [3] *Ant.* x. xi. 4 (x. 248, ed. Niese, ii, p. 384). Josephus' statement is
inspired, of course, by the same harmonistic purpose as the modern arguments with which we are dealing. He found no place in his secular sources
for the Darius the Mede of his Biblical source, and so he resorted to this
vague statement to mask the difficulty.   [4] *Op. cit.*, p. 154.

presented with a king whose throne-name is Darius, and this is the name employed in defining a date. Here is a contradiction of which we are offered no explanation, though it would surely be passing strange for the monarch's Prime Minister to be unaware of the contemporary usage of the king's name for dating events. For the essential issue is not whether Cambyses may have had two names, but whether he had two throne-names, and on that the answer is in no doubt.

(c) *Cambyses was not a Mede*

Boutflower here argues[1] that Cambyses may be said to have been 'of the seed of the Medes' since his mother was the daughter of Astyages, king of the Medes. For this statement he relies on the authority of Ctesias[2], who states that Cyrus married Amytis, daughter of Astyages, and that Cambyses was the fruit of that marriage. But according to Herodotus[3], the mother of Cambyses was Cassandane, daughter of Pharnaspes, while both Herodotus and Xenophon say[4] that the mother, not the wife, of Cyrus was the daughter of Astyages, the latter adding[5] the further information that Cyrus married his cousin, the daughter of his uncle Cyaxares II. Herodotus records[6] a further tradition, which, however, he rejects, according to which the mother of Cambyses was Nitêtis, the daughter of Apries of Egypt, and this same tradition is found in Dinon[7] and Polyaenus[8]. It is manifest, therefore, that the traditions recorded by the Greek writers are so diverse, that we can hardly select one as an authority, on its unconfirmed word.

---

[1] JTS xvii, 1915-16, pp. 51 f., and *In and Around the Bk. of Dan.*, pp. 152 f.
[2] See Müller, *Ctes. Cn. Frag.*, pp. 46, 48 (Frag. 29, 2. 10).
[3] *Hist.* ii. 1, iii. 2 (Loeb ed., i, p. 274, ii, p. 4).
[4] Herodotus, *Hist.* i. 107 f. (Loeb ed., i, p. 138); Xenophon, *Cyrop.* I. ii. 1 (Loeb ed., i, pp. 8 f.).   [5] *Cyrop.* VIII. v. 19 (Loeb ed., ii, p. 402).
[6] *Hist.* iii. 2 (Loeb ed., ii, p. 4).
[7] *Apud* Athenaeus, xiii, p. 560 E (see Müller, FHG ii, p. 91 b). Athenaeus also records a statement taken from Ctesias, that Nitêtis was sent, not to Cyrus, but to Cambyses. See xiii, p. 560 D (in Müller, *Ctes. Cn. Frag.*, p. 63).
[8] *Strategemata*, viii. 29 (ed. Wölfflin-Melber, p. 394).

Nor, indeed, were the case far advanced even if we could. For if the mother of Cambyses were a Mede, that would hardly make her son a Mede. And since the book of Daniel explicitly refers to Cyrus as 'the Persian'[1], we should need to have some clear proof that descent was reckoned through the female line before we could understand any reference to the son of Cyrus as 'the Mede'. The contrast between Cyrus the Persian and Darius the Mede is so definite that no one could possibly suppose the author to have known that they were father and son.

Boutflower further suggests[2] that the title Darius the Mede would be likely to gratify the Medes and to conciliate the Babylonians. But surely in that case it would have been more fitting to have used the title in the Babylonian texts, where, instead of the Median descent of Cambyses being mentioned, his relationship to Cyrus is alone noted.

(d) *Cambyses was not the son of Ahasuerus*

Josephus notes that Darius the Mede was the son of Astyages, and this Boutflower holds to approach very nearly to his claim that Astyages was the maternal grandfather of Cambyses. But while it is undoubted that Hebrew usage often employed 'son' for 'son's son', it is not established that 'son' might stand for 'daughter's son', where descent was not reckoned through the female[3].

Nor can Astyages be equated with Ahasuerus. Boutflower does not, indeed, attempt to make this equation, but argues[4] on the basis of Tobit xiv. 15 that the person intended is Cyaxares, the destroyer of Nineveh, and the father, therefore, of Astyages. But we need better authority than the Tobit passage can supply to assure us that Cyaxares was also called Ahasuerus—for Boutflower admits that the names cannot be identified[5]—and we need some secure

---

[1] Dn vi. 29 (EV vi. 28).   [2] *In and Around the Bk. of Dan.*, p. 152.
[3] I have discussed this point of Hebrew usage in JTS xxxii, 1930–1, pp. 20 f.   [4] Op. cit., p. 155.
[5] Wilson, however, attempts to identify them, suggesting that they are

parallels for the use of the word 'son' to mean 'son's daughter's son' before we can accept that sense here.

It would surely be strange that the person whom the contemporary records name as the son of Cyrus should also be called, in Josephus, the son of Astyages, and yet again, in Daniel, the son of Ahasuerus, to be identified with a third person, Cyaxares. And it would be a phenomenon for which we are offered no example and no explanation, if a monarch's first officer of state should attach to him a name, a nationality, and a paternity not only different from those assigned to him in the contemporary records, but without any recognizable relationship to them. In a rational world it is impossible to believe that *Cambyses*, the son of *Cyrus the Persian*, could be called by a well-informed contemporary *Darius the Mede*, the son of *Ahasuerus*[1].

Median and Persian forms of the same name (*Studies in the Bk. of Dan.*, p. 235. So, too, Stokmann (*Die Erleb. u. Ges. des Proph. Dan.*, p. 17). The same identification was proposed long ago by Willet (*Hex. in Dan.*, pp. 164, 265). Boutflower, however, rightly recognizes that the names cannot be equated. He says: 'It is, however, a mistake to seek to identify the name Cyaxares with the name Ahasuerus. Cyaxares is in the Old Persian Uvakhshatara; while Ahasuerus, Hebrew Achashverosh, appears in Old Persian as Khshayârsha, in Greek as Xerxes' (op. cit., p. 155).

[1] Winckler avoids the necessity for reconciling the paternity of Cambyses with that ascribed to Darius the Mede by the expedient of eliminating the name Ahasuerus from the text of Daniel as a gloss. He says: 'Wenn ix. 1 Darius als sohn von Ahasver bezeichnet wird, so ist das ein späterer zusatz, der sich sehr einfach erklärt' (*Altor. Forsch.*, 2 Reihe, ii, p. 214 n.). But textual emendation in the interest of a theory, and entirely without evidence, is never justified, and there is no reason whatever to suspect the originality of the text here.

II. DARIUS THE MEDE IS NOT GOBRYAS[1]

THIS identification is the favourite amongst modern writers, being adopted by Babelon,[2] Trochon,[3] Delitzsch,[4] Deane,[5] Pinches,[6] de Moor,[7] Vigouroux,[8] Hommel,[9] Wright,[10] J. D. Wilson,[11] R. D. Wilson,[12] Albright,[13] Stokmann,[14] Thilo,[15] and Möller[16]. That it has secured so many followers is evidence that it has, at any rate superficially, something to be said for it, but closer examination soon shows that it cannot be maintained[17].

The figure of Gobryas stands out in the light of modern research with considerable fullness. For he is known to us, not alone from the Greek writers, Herodotus and Xenophon, but also under the name Gubaru or Ugbaru, from many cuneiform texts[18]. According to Xenophon[19] he was an Assyrian prince, advanced in years, who revolted to Cyrus, with the district he governed, on account of the wanton

[1] A precursor of this view may be found in Des-Vignoles (*Chron. de l'hist. sainte*, ii, pp. 517 ff.), where it is held that Darius was a Median prince whom Cyrus rewarded for his services by making him king of Babylon, but without any attempt to identify him with any known person. Similarly Lenormant (*La Divination . . . chez les Chald.*, p. 181) and Rohling (*Das B. des Proph. Dan. übers. u. erk.*, p. 174).

[2] *Annales de phil. chr.*, New Series, iv, 1881, pp. 680 f.

[3] *Dan.*, p. 26.   [4] *Calw. Bibellex.*, 1885 ed., pp. 137 f.

[5] *Dan.: His Life and Times*, p. 100.

[6] Smith's *Dict. of Bible*, 2nd ed., I. i, p. 716, and Hastings's DB i, p. 559a.

[7] *Muséon*, xv, 1896, pp. 233 ff.

[8] *Dict. de la Bible*, ii, cols. 1298 f., and *La Sainte Bible polygl.* vi, p. 319.

[9] *Theol. Literaturbl.* xxiii, 1902, col. 147.

[10] *Dan. and his Proph.*, pp. 135 ff.

[11] *The New Schaff-Herz. Encyc.* iii, p. 350.

[12] *Studies in Bk. of Dan.*, chaps. vii–xii, and *Princeton Theol. Rev.* xx, 1922, pp. 177–211.   [13] JBL xl, 1921, p. 112 note.

[14] *Die Erleb. u. Ges. des Proph. Dan.*, pp. 15 ff.

[15] *Die Chron. des Danielb.*, pp. 39 ff.   [16] *Einl. in d. AT*, p. 254.

[17] For a full statement of this view, and criticism thereof, see Alfrink, in *Biblica*, ix, 1928, pp. 325–8.

[18] For the classic collection of all the material relating to Gobryas, see Schwenzner, *Gobryas*, in *Klio*, xviii, 1922, pp. 41–58, 226–52. Cf. also Lehmann-Haupt, *Gob. u. Bels. bei Xen.*, in *Klio*, ii, 1902, pp. 341–5.

[19] *Cyrop.* iv. vi. 1–7 (Loeb ed., i, pp. 390 ff.).

murder of his son by the king of Assyria (i.e. Babylonia). √
One of the cuneiform texts that has been deciphered has
been held to assert that he held high office under Nebuchadnezzar,[1] but the date of the text has been disputed[2]. Gubaru
figures in the Nabonidus Chronicle, where we learn that it
was he who pressed on in advance of Cyrus, and who η
occupied the city of Babylon,[3] while in Xenophon's legen-
dary account of the capture of the city, the final attack is
said to have been made by Gobryas and Gadatas[4]. The
Nabonidus Chronicle further informs us that Gubaru, who
was the governor of Gutium, appointed governors in ⸢
Babylon[5]. He also figures in another obscure event that
took place shortly after Cyrus entered the city of Babylon.
Unfortunately the tablet is injured, so that while some have
read it to state that on the eleventh of Marchesvan Gubaru
led an assault and slew the king's son (i.e. Belshazzar)[6],
others have found a statement that on that date Gubaru
died, and on a lost date the king's wife died[7]. It is very

---

[1] Cf. Scheil, in RAss xi, 1914, pp. 166–9; Langdon, in ET xxx, 1918–19, p.
462; Schwenzner, loc. cit., pp. 41 f., 250 ff. So, too, King, *Hist. of Bab.*, p. 281.

[2] Cf. Clay, in JAOS xli, 1921, pp. 466 f., where the text is assigned to the
reign of Cyrus.

[3] Col. iii, lines 15 f. (ed. Sidney Smith, *Bab. Hist. Texts*, pp. 113, 117).

[4] *Cyrop.* vii. v. 24 ff. (Loeb ed., ii, pp. 270 ff.).

[5] Col. iii, lines 15, 20 (ed. Sidney Smith, loc. cit.). In line 20 Gubaru
stands, and elsewhere in the text Ugbaru. Sidney Smith expresses doubt as
to whether these refer to the same person or to two different persons (ibid.,
p. 121 f.).

[6] So Hagen (in Delitzsch and Haupt's *Beitr. zur Ass.* ii, 1894, pp. 223,
247), and Delitzsch (ibid., p. 256), Lehmann-Haupt (*Klio*, ii, 1902, p. 342),
Prášek (*Gesch. der Med. u. Pers.* i, p. 230), Schwenzner (loc. cit., p. 42). This
reading is given in Driver's *Dan.*, p. xxx, where a note is appended stating
that this reading is considered the most probable by those who had most
carefully examined the tablet. Cf., too, Boutflower, op. cit., p. 129, and Wilson,
Studies in Bk. of Dan., p. 134. Pinches, who at first read the text as recording
the death of the king, i.e. Nabonidus (see TSBA vii, 1880, p. 167; and cf.
Hommel, *Gesch. Bab. u. Ass.*, p. 786, and Tiele, *Bab.-Ass. Gesch.* ii, p. 482)
later found it to refer to the death of the king's son, with the foregoing
scholars (cf. Smith's *Dict. of Bible*, 2nd ed. i. i, p. 390, and DB i, p. 559a;
also ET xxviii, 1916–17, p. 184).

[7] So Sidney Smith (*Bab. Hist. Texts*, p. 118). Scheil (RB ii, 1892, p. 253)
and Halévy (RS ii, 1894, p. 189) had earlier found the death of Gobyras here,
while Schrader (KB iii. ii, 1890, pp. 134 f.) had read it to record the death of

doubtful, however, whether this last reading can be sound, for there are texts which mention a Gubaru, who was governor of Babylon and Beyond the River, in the fourth year of Cyrus, in the accession year of Cambyses, and in the fourth year of Cambyses[1]. An admittedly uncertain reading is hardly sufficient evidence for the view that a second Gubaru appeared on the scene so soon after the first, and in the same office. Further, Herodotus mentions a Gobryas who was one of the principal counsellors of Darius Hystaspis on his assumption of the throne[2], and in the Behistun inscription we find a Gubaru figures[3].

It is claimed that here we have one who well fits the statements in the book of Daniel. The advanced years of Gobryas accord excellently with the sixty-two years of the book of Daniel; the appointment of governors in Babylon recalls the appointment of the one hundred and twenty satraps recorded in the book of Daniel; and the fact that Gubaru took the city and became its governor can without difficulty be found to agree with the statement that Darius the Mede 'received the kingdom'.

But despite these accordances, the identification founders on a number of difficulties, and its initial plausibility speedily vanishes when its claims are examined.

(a) *There is no evidence that Gobryas was called Darius*

Just as in the case of Cambyses, so here we find that the records, whether Greek or cuneiform, never mention anything that can be connected with the name Darius, but uniformly employ Gobryas or Gubaru (Ugbaru). Stokmann supposes[4] that when Cyrus installed him as vice-king

the king's wife. Dougherty (*Nab. and Belsh.*, p. 174), while acknowledging that the text is too uncertain for decisive conclusions, inclines to the view that the death of the king's wife is recorded.

[1] Cf. Schwenzner, loc. cit., pp. 239 ff., Montgomery, *Comm. on Dan.*, p. 64 n., and Alfrink, *Biblica*, ix, 1928, p. 326.

[2] *Hist.* iii. 70 ff. (Loeb ed., ii, pp. 90 ff.).

[3] §§ 68, 71. Cf. Weissbach, *Die Keilinsch. der Achäm.*, pp. 70 ff., and King and Thompson, *The Sculpt. and Inscr. of Darius*, pp. 76, 79.

[4] *Die Erleb. u. Ges. des Proph. Dan.*, p. 17. Similarly R. D. Wilson (*Studies*

in Babylon, he gave him the official honorific title of Darius. This assumption is not merely without foundation, but is demonstrably false. For in that case he would have been referred to in the cuneiform texts by this title.

Hommel adopts bold measures in dealing with the difficulty. He emends the text[1] of the book of Daniel to eliminate the name Darius in favour of Gobryas, supposing that it originally read גורוש, i.e. Guwaruwaš, or Gubaruwaš, but that this was corrupted to דריוש. But this wholly unsupported conjecture is not evidence, and even if it were accepted, it would still leave other difficulties unresolved.

(b) *There is no evidence that Gobryas was the son of Ahasuerus*

The Gobryas of the Behistun inscription is stated to be the son of Mardonia, a Persian[2]. If, then, the Gobryas of all the sources we have above referred to is one and the same person, his paternity is definitely established, and is not that ascribed to Darius the Mede. But it has been noted above that some scholars think that Gubaru died soon after the capture of Babylon, and this would involve the differentiation of the person mentioned on the Behistun inscription from the one named in the Nabonidus Chronicle. In that case we have no information whatever as to the name of the latter's father. But on the other hand, the period of his possible 'reign' in Babylon shrinks to vanishing point. Even if Gubaru did not die so soon after the capture of Babylon, it must be recognized to be possible that he is not to be identified with his namesake who appears in the Behistun inscription, and that the name of the father of the captor of Babylon is unrecorded in secular texts. Stokmann therefore builds on conjecture. He identifies Ahasuerus

---

in Bk. of Dan., p. 138, 234) thinks Gobryas may have assumed the regnal name of Darius.

[1] *Theol. Literaturbl.* xxiii, 1902, col. 147.

[2] § 68. See Weissbach, op. cit., pp. 70 f., King and Thompson, op. cit., p. 76.

with Cyaxares, and then maintains that Darius the Mede was the brother of Astyages, the last Median king[1]. A double improbability attaches to this conjecture. The equation of the names cannot be maintained, and if it were really the case that Gobryas was of such exalted rank, and related to the wife or mother of Cyrus, it would be very surprising that our records should contain no hint of it.

(c) There is no evidence that Gobryas was a Mede

Xenophon tells us that the Gobryas of his narrative was an Assyrian[2], by which we should probably understand a Babylonian. Herodotus, on the contrary, represents his Gobryas as a Persian[3], and makes it clear that he is not using the term to mean indifferently a Mede or a Persian, since he represents Gobryas as being indignant that 'we Persians' should be under the rule of the Mede, pseudo-Smerdis[4]. Moreover, the Gobryas of the Behistun inscription is a Persian[5]. Of a Median Gobryas there is no trace anywhere.

It is true that if the Gobryas of all our texts is the same person, either Xenophon or Herodotus must be inaccurate. And we should then have no difficulty in deciding between them, since the Behistun text would settle the issue. If, however, the Gobryas who took Babylon is a different person from the Gobryas of the Behistun inscription, we have only the conflicting testimony of Herodotus and Xenophon for the nationality of the former. But this would hardly justify us in setting aside the statements of both in favour of a view which rests on nothing more substantial than the requirements of a theory. Nor can we suppose that the identification of Darius the Mede with Gobryas is in any way supported by texts which are at direct variance with the Biblical statements.

---

[1] Op. cit., p. 17. Similarly Wilson, op. cit., p. 235.
[2] Cyrop. IV. vi. 1, 2 (Loeb ed., i, pp. 390 ff.).
[3] Hist. iii. 70 (Loeb ed., ii, p. 92).
[4] Ibid. iii. 73 (Loeb ed., ii, p. 96).   [5] Loc. cit.

(d) *There is no evidence that Gobryas bore the title of king*

This is the insuperable difficulty with which the theory has to contend, compared with which the previous ones are slight. For we read in Dn ix. 1 that Darius the Mede was 'made king over the realm of the Chaldaeans'. This is held to mean that he was made a subordinate king under the supreme authority of Cyrus. But we have already seen that in the first year of Cyrus, Cambyses occupied the position of subordinate king of Babylon. There is therefore no room for Gobryas in that position[1]. For neither before nor during the brief administration of Cambyses can Gobryas be fitted in.

(i) *Gobryas was not king of Babylon before Cambyses*[2].

Cambyses occupied the Babylonian throne in the first full year of Cyrus, and if the period of the authority of Gobryas is to be fitted in before this, he would be left with the few remaining months of the accession year of Cyrus as the whole expanse of his alleged reign. Since we possess a Babylonian contract tablet of the tenth of Marchesvan of that year, dated still by the reign of Nabonidus[3], this hypothetical reign of Gobryas would be limited to a period not exceeding four months.[4] And if Gobryas really died on the eleventh of Marchesvan, as some hold, the period of his possible rule would shrink to a maximum of a single day.

And not only so. For even though he had occupied the throne for four months of the accession year of Cyrus, it

---

[1] Cf. Dougherty, *Nab. and Belsh.*, p. 199: 'Gobryas . . . never occupied a regal position, although he exercised a very high administrative power'. Dougherty half favours the identification of Darius with Cambyses, but finally concludes that his identity is still an enigma.

[2] So Albright, JBL xl, 1921, p. 112 note.

[3] See KB iv, 1896, pp. 254 f. (No. lviii).

[4] Wilson (*Studies in Bk. of Dan.*, p. 135) attributes to him a reign of four months. He holds that he ruled, under Cyrus, over as much of the empire as was once under the Bab. and Ass. kings (ibid., p. 234). More recently, however, he says (*Princeton Theol. Rev.* xxii, 1924, p. 379): 'Gubaru, according to the cylinder, was made governor (in Aramaic *malka* 'king') of the city by Cyrus, a position which he seems to have held for at least twelve years.'

would still have been improper to date events by his first year[1]. They might, however, have been dated by his accession year. Yet this is precisely what we do not find in the cuneiform texts. In the accession year of Cyrus, documents are dated by the reign of Cyrus alone; in his first year the names of Cambyses and Cyrus both appear. But if Gobryas had held the position in the accession-year which Cambyses held in the following year, his name should have appeared beside that of Cyrus on the contract tablets, just as that of Cambyses does in the following year. For the name of the king of Babylon not to appear in the dating of Babylonian contracts would be an anomaly requiring more elucidation than has yet been offered.

(ii) *Gobryas was not king of Babylonia while Cambyses was king of Babylon.* Keil argued[2] that Darius the Mede must have reigned for two years, since by his calculations the Babylonian kingdom collapsed sixty-eight years after the commencement of the Exile, and according to 2 Chron. xxxvi. 22 f., and Ezra, i. 1, the seventy years of the Exile were completed in the first year of Cyrus. Stokmann's argument is the same, but his calculations different, and hence he assumes for Darius a reign of four years[3]. In this case he must be fitted in somewhere beside Cyrus and Cambyses, and Babylon must be assumed to have had a galaxy of sovereigns at the time.

Clearly Darius was not a subordinate of Cambyses, or he could not have made the decree with which he is credited in the book of Daniel. Equally clearly he was not joint

---

[1] As in Dn ix. 1, xi. 1. The Hebrew system of reckoning seems to have counted the accession year as the first year, however, so that Dn ix. 1 might be accounted for in this way, if it be assumed that it was actually written down during the brief four months' reign. But this would not account for xi. 1. For it would be a strange anomaly to refer in retrospect to the first year of a reign which lasted for but four months.

[2] *Bk. of Dan.,* ET, pp. 198 f. Similarly Alfrink, in *Biblica,* ix, 1928, pp. 338 f.

[3] *Op. cit.,* p. 16. Sulpicius Severus assigned an even more generous allowance of eighteen years to Darius (*Hist. Sac.* II. vii, ix, ed. Migne, cols. 132 f., or ed. Halm, pp. 62, 64; ET, pp. 100 f.).

under-king of Babylon, beside Cambyses. For not only would the same consideration debar that view, but the non-mention of his name on the contract tablets also. For joint kings would have had the same mention there. Equally certainly he was not over Cambyses, exercising the rule over the province of Babylonia, while Cambyses ruled over the city of Babylon. For again he would not have been ignored in the cuneiform texts, but would have been associated with Cyrus and Cambyses in them.

Every possible variety of the theory[1] must stumble over the fact that whereas in the book of Daniel events are dated by the reign of Darius the Mede, in the contemporary texts events are nowhere dated by the years of any one who can be equated with Gobryas, and since there are many texts from the years in which the reign of Darius the Mede is placed, we have a vital disagreement with contemporary usage, of which no explanation is even attempted.

(e) *That Gobryas was governor of Babylon is sufficiently attested, but wholly irrelevant to the Biblical narrative*

Wilson claims[2] that the Aramaic word *malka* may render the Akkadian *paḫatu*. The Nabonidus Chronicle tells us that 'Gubaru, his governor, appointed governors', where the word *paḫatu* stands[3]. Further, it has already been said that there are texts mentioning a Gubaru who was *paḫatu* of Babylon and beyond the River at various points in the reigns of Cyrus and Cambyses. If then *paḫatu* may be rendered by *malka*, have we not the clearest evidence that Gubaru could be referred to in an Aramaic text as *malka* of Babylon and Beyond the River?

---

[1] De Moor (*Muséon*, xv, 1896, p. 239 n.) held that Gobryas became king of Chaldaea *after* Cambyses' temporary occupation of the throne. This view accords neither with our Biblical nor with our extra-Biblical sources. For in the book of Daniel the reign of Darius is represented as the direct consequence of the fall of Belshazzar, while had he succeeded Cambyses in the same position, he would have had the same mention in the contract tablets.

[2] *Studies in Bk. of Dan.*, p. 134, and *Princeton Theol. Rev.* xx, 1922, p. 186.

[3] Col. iii, line 20 (see Sidney Smith, *Bab. Hist. Texts*, pp. 113, 118).

It is unfortunate for this argument that we find the word פֶּחָה, the exact equivalent of *paḥatu*, in Dn iii. 2, 3, 27, vi. 8, and there is therefore no reason whatever why the same word should not have been used of Darius, if the author had known that he was really *paḥatu*, and not king. To this Wilson replies that פֶּחָה is a loan-word, and not genuine Aramaic, and hence, while the author might have used it if he had chosen, he could equally use the best Aramaic equivalent[1].

But it is clear that, while Wilson admits that Darius was not really king, the author of the book of Daniel conceived Darius as one who was. For he dates events by the years of his reign, and represents him as exercising sovereign prerogatives, and issuing royal edicts. Wilson discounts the absence of any cuneiform texts dated by his years with the remark that the same argument would be equally valid against the reign of Gobryas.[2] But this neatly confuses the issue by implying that Gobryas was king, despite the admission already made that he was not—a confusion Wilson repeats when he explains the identification of Gobryas and Darius by the remark that many kings in ancient and modern times had two names[3]. The fundamental difficulty is to equate a Gobryas who was certainly a governor, but not a king, with a Darius who is certainly portrayed as a king, and not a mere governor. For if Darius were of lesser rank than king, how could he venture to issue a decree that for thirty days no one might ask any petition of god or man, save of himself? Whoever makes such a decree claims to be, not less than a king, but more.

Moreover, in the first year of the governorship of Gobryas, Cambyses was king of Babylon, and Gobryas must therefore have been the subordinate of a subordinate king. See, then, to what narrow proportions the figure of Daniel himself shrinks. For instead of being the Prime Minister of an

[1] *Princeton Theol. Rev.*, loc. cit., pp. 186 ff.
[2] *Studies in Bk. of Dan.*, p. 137.
[3] Ibid., p. 138.

imperial monarch, as the simple reader would suppose, Wilson reduces him to the subordinate of the subordinate of a subordinate[1]. Is the historical accuracy of the book of Daniel really saved by a theory that the author expressed himself in a way that could only give to his readers an utterly false idea of the events of his own time? If Daniel really lived in the sixth century B.C., and really knew that Cyrus was 'king of lands', and Cambyses sub-king of Babylon, and Gobryas his governor, and he himself Gobryas' appointee and chief subordinate, and if he really wrote the words of Dn vi. 2–4 (EV vi. 1–3) to define his position, he could only be pronounced a hollow braggart, and instead of the historicity of the chapter being at issue, it would be the veracity of the author. The theory which endeavours to reconcile the book of Daniel with history by fathering on Daniel such disregard of the facts he is presumed to have known resolves itself into a serious attack on the character of Daniel.

A further consideration tells against this theory. For how many years was Gobryas the governor of Babylon? If he was not the person who died on the eleventh of Marchesvan in the accession year of Cyrus—and if he was that person

---

[1] Ibid., p. 234, where Wilson says that Darius-Gobryas was under Cyrus, and probably under Cambyses. Of course, if the view be taken, as apparently by Wilson on p. 135, that Darius was succeeded by Cambyses at the end of the accession year of Cyrus, their tenure of office would not be simultaneous. But it has already been said that the Biblical text, by its reference to the first year of Darius, in retrospect, implies a longer rule for Darius, while the cuneiform texts present us with Gobryas in the character of Governor after the accession year of Cyrus. In his latest article on the subject, Wilson appears to have some doubt as to the identification of Darius with Gobryas. but plunges into yet greater improbabilities. He says (*Princeton Theol. Rev.* xxii, 1924, p. 383): 'Most probably he (i.e. Darius the Mede) was either the same as Gubaru, to whom Cyrus entrusted the Government of Babylon immediately after its capture, or a greater sub-king who ruled over Media as well as Assyria and Babylonia and Chaldea, or a subordinate of Gubaru'. The last alternative would reduce Daniel to the subordinate of a subordinate of Gubaru, who was himself the subordinate of Cambyses, the king of Babylon, who was the subordinate of Cyrus. This is to make Daniel a minor Civil Service clerk, in the completest contradiction of the Biblical account, whose historicity Wilson is defending!

we have seen that his governorship would vanish altogether —there is no reason to suppose that he was not the person who continued to be governor on into the reign of Cambyses. How then can the reign of Cyrus be placed after his governorship in the way we find in the book of Daniel? For indeed the first year of his governorship would coincide with the first year of the reign of Cyrus. Yet no reader of the book of Daniel could suppose such a thing. In a vision which is located in the third year of Cyrus, one comes to Daniel and says: 'As for me, in the first year of Darius the Mede, I stood up to strengthen and confirm him'[1]—as though the reign of Darius the Mede were a different period of reckoning from the already mentioned reign of Cyrus.

This theory, then, labours under the threefold difficulty that it would be unusual to date events by the years of one of lower rank than king, and out of harmony with the known contemporary usage; that it accords to Daniel but a shadow of the authority he appears to claim, and makes the decree of Darius an impossible piece of presumption; and that it makes the reign of Cyrus to synchronize with but a portion of the governorship of Darius, and reduces the chronology of the book of Daniel to a chaotic jumble. Nor can it produce the slightest evidence to show that Gobryas bore the name Darius, or belonged to the race ascribed to him, or was the son of the parent ascribed to him.

[1] Dn xi. 1.

III. DARIUS THE MEDE IS NOT ASTYAGES

THIS view, which was anciently held by Syncellus[1], has never commanded any wide support. It was maintained in the eleventh century, however, by Cedrenus[2], and in the seventeenth by Lightfoot[3] and Marsham[4], and in more modern times it has been held by Winer[5], Niebuhr[6], Westcott[7], and Unger[8]. Quite recently it has been revived by Alfrink in the course of the very valuable paper to which reference has already been made several times[9].

Herodotus tells us that Astyages was the last of the Median kings[10]. He was without male issue[11], but gave his daughter Mandane in marriage to a Persian, Cambyses, and Cyrus was born of this union[12]. Fearing lest Cyrus should rob him of his throne, Astyages gave orders for the murder of the lad. The order was not carried out, however, and Cyrus grew to manhood, when he led the Persians in revolt against the Medes, and displaced Astyages from the throne. But although Astyages fell into his hands,

---

[1] *Chron.*, p. 231 C D (ed. Dindorf, i, pp. 438 ff.). Cf., too, Jerome on Dn v. 1, vi. 1 (ed. Migne, cols. 518, 525), where it is said that Darius the Mede is the uncle of Cyrus, whom some Greek writers identify with Astyages, and some with the son of Astyages. Petrus Comestor (*Hist. Lib. Dan.*, ed. Migne, col. 1454) after naming Darius, the son of Ahasuerus, adds *qui et Astyages dictus est*, where it is not certain whether Astyages is equated with the father or the son. Nikel (*Einl. in das AT*, p. 204) is content to assume, without closer identification, that Darius was an elder relative of Cyrus, who was made vice-king of Babylon.

[2] Migne, PG cxxi, cols. 241, 284.

[3] *Works*, i, p. 135.   [4] *Can. Chron.*, p. 605.

[5] *Bib. Realw.*, 3rd ed., i, p. 250. Cf. 2nd ed., i, p. 292, where Winer had said Darius is *not* Astyages, but Cyaxares.

[6] *Gesch. Ass. u. Bab.*, pp. 45, 92 f.

[7] Smith's *Dict. of Bib.*, 1st ed., i, pp. 298 f.

[8] *Abhand. der phil.-phil. Cl. der kön.-bay. Ak. der Wiss.* xvi, 1882, pp. 262–7.

[9] *Biblica*, ix, 1928, pp. 328 ff.

[10] *Hist.* i. 109 (Loeb ed., i, p. 140). So, too, Eusebius, *Chron.* I. xv. 7 (ed. Migne, col. 141; ed. Schoene, i, col. 67; ed. Mai, p. 47).

[11] Herodotus, loc. cit. So, also, Justin, *Hist. Phil.* I. iv. 7 (ed. Gronovius, i, p. 51).

[12] Herodotus, *Hist.* i. 108 (Loeb ed., i, p. 138). So Justin, loc. cit.

he did him no injury, but maintained him at his court for the rest of his life[1].

Xenophon agrees that Cyrus was the son of Cambyses and Mandane, the daughter of Astyages[2], but relates that Astyages died when Cyrus had grown up, being succeeded on the throne of Media by Cyaxares, the uncle of Cyrus[3]. The figure of this Cyaxares will come before us in the following section, and does not further concern us here.

Ctesias gives a very different account. According to the fragments of his story that have reached us through Nicolaus of Damascus and Photius, Cyrus was in no way related to Astyages, but was the son of a bandit[4] and a girl who tended goats. He became a menial in the palace of Astyages, but rapidly rose to distinction. He now plotted against his royal master, who, too late, learned of the plot, after Cyrus had left to head the insurrection. Astyages took the field against the rebels, and in the first encounter killed the father of Cyrus. In a second battle at Pasargadae, however, he was less fortunate, and soon found himself deserted and alone[5]. He therefore fled to Ecbatana, where his daughter Amytis and her husband concealed him, until Cyrus ordered them and their children to be tortured[6]. Astyages, being now given up, was cruelly treated for a time, but afterwards given the government of a mountain tribe[7], while Cyrus married Amytis, after putting her husband to death[8]. Later, however, Astyages perished through the treachery of Oebares, the companion of Cyrus[9].

From these accounts our knowledge of Astyages is

---

[1] Herodotus, *Hist.* i. 125–30 (Loeb ed., i, pp. 162–70).
[2] *Cyrop.* I. ii. 1 (Loeb ed., i, pp. 8 ff.).
[3] Ibid. I. v. 2 (Loeb ed., i, p. 76).
[4] The bandit is named Atradates. The story is not wholly unconnected with that of Herodotus, which tells that Cyrus was brought up in the home of a herdsman named Mitradates (*Hist.* i. 110, Loeb ed., i, p. 142).
[5] See Müller, FHG iii, pp. 397 ff. (Frag. 66).
[6] See Müller, *Ctes. Cn. Frag.*, p. 45 (Frag. 29, 2).
[7] Ibid. Cf. Justin, *Hist. Phil.* I. vi. 16 (ed. Gronovius, i, p. 55).
[8] See Müller, *Ctes. Cn. Frag.*, p. 46.   [9] Ibid. (Frag. 29, 5.)

neither considerable nor sure. They all agree in representing Cyrus as having spent part of his early life at the court of Astyages, whether related to him or not. But whereas Xenophon brings Astyages to a peaceful end, and postpones the transfer of the Median kingdom to the control of Cyrus until the following reign, the others agree that Cyrus led a successful revolt against Astyages, ending in his capture. They further agree that Cyrus spared the life of Astyages, but differ as to his subsequent life.

The cuneiform sources tell us nothing of the relationship of Cyrus to Astyages, or as to the youth of Cyrus having been spent at the Median court[1]. But they do tell us that Astyages 'marched against Cyrus, king of Anshan . . . and Ishtumegu's (i.e. Astyages') army mutinied and he was captured, and they gave him up to Cyrus', and that Cyrus thereafter looted Ecbatana[2]. Another inscription gives us Nabonidus' account of a dream, in which Marduk assured him that in three years the Umman-Manda should no longer be, but that Cyrus, king of Anshan, with his small army, should overthrow them and carry Ishtumegu captive to his land.[3]

It is difficult to see how, on the basis of these sources, a theory that identifies Darius the Mede with Astyages can be established. Indeed, the argument of Alfrink appears to be rather that we have no reason to know that they could not be identified than that we have definite indications pointing to their identification. As a matter of fact, however, while there is nothing whatever to connect the Biblical narratives with Astyages, there is ample evidence that he can never have occupied the position which is here assigned him.

---

[1] They definitely dispose of Ctesias' story of his parentage, however, for they tell us unequivocally that Cyrus was of royal line, his father, grandfather, and great-grandfather having been kings of Anshan before him. Cf. Cyrus Cylinder, lines 20 f. (see Rogers, *Cun. Parallels*, p. 382).

[2] See Nabonidus Chron., col. II, lines 1–4 (ed. Sidney Smith, in *Bab. Hist. Texts*, pp. 111, 115).

[3] See Langdon, *Neubab. Königsinsch.*, pp. 218–21 (No. 1, col. 1, lines 18–32).

(a) *Astyages was not the son of Ahasuerus*

The father of Astyages was Cyaxares, whereas Ahasuerus is the equivalent of the Persian name which is commonly known in its Greek form of Xerxes. Alfrink[1], following Lenormant[2], argues that the Hebrew for the name Cyaxares might be expected to be אוחש(ת)ר, for which the better known name אחש(ו)ר(ו)ש might easily be substituted by a copyist. He also notes that in Tobit xiv. 15, where the reference is clearly to Cyaxares[3], the Greek has Ahasuerus. What Alfrink does, therefore, is to postulate textual corruption to remove the difficulty. It may be agreed that far more serious textual corruptions are found in the old Testament, and if no greater difficulty than this stood in the way of the theory, little complaint could be made. But before the text is altered to make it conform to a theory, the theory must be asked to produce some positive evidence in its own favour, and until it does so, it must be remembered that the present text is definitely against it.

(b) *Astyages cannot be equated with Darius*

Alfrink does not claim that the names can be equated, but again suggests that textual corruption may have been at work, and that the unfamiliar Astyages may have been replaced by the more familiar Darius, perhaps owing to the fact that Darius was known to be related to Xerxes (Ahasuerus), albeit as father and not as son[4]. But since the only consideration that could lead us to suspect this replacement is the theory the supposition is designed to serve, it cannot bring it any support. Nor does Alfrink feel any real confidence in the supposition himself. For he suggests as

[1] *Biblica*, loc. cit., p. 330.
[2] *La Divination . . . chez les Chald.*, p. 179 n.
[3] Cf. Gadd, *Fall of Nin.*, pp. 34 f. and 39 f. (lines 38 ff. of text). The name Cyaxares stands complete in line 47, as Umakištar. Cf. Eusebius, who wrongly calls the Median king at the fall of Nineveh Astyages, on the authority of Polyhistor (*Chron.* I. v. 3, ed. Migne, col. 119; ed. Schoene, i, col. 29; ed. Mai, p. 21). Cf. also Syncellus (*Chron.*, p. 210 B, ed. Dindorf, i, p. 396) and Abydenus (*apud* Eusebius, *Chron.* I. ix. 2, ed. Migne, col. 124; ed. Schoene, cols. 37 f.; ed. Mai, p. 25).   [4] *Biblica*, loc. cit., pp. 332 f.

another alternative that Astyages may have taken the royal style of Darius when he became king of Babylon[1]. This suggestion we have seen to be part of the regular stock-in-trade of all the theorists, whoever may be the person with whom they identify Darius. It can show as little evidence in the present case as in any of the others, and it remains sheer baseless conjecture, contributing nothing whatever to the weight of any theory.

(c) *A Babylonian reign of Astyages is irreconcilable with the Greek sources*

If positive arguments in favour of the theory that Darius the Mede is Astyages are lacking, there are not wanting such arguments to demonstrate the impossibility of the identification. These are supplied alike by the Greek and by the Babylonian sources.

Xenophon's story that Astyages died in a peaceful old age, passing on his kingdom to his son prior to the transfer of the realm to Cyrus, may be dismissed. The cuneiform evidence is fatal to its credibility. We are left, however, with the other Greek accounts, which agree in telling us that the life of Astyages was spared when he was captured. The Nabonidus Chronicle tells us nothing about him beyond his capture, and so puts no obstacle in the way of the credibility of their statement. Indeed, it would be fully in accord with what is elsewhere recorded of the character of Cyrus for him to be magnanimous to a beaten foe. But neither of the Greek writers allows room for Astyages to be placed upon the throne of Babylon. For while one of them tells us that Cyrus maintained him at his own court for the rest of his life, the other tells us that he placed him over a distant province. But that province was not Babylon. It is true that both of these accounts cannot be right, but it must be realized that if we set them both aside, we have nothing more substantial than conjecture on which to base the

---

[1] Ibid., p. 333.

Babylonian rulership that is substituted. Moreover, had Cyrus done so boldly magnanimous a deed as to entrust the important province of Babylon to the ex-king of Media it is incredible that the account should have been so garbled by the Greek writers, and still more incredible that Xenophon, who delighted to dwell on the noble qualities of Cyrus, should have passed it without mention. For so remarkable a stroke of policy could hardly have failed to be remembered.

In every particular so far, therefore, the theory requires us to set aside the evidence we have, whether Biblical or extra-Biblical, as untrustworthy, while it presents us with no evidence whatever for the hollow suppositions we are offered in its place.

(d) *A Babylonian reign of Astyages is definitely debarred by the cuneiform sources*

The omission of his name from the contract tablets alone makes it absolutely certain that Astyages was not king of Babylon. For we have seen that in the first year of Cyrus, his son Cambyses was temporarily associated with him on the throne as king of Babylon, but within a year Cyrus had himself superseded him, and assumed the title of king of Babylon. There is therefore no room for a reign of Astyages. Alfrink takes comfort in the thought that all the treasures of the Babylonian soil have not been yielded up, and some fortunate find may yet provide us with the mention of Astyages[1]. But our existing texts leave no gap into which a reign of Astyages between Nabonidus and Cyrus could be fitted.

Alfrink meets this by suggesting that when Cyrus installed Cambyses as sub-king of Babylon, he may have made Astyages regent, on account of the youth and inexperience of Cambyses[2]. For this groundless suggestion there is no antecedent probability, and of a regency of

---

[1] *Biblica*, loc. cit., p. 334.   [2] Ibid., p. 331.

Astyages there is as little trace as of his reign in Babylon. We find mention of Cyrus and Cambyses, and even of Gobryas, yet Astyages, whose rank and authority would have been so much higher than those of Gobryas, is unmentioned.

And not only so. The suggestion does not suffice for the work Alfrink would make it do. For he goes on to add that the early end of Cambyses' association with his father on the throne may have been due to the death of Astyages[1]. But Alfrink's chronology requires for Darius the Mede a regency of two years[2], whereas the association of Cambyses with his father lasted for less than one year.

Finally, this supposed regency of Astyages could not be harmonized with the references to Darius the Mede in the book of Daniel. For there Darius is clearly conceived of as one who was more than a regent, since events are dated by the years of his reign. And we know with full certainty that events were not dated in Babylon by the years of Astyages, during Cambyses' occupancy of the Babylonian throne, but by the reign of Cambyses and of Cyrus.

The case for Astyages rests from beginning to end, therefore, on unsupported conjecture. Not a single trace of his reign or regency can be found anywhere. For his reign neither Greek nor cuneiform texts allow room, while a regency is in itself improbable and insufficient to meet the case. The theory requires us not alone to set aside all the Greek accounts as untrustworthy, but in addition to dismiss the cuneiform records, and to assume that the Biblical text is untrustworthy, at least so far as the name and paternity of Darius are concerned. Where evidence is conflicting we must often make a choice. But we can hardly be asked to set aside all our evidence in favour of ungrounded fancy.

[1] Ibid.   [2] Ibid., pp. 338 ff.

IV. DARIUS THE MEDE IS NOT CYAXARES

JOSEPHUS represents Babylon as having been taken by Cyrus, and a few lines below says it was taken by Darius, who with Cyrus put an end to the Babylonian kingdom[1]. He adds that Darius was the son of Astyages, and had another name amongst the Greeks. It has already been said that whereas Herodotus and Ctesias represent Astyages as the last Median king, and the former states explicitly that he had no son, Xenophon ascribes to him a son Cyaxares, who is said to have succeeded him on the throne. It would seem that Josephus was aware of this tradition, and until modern times the dominant view was that Darius the Mede was no other than this Cyaxares II[2]. Prideaux confidently justified this view[3], and it has been held by Lowth[4], Hengstenberg[5], Rosenmüller[6], Hävernick[7], Dereser[8], Kranichfeld[9], Kliefoth[10], Füller[11], Keil[12], Zöckler[13], Watson[14], and Knabenbauer[15], amongst very many others. In recent years, however, its impossibility has been generally recognized, and it has been almost universally

[1] *Ant.* x. xi. 4 (x. 247 f., ed. Niese, ii, pp. 384 f.)

[2] Venema (*Diss. ad Vat. Dan. emb.*, pp. 79 ff., esp. p. 85) held Cyaxares to be the same as Nabonidus, and both to be identified with Darius the Mede. (Cf. Syncellus, *Chron.*, p. 209, ed. Dindorf, p. 393, where the equation Astyages = Darius = Nabonidus is made.) Venema thought Xenophon in error, however, in making Cyaxares the son of Astyages, but held him to be really his brother. For the last suggestion, cf. Zündel, *Krit. Unters.*, pp. 36 f.

[3] *O and NT Connected*, i, pp. 66 f., 120 ff. Prideaux held Cyaxares II to be the son of Astyages and Aryênis, the daughter of the Lydian king Alyattes (cf. Herodotus, *Hist.* i. 74, Loeb ed., i, p. 92). But in that case Cyaxares could not have been sixty-two years old at the time of the capture of Babylon. For the marriage took place in 585 B.C.—the date being determined by the eclipse mentioned by Herodotus (cf. Dougherty, *Nab. and Belsh.*, p. 33; CAH iii, p. 512).

[4] *Comm. on Proph.*, p. 366a.   [5] *Gen. of Dan.*, ET, pp. 40 ff.

[6] *Schol. in VT*, Part x, pp. 195 f.   [7] *Comm. über das B. Dan.*, pp. 210 ff.

[8] *Ezech. u. Dan.*, pp. 346 f.   [9] *Das B. Dan. erk.*, pp. 39–47.

[10] *Das B. Dan. übers. u. erk.*, pp. 155 ff.   [11] *Der Prof. Dan. erk.*, pp. 140 ff.

[12] *The Bk. of Dan.*, ET, pp. 193 ff.   [13] *The Proph. Dan.*, ET, pp. 30, 35.

[14] *Dar. the Med. ident.*, chap. vi.

[15] *Comm. in Dan. Proph.*, 1891, pp. 171 ff. (The 2nd ed., 1907, I have not seen.)

abandoned. Since its advocacy has been carried into the present century by Auchincloss[1], however, the reasons for its rejection fall to be set forth.

The story of Xenophon is that Cyrus spent his childhood with his father in Persia, but in his early teens lived at the Median court with his grandfather Astyages. Here he remained for some years, winning all hearts by his attractive disposition[2]. After the death of Astyages, his son Cyaxares, the uncle of Cyrus, became king[3], and Cyrus is found somewhat later as the general of his army[4]. Xenophon knows nothing here of the capture of Ecbatana by Cyrus—though elsewhere he shows that he is not ignorant of a truer record[5]. Cyaxares is represented as still alive and on the throne of Media at the time of the fall of Babylon, and Cyrus but adds his conquest to his uncle's empire. He goes to visit Cyaxares to tell him that he has set aside a palace for him in Babylon, so that he may have a residence of his own whenever he goes there[6]. Cyaxares thereupon gives his daughter in marriage to Cyrus, and makes him heir to the Median throne[7].

Here, then, we seem to have a tradition which fits well with the Biblical account. For Cyaxares would appear to be a Median sovereign, who ruled over Babylon for a period between the capture of the city by Cyrus and the actual reign of Cyrus. The fact that he was the uncle of Cyrus would suggest that he was of advanced years, like the Darius the Mede of the book of Daniel. But once more we find that examination reveals many difficulties, and modern

---

[1] *Dar. the Med.*, in *Bibliotheca Sacra*, lxvi, 1909, pp. 536 ff., and *The Bk. of Dan. Unlocked*, pp. 48, 95 ff. Auchincloss is scarcely a writer of sufficient importance to be taken note of, were it not that his identification has so many older scholars on its side. Moreover, Knabenbauer, in the second ed. of his Commentary, has also carried this view into the present century.

[2] *Cyrop.* I. iii. 1, iv. 1 (Loeb ed., i, pp. 26, 44).

[3] Ibid. I. v. 2 (Loeb ed., i, p. 76).   [4] Ibid. I. v. 5 (Loeb ed., i, p. 78).

[5] Cf. *Anab.* III. iv. 8, 11, 12 (Loeb ed., i, pp. 466 ff.) where Xenophon refers to the military overthrow of the Median kingdom by the Persians.

[6] *Cyrop.* VIII. v. 17 (Loeb ed., ii, p. 402).

[7] Ibid. VIII. v. 19 (Loeb ed., ibid.).

research has provided conclusive reasons against the identification.

(a) *The lack of equation of the names again provides a difficulty*

Cyaxares II, if there were such a person, was the son of Astyages, and we can neither equate his own name with Darius nor his father's with Ahasuerus. Keil has attempted to effect some equation by claiming that the meaning of Cyaxares is similar to that of Darius, and that Ahasuerus is a Persian dynastic name which corresponds to Astyages, which is a Median dynastic name[1]. Hengstenberg, on the contrary, claims that the two names Cyaxares and Astyages are identical, and then supposes that Xenophon has confounded the names of father and son[2]. He also quotes with approval Scaliger's claim that Cyaxares is identical with Ahasuerus, which is the Greek Xerxes[3].

Similarly Auchincloss argues[4], on the basis of the already noted Tobit xiv. 15, that Ahasuerus is to be identified with Cyaxares. He then further argues that Darius and Ahasuerus are to be identified, on the ground that in Ezra vi. 14 f. we find the order of the Persian kings given as Cyrus, Darius, Artaxerxes, Darius, whereas in Ezra iv. 5, 6, 7, 24 we find the order given as Cyrus, Ahasuerus, Artaxerxes, Darius. The way is then clear for the identification of Cyaxares with Darius, since both are to be equated with Ahasuerus. The argument is quite worthless, however. Its uncritical acceptance of the order of Ezra iv, despite the difficulties that beset that chapter, would alone make it useless, as would equally the failure to recognize that the

---

[1] *The Bk. of Dan.*, ET, p. 200; cf. Zöckler, *The Proph. Dan.*, ET, pp. 35 ff. It has been noted above that Wilson (*Studies in Bk. of Dan.*, p. 235) similarly —and as groundlessly—claims that 'Xerxes and Cyaxares are the Median and Persian forms of the same name'.   [2] *Gen. of Dan.*, ET, p. 42.

[3] *Ibid.*, p. 43. The reference to Scaliger is given as *De emend. temp.* vi, p. 587, and is to the ed. of 1629 (= p. 282 of 1583 ed., or p. 550 of 1598 ed.).

[4] *Bibliotheca Sacra*, loc. cit.

fact that two names are confused constitutes no proof that they were identical.

These wholesale identifications are manifestly unscientific, for they could only lead to the conclusion that all Persian names are identical, and we may as well call any one by any name we happen to fancy at the moment. In fact, they cannot be maintained, and we can only recognize that the name and paternity of Cyaxares differ from those of Darius the Mede, and that we have no reason to suppose that either Cyaxares or his father bore both of the names that are attributed to them.

(b) *The lack of accord with the book of Daniel provides a difficulty*

Even if Cyaxares could be equated with Darius, Xenophon can in no way be brought into agreement with the story of Daniel. For Xenophon does not make Cyaxares become the king of Babylon. He makes Cyrus become its king. For he tells us that the father of Cyrus was still living —whence we may infer that Cyrus had not yet inherited his kingdom—yet Cyrus assumed the style of king on his capture of Babylon. Of what state? Clearly, of the conquered Babylonian kingdom. For after visiting his father and his uncle he returned to Babylon, and thereafter conducted himself as a king[1]. He even appointed satraps, we are told, and set them over the conquered empire—in direct contradiction of Dn vi. 2 (EV vi. 1), where this is attributed to Darius the Mede. A work which disagrees so specifically with the book of Daniel can hardly be appealed to in support of the accuracy of that book.

Nor does the case rest there. For, on this view, it must be held that Cyrus reigned in Babylon as the nominal subordinate of Cyaxares, or Darius, and that his kingdom was in reality but a part of the larger empire of Darius. We should then have to assume with Josephus that Daniel was

[1] *Cyrop.* VIII. vi. 1 ff. (Loeb ed., ii, pp. 408 ff.).

removed by Darius to Media[1]. For if Darius made Daniel his Prime Minister, in the way recorded in Dn vi. 2 (EV vi. 1), it cannot be supposed that Daniel would reside anywhere but at the capital. And that he did live at the capital is clear from the story of Dn vi. Yet there is no shadow of suggestion in Xenophon that Cyaxares moved his capital to Babylon, and no shadow of suggestion in the book of Daniel that the scene is shifted from Babylon. But this brings a further difficulty. For Daniel dates events by 'the first year of Darius'. It is inconceivable that Cyaxares should begin again to number the years of his reign from the time he annexed Babylon, when he had already reigned for a number of years, according to Xenophon. It may, of course, be replied that the Babylonians would count his years from the time he began to rule over them, but it may be taken as certain that his Prime Minister, living not in Babylon, but at the Median king's court, would follow the Median reckoning.

(c) *The lack of accord with the inscriptions provides a fatal difficulty*

Even in ancient times it was perceived that Xenophon's *Cyropaedia* was no more than a historical romance, written for didactic purposes. This recognition of its character appears not only in the oft-quoted passage from Cicero[2], but also in Diogenes Laertius[3], who refers to Plato[4] for support, and in Ausonius[5]. Modern research has abun-

---

[1] *Ant.* x. xi. 4 (x. 249, ed. Niese, ii, p. 384).

[2] *Cyrus ille a Xenophonte non ad historiae fidem scriptus sed ad effigiem justi imperii* (*Ad Quint. Frat.* I. i. 8, Loeb ed., *Letters to Friends*, iii, pp. 410, 412).

[3] Καὶ ἐν τοῖς Νόμοις ὁ Πλάτων πλάσμα φησὶν εἶναι τὴν Παιδείαν αὐτοῦ (i.e. Κύρου)· μὴ γὰρ εἶναι Κῦρον τοιοῦτον (*Vit. Phil.* iii. 24 (34), ed. Cobet, p. 77).

[4] The reference to Plato is to *De Leg.* iii. 12 (694 C, ed. Schneider, ii, p. 311, or Loeb ed., i, p. 226): Μαντεύομαι δὴ νῦν περί γε Κύρου τὰ μὲν ἄλλ' αὐτὸν στρατηγόν τε ἀγαθὸν εἶναι καὶ φιλόπολιν, παιδείας δὲ ὀρθῆς οὐχ ἧφθαι τὸ παράπαν οἰκονομίᾳ τε οὐδὲν τὸν νοῦν προσεσχηκέναι.

[5] *Xenophon Attice . . . tu, qui ad Cyri virtutes exequendas votum potius quam historiam commodasti: cum diceres, non qualis esset, sed qualis esse deberet* (*Grat. Act. pro cons.* xv, ed. Peiper, p. 371, or Loeb ed., ii, p. 258).

dantly confirmed this judgement[1]. For the inscriptions support Herodotus' statement that Astyages was the last Median king, and leave no room for this fictitious Cyaxares II. He is a mere figment of Xenophon's imagination. Xenophon makes Cyrus the general of his uncle Cyaxares, and in the *Cyropaedia* knows nothing of the revolt of Cyrus and capture of Ecbatana; but this is now certainly established by the Nabonidus Chronicle. Xenophon makes Cyrus assume the style of king first after the capture of Babylon; the inscriptions show that he was already styled King at least a dozen years before the fall of Babylon. Xenophon makes the father and uncle of Cyrus live and rule until after the capture of Babylon, Cyrus inheriting their realms on their death; the only royal title Cyrus gives to his father is 'king of Anshan', yet that is the title he himself bears long before his conquest of Babylon, and we must therefore conclude that his father was already dead, and that he had succeeded to the throne. Xenophon represents Cyrus as the nominal subordinate of Cyaxares after the fall of Babylon; yet Cyrus himself, in his inscriptions, proclaims himself 'king of lands' in a way that leaves no doubt that he is no underling. Xenophon calls the father of Cyrus the 'king of Persia'; Cyrus does not give this title to his father, and since he himself first appears as 'king of Anshan', in Elam, and later as 'king of Persia', we must, conclude that Cyrus himself added the kingdom of Persia, either by conquest or by inheritance[2].

[1] Cf. Meyer (JE iv, p. 403 a): 'The *Cyropaedia* has no value for the historian', and von Christ (*Gesch. der griech. Lit.*, 6th ed., i, p. 516): 'Das Werk ist also ein pädagogisch-politischer Tendenzroman. Mit der überlieferten Tatsachen wird sehr frei umgesprungen.' So, too, Weissbach in PW, Supp. vol. iv, col. 1130.

[2] That Cyrus was a Persian may be taken as certain (cf. Rogers, *Hist. of Anc. Pers.*, p. 36). Driver (*Dan.*, p. xxx) states that he was not a Persian, and this view has been widely held. But it cannot be maintained. For Darius Hystaspis emphasizes his own Persian origin, yet claims Cambyses, Cyrus' son, as belonging to his own family (cf. CAH iv, p. 4). It has been noted that Cyrus traces his own ancestry back to Teispes, king of Anshan, while Darius Hystaspis traces his back to Teispes, son of Achaemenes, and claims that

The thoroughly unhistorical character of Xenophon's story is thus sufficiently demonstrated. No Cyaxares II ruled in Media after Astyages, but Cyrus succeeded to the throne by right of conquest. No Cyaxares II ruled in Babylon after the collapse of the Neo-Babylonian empire, for again Cyrus inherited the throne by right of the sword. No imperial monarch interposed his rule between Nabonidus and Cyrus, for ere the month in which Cyrus entered Babylon had run its course, contracts were being dated by his reign.

eight of his family had been kings before him, and that they were kings in two lines. Probably, therefore, Teispes was a common ancestor of Cyrus and Darius; and Anshan and Persia, both minor states at the time, were ruled by different branches of the one family. But since Hystaspes, the father of Darius, did not occupy the throne, for some unspecified reason, Cyrus would seem to have united the two kingdoms under his rule. Cf. Hall, AHNE, 7th ed., pp. 553 ff.; Gray, CAH iv, pp. 5 f.; Sayce, DB i, p. 542. Hystaspes was still living in the reign of his son. Cf. Beh. inscr., § 36 (King and Thompson, *Sculp. and Inscr. of Darius*, p. 42).

V. THERE IS NO RELIABLE EVIDENCE FOR ANY DARIUS THE MEDE

THERE are some arguments presented in support of the contention that there was a Darius the Mede, as portrayed in the book of Daniel, which do not depend on any particular identification, and of these some are common to many defenders of the historicity of the Biblical narrative. It is necessary, therefore, to traverse these to show that they are invalid.

(a) *The alleged traces in Greek writers of an older Darius, before Darius Hystaspis, are untrustworthy*

Prideaux notes[1] that the coin known as the daric is said to have been named after a Darius who reigned before Darius Hystaspis, and this evidence has been repeated by many others[2]. Hengstenberg strove to reinforce this by adducing[3] further evidence, from Eusebius, pointing to the existence of this older Darius, and this also has been taken up by many apologists[4]. The fullest collection of this supposed evidence is found in Alfrink's paper, where the argument is presented afresh[5].

It is pointed out that Harpocration, in his Lexicon, s.v. Δαρεικός, notes that this coin was named, not after Darius the father of Xerxes, as most have maintained, but after an older Darius[6]. A scholion on Aristophanes' *Ecclesiazusae*, line 602[7], which states the same fact, apparently on the authority of Harpocration, is also adduced, though this

---

[1] *O and NT Conn.* i, p. 123. So, earlier, Marsham, *Can. Chron.*, p. 604.

[2] So, e.g., Hengstenberg, *Gen. of Dan.*, ET, p. 42 ; Quatremère, *Mél. d'hist. et de phil. orient.*, p. 382 ; Pusey, *Dan. the Proph.*, 8th ed., p. 126; Keil, *The Bk. of Dan.*, ET, p. 200 n. ; Deane, *Dan.: His Life and Times*, p. 101.

[3] Op. cit., p. 41.

[4] So, e.g., Pusey, op. cit., p. 126; Keil, op. cit., pp. 193, 199 n.

[5] *Biblica*, ix, 1928, pp. 333 f.

[6] *Lex. in dec. or. att.*, ed. Dindorf, i, p. 84: ἐκλήθησαν δὲ Δαρεικοὶ οὐχ ὡς οἱ πλεῖστοι νομίζουσιν, ἀπὸ Δαρείου τοῦ Ξέρξου πατρός, ἀλλ᾽ ἀφ᾽ ἑτέρου τινὸς παλαιοτέρου βασιλέως.

[7] See Dübner, *Schol. Gr. in Aristoph.*, p. 540: οὐκ ἀπὸ Δαρείου τοῦ Ξέρξου πατρός, ἀλλ᾽ ἀφ᾽ ἑτέρου τινὸς παλαιοτέρου βασιλέως ὠνομάσθησαν.

adds no independent weight to the testimony. A similar statement is found in Suidas[1]. But evidence of such late origin[2] has scant value, and no one would dream of adducing it unless he had a manifestly weak case to make out. Hengstenberg, who borrows the evidence from Prideaux, confesses his doubt as to its value, though holding it not to be despised. Of even less weight is the reference in Xenophon's *Cyropaedia* to 'darics' in a speech represented as made to Cyrus by one of his officers before the fall of Babylon[3]. For such an anachronism is a trifling matter in such a romance. Similarly, Révillout adduces[4] Ezra i. 69 to prove that darics were struck in the reign of Cyrus. As well might the Chronicler's more glaring anachronism[5] be adduced as serious evidence to prove that darics were current in Israel in the time of David.

It is, indeed, probable that 'darics' were first issued in the reign of Darius Hystaspis[6], though Hoffmann has cast doubt

---

[1] *Lex.*, ed. Bernhardy, i, p. 1174, s.v. Δαρεικούς: οὐκ ἀπὸ Δαρείου τοῦ Ξέρξου πατρός, ἀλλ᾽ ἀφ᾽ ἑτέρου τινὸς παλαιοτέρου βασιλέως ὠνομάσθησαν.

[2] Harpocration may possibly belong to the second century A.D., but some authorities would place him much later, while Suidas probably belongs to the tenth century A.D.

[3] *Cyrop.* v. iii. 3 (Loeb ed., ii, p. 42). De Moor attached much weight to this 'proof'. He confessed that it was an anachronism to represent darics as already in existence before 'Darius' became king, but found in the anachronism evidence that there was a king Darius about this time (*Muséon*, xv, 1896, p. 234). But a confessed anachronism can yield no evidence for chronology.

[4] *Ann. de la soc. fr. de num.* viii, 1884, p. 121. Madden (*Coins of the Jews*, p. 47), while accepting the evidence of the books of Ezra and Nehemiah 'to show that coins of a similar name were current during the reigns of Cyrus, Cambyses and Darius Hystaspis' doubts if the coin called daric is intended by those mentioned during the reign of Cyrus, believing that 'the daric proper was probably not in circulation till the reign of Darius, son of Hystaspes'.

[5] 1 Chron. xxix. 7.

[6] Cf. Head, *Coinage of Lyd. and Pers.*, p. 24, and *Hist. Num.*, p. 825; Babelon, *Les Perses Ach.*, p. iii; Kennedy in DB iii, p. 421a; Hultsch in PW iv, Part 2, col. 2181; Meyer in JE iv, p. 441b, and in EBrit, 14th ed., vii, p. 59 a and xvii, p. 570 a; Prášek, *Gesch. d. Med. u. Pers.* ii, p. 135; CAH iv, p. 129. But cf. Gardner, *Hist. of Anc. Coin.*, pp. 87 f., where it is held that the connexion of the name with Darius does not prove that darics were not issued before the accession of Darius, and where the institution of the coins is attributed to Cyrus. But of this no evidence is adduced. Cf., too, Hill, *Hist. Gr. Coins*, p. 27, where it is held that evidence is insufficient to establish that it was in the reign of Darius that the coins were first issued.

on the connexion of the word 'daric' with the name of Darius[1]. If the similarity rests on no philological connexion but is purely fortuitous, then the whole argument collapses, while even if the name is derived from Darius, it cannot of itself prove when that Darius lived and ruled. Nor can a late, post-Christian, tradition establish it. Certainly so slender a case can oppose nothing to the definite evidence already noted, which leaves no room for a Darius immediately before Cyrus.

The other ancient reference that has been brought forward is a fragment preserved by Eusebius, which relates that Darius removed Nabonidus from Carmania, whither Cyrus is said to have sent him as governor[2]. But again, whatever truth there may be in the story[3], it is altogether without evidential value for an earlier Darius. It might just as well have been Darius Hystaspis, so far as the fragment goes. It neither says it was an earlier Darius, nor requires us to posit one.

Alfrink adduces a further statement from Suidas, who records, s.v. Θαλῆς, that Thales predicted an eclipse in the time of Darius[4]. Cicero[5] and Eusebius[6] tell us that this eclipse was in the time of Astyages, however, whence Alfrink finds some support for his identification of Darius

---

[1] ZA ii, 1887, pp. 49, 56. Cf. Prince, *Comm. on Dan.*, p. 265, and Meyer in EBrit, 14th ed., vii, p. 59a and xvii, p. 570a. It is probable that the word is connected with the Persian word ‏ﻰﺟ‎ = gold. Cf. Révillout's derivation from the Akkadian *darag mana* = *degree, or one sixtieth, of a mina* (*Ann. de la soc. fr. de num.*, viii, 1884, p. 119). Hill, on the contrary, regards the word as a pure Greek formation from Δαρεῖος, and holds it doubtful whether it corresponds to any Persian word (op. cit., p. 27). Meillet (*Gram. du vieux perse*, p. 67) held that the Gk. δαρεικός was the source of the Persian word for *gold*, and not *vice versa*, but Benveniste has deleted this from the second ed. (p. 78).

[2] *Chron.* I. x. 3 (ed. Migne, col. 126, or ed. Mai, p. 28, or ed. Schoene i, col. 41).

[3] Prášek (*Gesch. d. Med. u. Pers.* i, p. 230 n.) doubts the whole tradition that Nabonidus was sent to Carmania. This tradition, without the story of his later removal, is also recorded in Josephus, *Contra Ap.* i. 20 (i. 153, ed. Niese, v, p. 29), on the authority of Berossus.

[4] *Lex.*, ed. Bernhardy, i, col. 1105.

[5] *De Div.* I. xlix (112), (Loeb ed., p. 344).

[6] *Chron.*, ed. Migne, col. 464, or ed. Mai, p. 331, or ed. Schoene, ii, col. 94.

with Astyages. But it may be noted that, according to Herodotus[1], the eclipse took place in the reign of Cyaxares, and it is dated by astronomers in the year 585 B.C. It is manifest that Suidas has here no evidential value whatever, especially since Alfrink himself suggests that either the name Darius in the text of Daniel is due to scribal change, or it was assumed by Astyages after ascending the throne of Babylon. Alfrink himself agrees, therefore, that Darius the Mede was not known by that name in 585 B.C., and his willingness to regard the name as not original in Daniel is the mark of his distrust of the evidence of Suidas. Even if Suidas could be relied on, there would be less reason to equate his Darius with Astyages than with Cyaxares, the father of Astyages and the conqueror of Nineveh, who had certainly died long before the fall of Babylon, and who could not therefore be connected with the Darius the Mede of the book of Daniel.

(b) *The spelling of the name of Darius in the book of Daniel is of no special significance*

Tisdall has drawn attention[2] to the agreement of the spelling found in the book of Daniel with that found in the oldest of the Papyri from Elephantine, and has claimed that this is an argument for the early origin of the book of Daniel. Boutflower has also drawn attention to the same point[3].

In a papryus[4] of 495 B.C., dated in the twenty-seventh year of Darius—who must therefore be Darius Hystaspis —we find the name spelt דריוש. But in papyri which date from the reign of Darius II, bearing dates from 420 B.C., to 408 B.C., we find the spellings דריוהוש[5] and דריהוש[6], and the former stands also in the fragments of papyri containing a translation of the Behistun inscription[7], which Cowley

---

[1] *Hist.* i. 74 (Loeb ed., i, pp. 90, 92).   [2] JTVI liii, 1921, p. 245.
[3] *Dadda-'Idri*, p. 42.   [4] Cowley, *Aram. Pap.*, p. 1 (1: 1).
[5] *Ibid.*, p. 57 (20: 1), p. 62 (21: 3), p. 85 (25: 1), p. 99 (27: 2), p. 103 (28: 1), p. 107 (29: 1, 5), p. 111 f. (30: 2, 4), pp. 119 f. (31: 2, 4, 19), p. 123 (32: 7).
[6] Ibid., pp. 112 f. (30: 19, 21, 30).
[7] Ibid., p. 253 (Beh: 37) and p. 266, last line.

dates on independent grounds *circa* 420 B.C.[1] So far as Egyptian Aramaic is concerned, therefore, we have indisputable contemporary evidence that whereas in the reign of the first Darius the name was spelt as in the book of Daniel, in the reign of the second it was spelt differently. G. R. Driver has suggested[2], with much probability, that the ה was a *litera prolongationis*, of which he adduces some other examples.

Nor is this later form found only in Egyptian Aramaic. For in Babylonian Aramaic of the time of the second Darius we find[3] the spelling דריהוש. It would certainly be surprising for an older spelling to be subsequently restored, and since in the days of Darius II the later spelling was so widely spread, there would seem to be a strong *prima facie* case for holding that as we find the old spelling in the book of Daniel, it must have been written before the days of the second Darius. This consideration could not, of course, directly prove that there was a Darius the Mede, but if it is valid evidence that the book of Daniel was written somewhere about the time of the earliest papyri, it adds no little weight to the testimony of that book for a Darius the Mede.

It is to be noted, however, that in Neh. xii. 22 we find the same spelling as in the book of Daniel, yet it is impossible to place the composition of the book of Nehemiah earlier than the reign of the second Darius, and since the reference in the verse just mentioned appears to be to Darius III, it must be a great deal later. The only Old Testament books in which we find the name Darius are Haggai, Zechariah, Ezra, Nehemiah and Daniel, and in every instance we find the same spelling, which is the old spelling we have seen to be independently authenticated for the reign of Darius I. But a simple explanation lies to hand. Haggai and Zechariah were prophets contemporary with Darius Hystaspis,

---

[1] Ibid., p. 250.   [2] JBL xlv, 1926, pp. 323 ff.
[3] Clay, *Aram. Indorsements*, in *OT and Sem. Stud.* i, p. 307 (No. 22) and p. 308 (No. 26).

and it is not therefore surprising to find the name spelt in their books precisely as in the only papyrus that belongs to the same reign. When the Chronicler came to write Ezra-Nehemiah he adopted the spelling he found in those books, which by this time belonged to the sacred canon. And similarly the author of the book of Daniel based his spelling of the name on the same source.

The validity of this explanation may be tested by reference to two other names. In papyri dated from 465 B.C. to 441 B.C., and belonging therefore to the reign of Artaxerxes I, we find that monarch's name spelt ארתחששׁסׁט[1]. The same spelling is found in a text on sandstone, which de Vogüé[2] and Lidzbarski[3] date in the same reign. Again in the Sardis bilingual inscription[4], which Torrey[5] assigns to the reign of the first Artaxerxes, but which S. A. Cook[6] inclines to place rather in the reign of the second or third Artaxerxes, we find the same name spelt still in the same way. In the Old Testament the name is found only in Ezra and Nehemiah. If these two men were contemporaries of one another, then all the references in the books which bear their names would appear to be to Artaxerxes I, while if, as some hold,[7] Ezra is to be placed fifty years later than Nehemiah, then

---

[1] Cowley, op. cit., p. 16 (6: 2), p. 19 (7: 1), p. 22 (8: 1), p. 26 (9: 1), p. 29 10: 1), p. 37 (13: 1), p. 42 (14: 1).

[2] *Comptes rendus*, 1903, pp. 273, 275.

[3] *Eph. für sem. Epig.* ii, p. 221.

[4] Aramaic text, line 1. The inscription was first published by Littmann in *Lydian Inscriptions*, in *Sardis*, VI. i, pp. 23–38.

[5] AJSL xxxiv, 1917–18, p. 192.

[6] JHS xxxvii, 1917, p. 81.

[7] So Van Hoonacker, *Néh. et Esd.*, and *Néh. en l'an 20*; also RB x, 1901, pp. 5 ff., 175 ff., xxxii, 1923, pp. 481 ff., xxxiii, 1924, pp. 33 ff. So also Batten, *Comm. on Ezr. and Neh.*, pp. 28 ff.; Browne, *Early Jud.*, chap. x; Albright, JBL xl, 1921, pp. 119 ff. (but recanted in *Arch. of Pal.*, p. 219; cf. JQR xxiv, 1933–4, p. 371); Barnes, in *People and Bk*, pp. 293 f.; Lofthouse, *Isr. after Ex.*, p. 198; Oesterley, *Hist. of Isr.* ii, chap. x (cf. Oesterley and Robinson, *Intro. to OT*, pp. 127 ff.); Ricciotti, *Stor. d'Isr.* ii, pp. 125 ff. The earliest suggestion of this view I have found is in the form of a query in Vernes, *Précis d'hist. juive*, p. 582 n. Sellin (*Gesch. d. isr.-jüd. Volkes*, ii, pp. 134 ff.) still holds to the view that Ezra and Nehemiah belong to the reign of Artaxerxes I, as also do Kittel (*Gesch. des V. Isr.* iii, pp. 567 ff., 608 ff.), Schaeder (*Esr.*

E

some of the references would be to Artaxerxes II. Yet the spelling of the name here is ארתחשסתא or ארתחששתא[1], and is different, therefore, from that found in contemporary documents, either in Egypt or in Asia Minor. While in the case of Darius, then, the Chronicler followed the correct old spelling, because he found it standing in the sacred canon, in the case of Artaxerxes he followed the spelling of his own day, since he had no guidance here from an older canonical work, contemporary with Artaxerxes.

Similarly again with the name Xerxes. The oldest papyrus of this king's reign, dated in 484 B.C., spells the name חשירש[2], but in other texts we find חשיארש[3]. The latter stands also on a tablet from Memphis[4], dated in 482 B.C. In the Old Testament the name is found in Ezra, Esther, and Daniel, where it is spelt אחשורוש or אחשרש. Although the book of Esther narrates a story which is laid in the reign of Ahasuerus, it makes no pretence to have been written in that reign. Similarly the book of Ezra cannot have been written until long after the reign of Xerxes. It is not to be wondered at, therefore, that here we do not find the spelling that was contemporary with Xerxes. Whether the book of Esther is older than the book of Daniel is disputed, but the book of Ezra is almost certainly older, and it doubtless provided the author of Daniel with his spelling of the name.

It is surely significant that of the three names the only one that is spelt in the Old Testament in the authenticated contemporary manner is the one which stands in acknowledged

der Schreib.), Eissfeldt (Einl. in d. AT, p. 597) and Möller (Einl. in d. AT, pp. 262 f.). Some have held that Nehemiah preceded Ezra, though both belonged to the reign of Artax. I. So Kosters (Het Herstel., pp. 124–41 = Wiederherst., pp. 103–17), Bertholet (Esr. u. Neh., pp. 30 f., and RGG, 1st ed., ii, col. 636), Albright (Arch. of Pal., l.c.).

[1] Oesterley thinks the two spellings were intended to distinguish two kings (op. cit., p. 96 n.). Cf. de Vogüé, loc. cit., p. 272. So, earlier, Imbert (Muséon, vii, 1888, p. 223) and Torrey (Ezr. Stud., p. 170).

[2] Cowley, op. cit., p. 4 (2: 1).

[3] Ibid., p. 10 (5: 1) and p. 168 (64 No. 20).

[4] CIS ii, 122: 3 (vol. i, p. 124), or Cooke, N. Sem. Inscr., p. 200 (71: 3).

contemporary works, from which, therefore, it may have been derived by the author of Daniel and the Chronicler.

(c) *The authority of Darius in the book of Daniel is not represented as delegated*

Many of the writers who have identified Darius with the various persons discussed above, recognizing that on the fall of the Neo-Babylonian empire the real power passed into the hands of Cyrus, and that Darius, whether nominal suzerain or subordinate of Cyrus, exercised no independent authority, have sought to show that in the book of Daniel this is precisely what we find. We read that Darius the Mede was 'made king over the realm of the Chaldaeans',[1] and that he 'received the kingdom'[2]. It is argued that these phrases imply that Darius received the kingdom from another, by whom he was made king, and show that the author knew the authority of Darius was but delegated[3].

That this contention is unwarranted needs little demonstration. Kliefoth recognized[4] that the phrase קבל מלכותא in vi. 1 merely states that the kingdom passed to Darius, without the slightest indication as to the manner of the transfer. In vii. 18 the phrase is used of the saints' receiving the kingdom from God, and we find it again in a similar sense in the Peshiṭta version of Heb. xii. 28. The same phrase is well authenticated in Syriac usage to indicate ordinary succession to the throne. Bevan adduced a passage where the phrase describes the accession of Julian the Apostate[5], to which Charles has added another recording the accession of Ucataeus[6]. To these may be added a third,

---

[1] Dn ix. 1. [2] Dn vi. 1 (EV v. 31).
[3] So Venema, *Diss. ad vat. Dan. emb.*, pp. 82 f.; Pusey, *Dan. the Proph.*, 8th ed., pp. 124 f.; Keil, *Bk. of Dan.*, ET, p. 198; Wright, *Dan. and his Proph.*, p. 136, and *Dan. and its Crit.*, p. 97; Wilson, *Stud. in Bk. of Dan.*, p. 134, and *Princeton Theol. Rev.* xx, 1922, p. 186, xxii, 1924, pp. 377 f.; Boutflower, *In and Around Bk. of Dan.*, p. 143.   [4] *Das B. Dan. übers. u. erk.*, p. 155.
[5] See Hoffmann, *Jul. der Abtr.*, p. 5, line 10 (adduced in Bevan, *Short Comm. on Dan.*, p. 20 n.).
[6] See Bernstein, *Chrest. Syr.* i, p. 110, lines 1 f. (adduced in Charles, *Crit. Comm. on Dan.*, p. 140).

from the ancient Syriac version of the *Ecclesiastical History* of Eusebius[1], which reads: ܟܕ ܕܝܢ ܗܘ ܐܘܓܘܣܛܘܣ ܒܬܪ ܩ̈ܕܡܝܢ ܒܬܪܗ ܩܒܠ ܒܪܗ ܠܗܪܘܕܣ ܐܪܟܠܐܘܣ ܒܡܠܟܘܬܐ. It may also be noted that Mrs. Margoliouth records[2] the phrase ܡܩ̈ܒܠܢܐ ܘܝܪ̈ܬܐ with the meaning *successors and heirs*. The expression in our passage therefore means that Darius received the kingdom from Belshazzar, and may be rendered 'succeeded to the kingdom'. It was so rendered by Jerome, *successit in regnum*, while the rendering of the LXX and of Theodotion, παρέλαβε τὴν βασιλείαν, has the same significance[3]. Moreover, in 4 Macc. iv. 15 we find[4]: ܟܕ ܕܝܢ ܡܝܬ ܣܠܘܩܘܣ ܡܠܟܐ ܡܩܒܠ ܠܗ ܒܪܗ ܐܢܛܝܘܟܘܣ ܕܡܬܩܪܐ ܐܦܝܦܢܣ ܡܠܟܘܬܗ, and in the Syriac version of 2 Macc. iv. 7 there stands[5] the phrase ܩܒܠ ܡܠܟܘܬܐ, used of the succession of Antiochus Epiphanes, while in the Syriac version of Bel and the Dragon, verse 1, the same phrase is used[5] of Cyrus' receiving the kingdom from Astyages. Where there is such abundance of evidence for the use of the idiom to express either normal inheritance or inheritance by the sword, it is idle to pretend that in the book of Daniel it must denote a delegated authority.

As little can the expression הָמְלַךְ עַל מַלְכוּת, found in Dn ix. 1, be used to prove that Darius reigned by the grace of another. That expression is unique, the Hophʿal occurring nowhere else. In the Peshiṭta version it is rendered by ܐܡܠܟ ܒܡܠܟܘܬܐ, with which accords the Vulgate *qui imperavit*. The LXX similarly has ὃς ἐβασίλευσεν, while Theodotion reads the plural οἳ ἐβασίλευσαν. Montgomery therefore suggests[6] with great probability that we should read the Hiphʿil instead of the Hophʿal, and that we have here an

[1] iii. 13 (ed. Wright and McLean, p. 139, lines 1 f.).

[2] Supp. to the *Thesaurus Syr.*, p. 291a.

[3] Charles adduces, in proof of this, *Bel and Drag.*, verse 1, 2 Macc. iv. 7, x. 11, and Josephus, *Ant.* x. xi. 2 (x. 229, ed. Niese, ii, p. 381). We may add Herodotus, *Hist.* ii. 120 (Loeb ed., i, p. 412), and Boeckh, CIG ii, p. 880 (3595: 3, 17) and iii, p. 335 (4697: 1).

[4] Cf. Bensly, *4 Macc. in Syriac*, p. 13 of Syriac text.

[5] As given in Walton's *Bib. Sac. Polygl.*

[6] *Comm. on Dan.*, pp. 360 f.

Aramaism, the Hiph'il being employed in the sense of the Syriac Aph'el, which has the same meaning as the Hebrew Ḳal, but that the Massoretes mistakenly treated it as a unique Hoph'al. Even if the pointing of the MT is accepted, the phrase in no way implies a reference to Cyrus as the king-maker, but simply states that Darius was established on the throne.

That the authority of Darius was conceived as real and absolute is clear from the whole tenor of the narrative concerning him which our book contains. He issues decrees to 'all the peoples, nations, and languages, that dwell in all the earth'[1], precisely as Nebuchadnezzar is represented as having done[2]. Clearly his empire and his authority are regarded as being fully equal to those of Nebuchadnezzar. His dominions are so vast that they can be divided into a hundred and twenty satrapies[3]. It is not merely Babylonia that has come under his sway, but the entire Neo-Babylonian empire, and within his kingdom a monarch who forbids any petition of god or man will brook no interference. The book of Daniel is not concerned to tell how underlings and subordinates were compelled to recognize the power of the God of the Jews. It desires to set before its readers how the mightiest of monarchs and the proudest of potentates were brought to humble recognition of His power. And the reduction of the fictitious Darius the Mede to be a mere nominee of the all-powerful Cyrus would but make him an irrelevance in the book of Daniel.

[1] Dn vi. 26 (EV vi. 25).   [2] Dn iii. 31 (EV iv. 1).
[3] Dn vi. 2 (EV vi. 1).

VI. DARIUS THE MEDE IS A CONFLATION OF CONFUSED TRADITIONS[1]

I HAVE argued elsewhere[2] that the author of Daniel confused the fall of Babylon in 538 B.C. with that in 520 B.C., and the same view has often been taken by others. The former fall brought to an end the Neo-Babylonian empire, whose administration had been for many years in the hands of Belshazzar, while the latter was achieved by Darius Hystaspis. By confusing these events, our author arrived at his view of the kingdom passing from Belshazzar to Darius. Again, Darius Hystaspis organized the empire, and divided it into satrapies. But whereas Herodotus tells us[3] that he divided it into twenty satrapies, while his own inscriptions variously mention[4] twenty-one, twenty-three, twenty-four and twenty-nine divisions of his dominions, our author gives the number as a hundred and twenty[5]. Probably the number was thus swollen under the influence of Est. i. 1, which attributes to Xerxes an empire of a hundred and twenty-seven satrapies.

But it is not sufficient to suppose that Darius Hystaspis is the original of the Darius of the book of Daniel, and that our author has transposed Darius and Cyrus.[6] His con-

---

[1] Cf. Kamphausen, *Das B. Dan. u. die neu. Geschichtsf.*, p. 29; Prince, *Mene Mene*, pp. 42 ff.; Haupt, in Kamphausen, *Bk. of Dan.*, p. 29; Montgomery, op. cit., p. 65; Charles, op. cit., p. 145 f. Wilson argues at length (*Studies in Bk. of Dan.*, chap. xi) that Darius the Mede cannot be a reflection of Darius Hystaspis, since his name, race, &c., do not agree. This would be valid against the view that Darius the Mede *is* Darius Hystaspis, and that the error is merely chronological, but is irrelevánt against the view that the former is a *confused* reflection of the latter.

[2] *Expositor*, 9th series, ii, 1924, pp. 267 ff.

[3] *Hist.* iii. 89 (Loeb ed., ii, p. 116).

[4] Cf. Paton, *Comm. on Est.*, p. 124, and Rogers, *Hist, of Anc. Pers.*, p. 106; also Kliefoth, *Das B. Dan. übers. u. erk.*, p. 164.

[5] Dn vi. 2 (EV vi. 1). Lenormant found here the hand of a glossator, who thought of Darius Hystaspis, but introduced an exaggerated number. See *La Divination . . . chez les Chald.*, p. 218 f.

[6] The identification of Darius the Mede with Darius Hystaspis was main-

fusion is much more complex than that. For Darius Hystaspis cannot be supposed to have been sixty-two years of age[1]. The fact that his father was still alive at his accession[2], and that he himself lived for a further thirty-six years[3] would render such a supposition very improbable[4]. But it would appear that Cyrus was in the neighbourhood of sixty-two years of age at the time of his annexation of the Babylonian empire in 538 B.C.[5] For Cicero preserves a tradition[6] that he lived to be seventy years old, having reigned thirty years in all. Since his death appears to have taken place in the ninth year of his reign, according to the Babylonian reckoning from the annexation of the Babylo-

tained by Génébrard in the sixteenth cent. (cf. Des-Vignoles, *Chron. de l'hist. sainte*, ii, p. 515; Génébrard's work I have not seen), and more recently by Bosanquet (*Messiah the Prince*, pp. xv ff.), who held that Daniel prophesied from 575 B.C. to 492 B.C. But his chronology and his argument are alike negligible. Lagrange (RB, New Series, i, 1904, p. 501) also held that Darius the Mede is just Darius Hystaspis, and assumed that a series of textual alterations had introduced him between Belshazzar and Cyrus.

[1] Lagrange (ibid., p. 502) holds the sixty-two years to be the age of Daniel, and not of Darius.

[2] Cf. Herodotus, *Hist.* iii. 70 (Loeb ed., ii, p. 92) and the Behistun inscription §§ 35 f. (ed. King and Thompson, pp. 40 ff.).

[3] A tablet dated in his thirty-sixth year is given by Peiser in KB iv, pp. 308–11 (No. ix). Darius is also assigned a reign of thirty-six years by Syncellus (*Chron.*, p. 241, ed. Dindorf, p. 457) and by Eusebius (*Chron.* I. xv. 7, xviii. 5, ed. Migne, cols. 142, 177, or ed. Mai, pp. 48, 87, or ed. Schoene, i, cols. 69, 125).

[4] Pinches puts his age at accession at about thirty-six (DB i, p. 559 a). This is probably correct; cf. Müller, *Ctes. Gn. Frag.*, p. 65 b. Herodotus, however, says that he was about twenty years of age at the death of Cyrus (*Hist.* i. 209, Loeb ed., i, p. 262).

[5] This was noted by Bengel (*Ordo temp.*, p. 181): *Habebat Darius annos 62: ac Cyrus prope totidem.*

[6] *De Divin.* I. xxiii (46), (Loeb ed., p. 274): *Nam ad septuagesimum pervenit, cum quadraginta natus annos regnare coepisset.* Cicero gives Dinon as his authority. Ctesias (see Müller, *Ctes. Cn. Frag.*, p. 63a) and Justin (*Hist. Phil.* I. viii. 14, ed. Gronovius, i, p. 60) also assign Cyrus a reign of thirty years, while Herodotus (*Hist.* i. 214, Loeb ed., i, p. 268) assigns him a reign of twenty-nine years, and Sulpicius Severus (*Hist. Sacr.* II. ix, ed. Migne, col. 133, or ed. Halm, p. 64, ET, p. 101) a reign of thirty-one years. Xenophon, as has been above said, allows Cyrus a reign of but nine years. For he says that he first assumed the style of king after the fall of Babylon, and inherited the Median throne two years later. But the worthlessness of Xenophon's romance for serious history has been sufficiently demonstrated above.

nian empire[1], if Cicero is to be relied on for his age at death, we should arrive at an age of sixty-one at the time of his overthrow of Nabonidus and Belshazzar. This is so near to the sixty-two years of Darius the Mede that it may well be that just as the author confused the two occupations of Babylon, so he transferred the age of Cyrus, which some tradition had preserved, to Darius. His reason for recording a detail of so little significance to his narrative is not apparent[2].

Further, when our author calls Darius the son of Ahasuerus[3], he is introducing a fresh confusion. This time it has nothing to do with Cyrus, however, but does curiously

[1] Gray (CAH iv, pp. 11, 15) assigns to Cyrus a reign over Babylon lasting from 539 to 529 B.C., as also do Nöldeke (*Aufs. zur pers. Gesch.*, pp. 22, 26), Hall (AHNE, 7th ed., pp. 559, 563) and Weissbach (in *Hilprecht Ann. Vol.*, Zeittafel, facing p. 290, and in PW, Supp. iv, col. 1131), the last named observing that the reign of Cyrus lasted for nine or ten months over nine years. This, however, would seem to be incorrect. For the last recorded date of the reign of Cyrus is in Ab of his ninth year (*Hilprecht Ann. Vol.*, loc. cit., and Clay, *Bab. Exp. of Univ. of Penn.*, Series A, vol. viii, part i, p. 79, No. 74), and in Elul the accession year of Cambyses had already begun (see KB iv, pp. 284 f., No. 1). Since Cyrus became king over Babylon in Marchesvan, he reigned for less than five months of his accession year, and since he died in Ab or Elul of his ninth year, he reigned for about eight years and five months after his accession year—making in all a year less than Weissbach reckons. (In the table facing p. 291 in the *Hilprecht Ann. Vol.*, Weissbach makes the last year of Cyrus 530–29, which would put his death in the Julian year 530, in disagreement with the previous page.) Oesterley (*Hist. of Isr.* ii, p. 468) correctly gives the length of Cyrus' reign as 538–29 B.C., as does Rogers (*Hist. of Anc. Pers.*, p. 65).

[2] Various fanciful suggestions have been noted above.

[3] We may note the curious view of Eusebius that Darius the Mede and Darius the son of Ahasuerus are two different people. In royal lists at the beginning of Book II of his *Chron.* (ed. Migne, cols. 331 f.) he assigns three years to the former and thirteen years to the latter. The same distinction appears in George, Duke of Manchester's *Times of Dan.*, p. 54. In this work history is freely reconstructed, and the order of the kings is held (pp. 51 ff.) to be (1) Neb. I (identified on pp. 128 ff. with Cyrus the Great), (2) Neb. II (identified on pp. 126 ff. with Cambyses), (3) Belsh. (represented on pp. 257 f., 269, to be a son of Neb. II, who only reigned during his father's lifetime), (4) Dar. the Mede (identified on pp. 81 ff. with Dar. Hyst.), (5) Ahasuerus of the book of Esther (identified on pp. 86 f. with Xerxes), (6) Cyrus, (7) Artaxerxes, (8) Dar. the son of Ahas. (identified on p. 87 f. with Dar. Noth.), (9) Dar. the Pers. (identified on p. 90 with Dar. Codom.). This defiance of all historical sources attributes to Daniel a somewhat prolonged life, from the days of Nebuchadnezzar (= Cyrus) to the days of Darius Nothus.

reverse the relationship that existed between Darius
Hystaspis and Xerxes. For Xerxes was the son of Darius.
It is exceedingly difficult to suppose that our author
imagined that Xerxes the Great was a Mede, or that he was
a predecessor of Cyrus, and it may well be, as Bevan holds[1],
that he merely fitted his supposed Median kings with
Persian names through ignorance of genuine Median names.
On the other hand, we have already noted so many confusions in Greek writers between the names of Median
kings and the names of the Persian kings that the confusion
may well be due, not to our author, but to an older source,
which attached a Persian royal name to one of the Median
kings[2].

More serious is the styling of Darius a Mede. For both
Cyrus and Darius Hystaspis were certainly Persians. But
if our author supposed that Darius preceded Cyrus, this
further mistake would naturally follow. For he might well
know that Cyrus established the Persian empire, and the
knowledge that there had been a Median empire earlier than
the Persian would lead him to call Darius a Mede. It has
been pointed out, and especially by Charles[3], that he would
be influenced in this confusion by Scriptural prophecy.
For Jeremiah had prophesied that Babylon should fall
before 'an assembly of great nations from the north'[4], and
had further specified them as the Medes[5]. So, too, Isaiah
xiii had predicted the overthrow of Babylon by the Medes[6].
It was indeed natural that the Hebrew prophets should look
for the downfall of the Chaldaean régime at the hands of the
Medes. For it was by them that Nineveh was destroyed, and
though Nebuchadnezzar was then, and remained, the ally
of the Medes, he seems to have felt a certain nervousness

---

[1] *Short Comm. on Dan.*, p. 109.
[2] Winckler assumes (*Altor. Forsch.*, 2 Reihe, ii, p. 214 n.) that the confusion
is due to a glossator. But there is no reason to suppose that the text is not
original to the work.
[3] *Crit. Comm. on Dan.*, pp. 141 ff. Cf. Bevan, loc. cit.
[4] Jer. l. 9, 41.   [5] Jer. li. 11, 28.   [6] Isa. xiii. 17.

of them; and when he used his good offices to bring about peace between Media and Lydia[1], his desire was probably to prevent his neighbour and ally from becoming too powerful. And at the beginning of the reign of Nabonidus we find that monarch forming an alliance with Cyrus, who was to revolt against Astyages[2]. Apparently at a later date the author of Isaiah xxi hailed Elam and Media as the prospective conquerors of Babylon[3]. This was doubtless written after Cyrus, king of Anshan, in south-west Elam, had brought the rest of Elam under his sway, when to the Hebrew observer it appeared likely that these two powers might unite in the destruction of Babylon. And since Elam is mentioned first, it is possible that the passage dates from a time after the absorption of Media by Cyrus. Already, then, hopes were moving from the Medes to Cyrus, on whom they soon became centred in the writings of deutero-Isaiah[4]. But the author of the book of Daniel, in the absence of any exact history of the period, seems to have been misled by the earlier hopes, and to have assumed that though the Persians shared in the overthrow of the Babylonian empire, the throne of Babylon fell to the Medes.

Fruin argues[5] that our author probably believed that two other Median kings followed Darius, but of this we have no evidence[6], and it is extremely unlikely. For when we read in vi. 29 (EV vi. 28) that 'Daniel prospered in the reign of Darius, and in the reign of Cyrus the Persian', the implication would seem to be that the reign of Cyrus is thought of as immediately succeeding that of Darius.

It may be noted that Bevan thinks the confusion with

---

[1] Cf. Herodotus, *Hist.* i. 74 (Loeb ed., i, p. 92).

[2] See Langdon, *Neubab. Königsinsch.*, pp. 218 ff.; Smith, *Bab. Hist. Texts*, pp. 44 f.; Dougherty, *Nab. and Belsh.*, pp. 144 f.

[3] Isa. xxi. 2.

[4] Isa. xli. 2, 25 ff.; xliv. 28; xlv. 1 ff.; xlvi. 1 f.; xlvii. 1 ff.; xlviii. 14.

[5] NTT xvi, 1927, p. 102, and xvii, 1928, pp. 225 f.

[6] It has been noted above that Eusebius, by making Darius the son of Ahasuerus to be the successor of Darius the Mede, invents one additional king; but this is scarcely serious evidence.

Darius Hystaspis improbable[1]. He points out that the author of Daniel knew four Persian kings[2], of whom the fourth is clearly Xerxes[3]. While there is some difference of opinion as to the identity of the intermediate two, it is generally felt that Darius Hystaspis must have been one of them. If, therefore, the author of the book of Daniel knew of Darius as a successor of Cyrus, he would hardly have made him also a predecessor. It may be allowed that he would not have done so consciously. But since his ideas of this period were so inexact, this has little weight. If he could confuse the two captures of Babylon, he could just as easily make the contrary error of supposing there were two Dariuses about that time. And if he could transfer some things that properly belonged to Cyrus to his Darius the Mede without erasing Cyrus from the page of history, he could equally transfer some of the things that properly belong to Darius Hystaspis to his Darius the Mede without removing Hystaspis from his own place as a successor of Cyrus.

Despite all the efforts to find a place in history for Darius the Mede, therefore, we are compelled to recognize that he is a fictitious creation. No Median king succeeded to the control of the Babylonian kingdom, and no person answering to this Darius is known, or could be fitted into the known history of the period. For his creation the author of the book of Daniel appears to have used some traditions belonging to Darius Hystaspis and some belonging to Cyrus, but all confused and distorted. The root of his confusion probably lay in the two falls of Babylon, and in the preconceptions he brought to history from Scripture. Yet Cyrus was to him a different person—though a person without individuality in his narrative—from this Darius around whom clung in his mind some of the things that properly belonged to Cyrus. The claim of the book of

---

[1] Loc. cit.   [2] Cf. Dn xi. 2.

[3] This passage will be discussed below, where it will be noted that many hold that Xerxes is there said to be the fifth king, and not the fourth. Nor is the view that the wealthy king of Dn xi. 2 is Xerxes quite unchallenged.

Daniel to be a work of history, written by a well-informed contemporary, is shattered beyond repair by this fiction of Darius the Mede. But if the work is of much more recent origin, and if its purpose was not scientific but practical, not the setting forth of history, but the encouragement of men to loyal endurance, its worth is unimpaired. The value of the parable of the Prodigal Son depends not on the historical accuracy of the story, but on the message it enshrines. And the value of Daniel vi depends, not on the title of Darius to a place in history, but on its message that men ought always to pray, for the treasures of a deep religious experience are of more worth than the favour of princes, and the power of God is able to laugh at the might of monarchs and the raging of wild beasts.

THE FOUR WORLD EMPIRES

IN the second chapter of the book of Daniel we have the account of a dream of Nebuchadnezzar's, in which he saw a great image, with head of gold, breast of silver, belly of bronze, legs of iron, and feet of iron and clay; together with Daniel's interpretation of the dream, in which it is said to represent four successive kingdoms. In the dream the image is struck on the feet by a stone cut without hands,[1] whereupon it collapses and is shattered, while the stone grows and becomes a great mountain that fills the earth. This is said in the interpretation to represent an enduring kingdom that the God of heaven shall set up on the ruins of the earlier kingdoms.

In the seventh chapter of the book we have the account of a vision of Daniel's seen in the first year of the reign of Belshazzar, in which the prophet beholds four great beasts coming up out of the sea, of which the fourth is a nameless monster with ten horns, amongst which springs up an eleventh that has eyes and a mouth speaking great things. The interpretation given to the seer declares them to represent four kings, or kingdoms, while the eleventh horn is said

[1] From early times it has been supposed by expositors that the Virgin Birth of Jesus was referred to in the stone cut without hands. So Chrysostom (*Op. omn.*, ed. Montfaucon, vi, p. 215 a, or ed. Migne, PG lvi, col. 207), Cosmas Indicopleustes (*Top. Christ.* ii (146), ed. Migne, col. 112, ET, p. 69), Theodoret (ed. Schulze in Migne, PG lxxxi, col. 1301), Victor of Antioch (in Mai, *Script. vet. nov. coll.* i, 1825 et 1831, p. 35), Rupert of Deutz (*Op. omn.* i, p. 615 a, ii, p. 540 a, or ed. Migne, PL clxvii, col. 1505, clxix, col. 1345), Hugo of St. Chère (*Op. omn.* v, p. 148 b), Nicolaus de Lyra (*Bib. Sac.* iv, p. 298 b, and in J. P. M(igne)'s *Script. sanct. curs. compl.* xx, col. 88), Luther (*Der Proph. Dan. Deudsch*, p. b ii b, and *Kurtze Erc. uber Dan.*, p. a iii b), Oecolampadius (*In Dan. lib. duo*, p. 31), Bullinger (*Dan. exp. hom. LXVI*, p. 21 b), Pintus (*In Dan. comm.*, p. 51 b), Cornelius a Lapide (*Comm. in quat. proph. maj.*, 1727, p. 1280), Vigouroux (*Sainte Bib. Polygl.* vi, p. 283). More (*Exp. of Vis. of Dan.*, p. 6) held the stone to be the Church, which shall at the last strike the image, but the Virgin Birth to be appropriately referred to in the stone's being cut without hands, since it was the supernatural origin of the Church.

to represent a king who shall make war with the saints, and speak insolently against the Most High. In this vision the climax is reached in the setting up of a throne, on which an Ancient of Days sits in judgement, followed by the destruction of the fourth beast, while the others have their lives temporarily spared, though they are shorn of their dominion. One like a son of man then comes with[1] the clouds of heaven and receives the everlasting dominion. The interpretation says that this means that the saints of the Most High shall receive the kingdom,[2] which shall endure for ever.

[1] The LXX here has ἐπί = on, for MT עַם = with = Theodotion's μετά, and Charles follows LXX, holding that MT represents a corruption of perhaps not earlier date than the beginning of the Christian era (cf. *Crit. Comm.*, on *Dan.*, p. 186). The fact that both the reading of MT and that of LXX are represented in the NT and in early quotations (see full references in Charles, loc. cit.) can scarcely be used to indicate that MT contains the corrupt form, but leaves the question as to which is original entirely open, to be decided on grounds of general probability. Since many Theodotionic readings appear in writings of earlier date than that ascribed to Theodotion, it has been suggested that there were two pre-Christian versions of Daniel, one of which is represented in the Chigi MS., and the other a pre-Theodotionic version, which was but slightly revised by Theodotion (see Swete, *Intro. to OT in Greek*, pp. 48 f., and Gwynn in DCB iv, pp. 974 ff.). If this view is correct, the two alternatives may have been current in these two Greek versions from before the beginning of the Christian era.

[2] The interpretation makes it clear that the one like a son of man is not here a Messianic figure, but that just as the four beasts represent four earthly empires, so he represents the coming empire, transcending them in honour and dignity as man transcends the beasts. Similarly the clouds of heaven belong to the symbolism. The other empires are from the sea, i.e. from below, while this comes from the clouds, i.e. from above. Just as the clouds come from one knows not where, even so this kingdom of God's ordinance should have its beginning. But while the term 'son of man' has not here a personal Messianic connotation, it early developed it, and it is found in 1 Enoch xlvi. 2 ff., xlviii. 2, and in the NT. Hence the older commentators generally read back the Messianic sense into this passage. In modern times this view has continued to be taken by Ewald (*Proph. of OT*, ET v, p. 252), Orelli (*OT Proph.*, ET, p. 459), Briggs (*Mess. Proph.*, p. 420), Knabenbauer (*Comm. in Dan.*, p. 196), d'Envieu (*Le Livre du proph. Dan.* ii, pp. 592 ff.), Behrmann (*Das B. Dan. übers. u. erk.*, p. 48), Böhmer (*Reich Gottes u. Mensch. im B. Dan.* pp. 139–44), Riehm (*Mess. Proph.*, ET, pp. 193 ff. *note*), Cornill (*Proph. of OT*, ET, p. 174), Volz (*Jüd. Esch.*, pp. 10 f.), Wright (*Dan. and its Crit.*, pp. 109 f.), Tillmann (*Der Menschens.*, pp. 86 ff.), Stokmann (*Die Erleb. u. Ges. des Proph. Dan.*, pp. 112 f.), Boutflower (*In and Around Bk. of Dan.*, pp. 58 ff.), Noth (TSK xcviii–ix, 1926, p. 152). Ephraem Syrus, while holding that the prophecy was fulfilled in Christ, held its primary reference to be to the Jews (*Op. omn.*, Syriac and Latin, ii, p. 215), and Ibn Ezra maintained

Both chapters, then, speak of four world empires, to be followed by an enduring kingdom of divine origin, and it a collective interpretation of the phrase (cf. *Mik. Ged.* xii, p. 69 a, or Gallé, *Dan. avec Comm.*, p. 80). With this view many modern scholars agree. So Hitzig (*Das B. Dan. erk.*, pp. 114 ff.), Drummond (*Jewish Mess.*, p. 229), Reuss (*Litt. pol. et polém.*, p. 256), Meinhold (*Das B. Dan. ausg.*, p. 301), Bevan (*Short Comm. on Dan.*, pp. 118 f.), Prince (*Crit. Comm. on Dan.*, pp. 137 f.), Driver (*Bk. of Dan.*, pp. 102 ff.), Marti (*Das B. Dan. erk.*, p. 52, and in HSAT, 4th ed., ii, p. 476), Schürer (GJV, 4th ed., ii, p. 590, ET II. ii, p. 137), Buttenwieser (JE viii, p. 508 a), Völter (*Die Menschensohnfrage*, p. 24), Andrews (in Peake's *Comm.*, p. 529), Holzinger (*Beitr. zur AT Wiss.*, p. 106), Baumgartner (*Das B. Dan.*, p. 21), Bousset (*Rel. des Jud. im späthell. Zeit.*, 3rd ed., pp. 265 f.), Willet (in *Abingdon Comm.*, p. 754), Peake (*Serv. of Yah.*, p. 221), Obbink (*Daniël*, p. 102). Some scholars, while holding that this is the primary reference, believe this does not exclude the thought of an individual, who not alone symbolizes the Kingdom, but is its head. Cf. Keil (*Bk. of Dan.*, ET, p. 235), Riessler (*Das B. Dan. erk.*, p. 70), Lagrange (RB, New Series, i, 1904, p. 506, and *Judaïsme av. JC*, pp. 66 f.), Bertholet (RGG, 1st ed., iv, col. 296), Buzy (RB, New Series, xv, pp. 419 ff., and *Les Symb. de l'AT*, pp. 291 ff.), Welch (*Vis. of End*, p. 131), Goettsberger (*Das B. Dan. übers. u. erk.*, p. 56). Schmidt's view (JBL xix, 1900, p. 26, and EB iv, col. 4710), that the 'son of man' is the angel Michael, has been followed by Cheyne (*Bib. Prob.*, pp. 216 ff.), Hirsch (JE xi, p. 462 b), Kittel (*Relig. of People of Isr.*, ET, p. 213), Barnes (*People and Bk.*, p. 315), Box (*Jud. in Gk. Per.*, p. 213). A number of scholars have held that the origin of the figure lies behind the book of Daniel in mythology. So Gunkel (*Schöpf. und Chaos*, p. 331), Hommel (ET xi, 1899–1900, pp. 341 ff., and *Theol. Literaturbl.* xxiii, 1902, col. 147), Zimmern (KAT, 3rd ed., p. 392), Gressmann (*Urspr. der isr.-jüd. Esch.*, pp. 340 ff.), Jeremias (*OT in Light of Anc. East*, ET i, p. 196), Meyer (*Urspr. und Anf.* ii, p. 199), von Gall (ΒΑΣΙΛΕΙΑ ΤΟΥ ΘΕΟΥ, pp. 412 ff.). The most recent extensive presentation of this view is by Gressmann (*Der Messias*, pp. 343–73), who holds that the term is of mythological origin, but in Daniel is definitely Messianic, standing not for a kingdom, but for an individual. Similarly Kraeling, *Oriental Stud.*, pp. 228 ff. Cf., too, Junker (*Unters. über lit. u. exeg. Prob. des B. Dan.*, pp. 55–65). This view is opposed and criticized by König (*Gesch. der AT Relig.*, pp. 528 ff.; cf. id., NKZ xvi, 1905, pp. 904–28). The argument which has often been brought against the representative view of the 'son of man' (e.g. by Auberlen, *Proph. of Dan. and Rev. of John*, ET, p. 41; Zöckler, *Bk. of Proph. Dan.*, ET, p. 157 b; Boutflower, *In and Around Bk. of Dan.*, p. 59; Kraeling, loc. cit.), that Dn vii. 21 proves that the 'son of man' cannot stand for the saints, since it shows that the saints were in the vision before the destruction of the Little Horn, and therefore before the appearance of the 'son of man', strangely misses the point that the 'son of man' is not held to stand for the saints, as such, but for the *Kingdom*, or *rule*, of the saints. Stier's objection (*Gott u. sein Eng. im AT*, p. 96 n.) that in vii. 14 the dominion is given to the 'son of man', and that therefore he cannot represent the dominion, might have some weight against the view that the 'son of man' represents the authority which is given to the saints, but has none against the view that the figure represents the rule of the saints, or *the saints as invested with authority*. Similarly Kraeling's further argument (loc. cit.) that the arrival on the clouds makes the collective interpretation incongruous is unconvincing,

has been agreed by the vast majority of writers that the four kingdoms of chapter ii are identical with those of chapter vii. A few have been found to dispute this, and to interpret the two chapters differently. Amongst these we may note Conring,[1] Dathe,[2] Hezel,[3] J. Jahn,[4] Lacunza,[5] Hitzig,[6] Merx,[7] Havet,[8] Meinhold,[9] and Eerdmans.[10] With such

since it merely confuses the symbolic and the actual. It would be as reasonable to argue that the lost piece of silver in Lk xv. 8–10 cannot symbolize lost souls, since these cannot be swept up with a broom.

[1] *Disc. ad Lamp. post.*, pp. 363 ff. Conring held the empires of chap. ii to be Nebuchadnezzar's, that of his successors, the Persian and the Greek, while those of chap. vii were the Median, the Persian, Alexander's, and that of Alexander's successors.

[2] *Proph. maj.*, pp. 608 f., 629. Dathe, following Harenberg, identifies the kingdoms of chap. ii with Nebuchadnezzar, Evil-merodach, Neriglissar, Laborosoarchod (Labashi-marduk), with Nabonidus as the mingled iron and clay. In chap. vii he finds the Babylonian empire of Nebuchadnezzar, the Persian empire of Cyrus, the Greek empire of Alexander, and the empire of Alexander's successors.

[3] *Die Bib. mit vollst.-erk. Anm.* vi, pp. 733 ff., 762 ff. Hezel's views are similar to those of Dathe.

[4] *Einl. in die göttl. B. des A. Bundes*, II. ii, pp. 611 f., 614 f. Jahn held the kingdoms of chap. ii to be the Chaldaean kingdom of Nebuchadnezzar the Median kingdom of Darius, the Persian kingdom of Cyrus, and the Greek kingdom of Alexander and his successors, and those of chap. vii to be the Chaldaean, the Medo-Persian, Alexander's, and that of Alexander's successors.

[5] *The Coming of Mess.*, ET i, pp. 136 ff., 162 ff. Lacunza held the four kingdoms of chap. ii to be the Chaldaeo-Medo-Persian, the Greek, the Roman, and the divided European states from the fifth cent. A.D., and the beasts of chap. vii to represent false religions, idolatry, Mohammedanism, false Christianity, and Deism.

[6] *Das B. Dan. erk.*, pp. 37, 99. Hitzig held the kingdoms of chap. ii to be Nebuchadnezzar's, Belshazzar's, the Medo-Persian, and the Greek, and those of chap. vii to be Belshazzar's, the Median, the Persian, and the Greek.

[7] *Cur in lib. Dan.*, pp. 19 f., 20 f. Merx held the kingdoms of chap. ii to be five in number, and to represent Nebuchadnezzar, Darius, Cyrus, Alexander, and Alexander's successors, while the four beasts of chap. vii he held to stand for Darius the Mede, the Persian empire, Alexander, and the Seleucids.

[8] *Le Christ. et ses orig.* iii, p. 306. Havet held the fourth kingdom of chap. ii to be the Macedonian and the stone to represent the Roman empire, while in chap. vii he held the fourth empire to be the Roman.

[9] *Das B. Dan. ausg.*, pp. 274, 306. Meinhold held the kingdoms of chap. ii to be the Neo-Babylonian, the Median, the Persian, and the kingdom of Alexander and his successors, and those of chap. vii to be the Neo-Babylonian, the Medo-Persian, Alexander's, and that of his successors.

[10] *Actes du xviii^e cong. des orient.*, pp. 199 f. and *Godsd. van Isr.* ii, pp. 49 ff. Eerdmans holds the kingdoms of chap. ii to be those of Nebuchadnezzar, Evil-merodach, Neriglissar, and Nabonidus, and those of chap. vii to be Egypt, Media, Lydia, and Babylonia.

relatively rare exceptions, however, it has been generally agreed that the two chapters are closely linked together. Not all, indeed, recognize the community of authorship of the chapters. For it has been already noted that a growing number of scholars hold the book of Daniel to be composite, and of these not a few divide the book at the end of chapter vi, or maintain chapter vii, though belonging to the first part of the book, to be an appendix from another hand. Many of the scholars[1] who maintain the composite origin of the book believe that chapter ii, or chapters ii and vii, were glossed in the Maccabean age, from which they hold the closing chapters to date. It would take us beyond our present purpose to discuss these questions. Nor is it necessary to do so. For the almost universal consensus of opinion that the four empires of the two chapters are to be identified alike makes it possible for us to examine their identification without such discussion. It will only be necessary, in dealing with the views of the scholars who differently identify the empires of the two chapters, to examine the proposed identifications in the light of the separate chapters to which each refers.

The point at which the discussion of these four empires impinges on the already discussed question of Darius the Mede is in the identification of the second empire. For a large number of scholars, especially since the beginning of the nineteenth century, have argued that the second empire is the Median, and so have found an historically false view of a Median empire, intermediate between the Neo-Babylonian and the Persian empires, inherent in the author's

[1] So Hölscher (TSK xcii, 1919, pp. 120 f., 122 f.), Sellin (*Einl. in das AT*, 6th ed., pp. 153 f., ET, p. 234), Haller (*Das Judentum*, 2nd ed., pp. 279 f., 295), Noth (TSK xcviii–ix, 1926, p. 155), Thilo (*Chron. des Danielb.*, pp. 33 ff.) Montgomery (*Comm. on Dan.*, pp. 176 f.), Scott (AJSL xlvii, 1931, p. 294). G. Jahn (*Das B. Dan. nach der LXX herg.*, pp. 22 f.) and Löhr (in Kittel's *Bib. Heb.*, 2nd ed.) also found glosses in chap. ii, but are not to be reckoned amongst those who divide the book into a Maccabean and a pre-Maccabean section. Similarly Junker (*Unters. über lit. u. exeg. Prob. des B. Dan.*, pp. 16 ff.), who holds the whole book to belong to the Persian period, but to have been glossed in the Maccabean age.

F

conception; and this error links with the conception of the
fictitious Darius the Mede that has been examined in the
foregoing study. Before this can be discussed, however, we
must first deal with the identification of the fourth kingdom.
It is here that discussion has principally concentrated
throughout the centuries of interpretation. For while the
traditional view has maintained the fourth kingdom to be
the Roman, there has been a long line of writers to maintain
that it is the Greek, and that the dream of Nebuchadnezzar
and the vision of Daniel reached their climax in the days of
Antiochus Epiphanes. This latter view does not necessarily
carry with it the further view that the second kingdom is the
Median, but it opens the way for that view. For if the Greek
view of the fourth kingdom fails, then the Median view of
the second kingdom fails with it.

I. THE FIRST KINGDOM IS THE NEO-BABYLONIAN

OF this there is little dispute. In Dn ii. 38 we read that Daniel specifically informed Nebuchadnezzar:'Thou art the head of gold.' There is therefore no uncertainty that in this chapter the first kingdom is either the reign of Nebuchadnezzar, or the Neo-Babylonian empire which he represents. A few have adopted the former view, but most the latter. The difference between them is not of great significance, but it will fall to be considered below in so far as it affects the identification of the second kingdom.

Similarly it is agreed by most that the first kingdom of chapter vii is the Neo-Babylonian. Hitzig, who identified the first kingdom of chapter ii with the reign of Nebuchadnezzar and the second with that of Belshazzar, found it necessary here to identify[1] the first beast with the reign of Belshazzar, since the vision was given in the reign of Belshazzar, when Nebuchadnezzar had already died. Eerdmans, again, holds[2] that the first beast of chapter vii represents Egypt, while Conring[3] and Merx[4] held the first beast to stand for the Median kingdom. But apart from a few such rare exceptions, there is a complete agreement that the Neo-Babylonian empire is again intended. Many writers, both in ancient and modern times, have found some confirmation of this in the terms of the description of the first beast. For of the winged lion it is said:[5] 'I beheld till the wings thereof were plucked, and it was lifted up from the earth, and made to stand upon two feet as a man, and a man's heart was given unto it.' It has been widely thought that this is a reference to the story of Nebuchadnezzar's madness, as recorded in chapter iv, where we are told that the monarch's heart was changed from a man's, and a

---

[1] Loc. cit.   [2] Loc. cit.   [3] Loc. cit.   [4] Loc. cit.   [5] Dn. vii. 4.

beast's heart given unto him, at the time of his affliction,[1] and that his understanding returned to him on his recovery.[2] This reference has been maintained by Jerome,[3] Hippolytus,[4] Aphraates,[5] Petrus Comestor,[6] Jephet Ibn 'Ali,[7] Nicolaus de Lyra,[8] Osiander,[9] More,[10] Hitzig,[11] Kliefoth,[12] Pusey,[13] Keil,[14] Meinhold,[15] Prince,[16] Wright,[17] Bertholet,[18] Hertlein,[19] Montgomery,[20] and Goettsberger.[21] It is therefore common to writers of all schools, and is represented amongst apologists and critics alike. Charles,[22] however, contests this view, though he agrees in the identification of the first beast with the Neo-Babylonian empire.

It should, perhaps, be noted that Ewald[23] held that Daniel lived at Nineveh in the days of the Assyrian Empire, and that a writer of the period of Alexander the Great composed a work in which prophecies concerning four world empires were attributed to this Daniel. In this work the four empires were conceived of as the Assyrian, the Chaldaean, the Medo-Persian, and the Greek. A later writer, of the Maccabean age, is then held to have re-edited this book, and since he now placed Daniel in the period of the Neo-Babylonian empire, he began with Nebuchadnezzar. This necessitated the separation of the Median from the Persian empire for the purpose of maintaining the number of the empires,

---

[1] Dn iv. 13 (EV iv. 16).   [2] Dn iv. 31 (EV iv. 34).
[3] On Dn vii. 4 (ed. Migne, col. 528).
[4] Cf. Bonwetsch, *Hippolyt's Komm. zum B. Dan.*, p. 188, or ed. Migne, cols. 644, 681; ET in *Ante-Nic. Chr. Lib.* ix, p. 107.
[5] Homily v. 13, ed. Wright, pp. 92 f., German tr. by Bert, p. 81, or ed. Parisot, in PS I. i, cols. 216 f., ET by Gwynn, p. 358. (The reference in Parisot and Gwynn is v. 16.)   [6] *Hist. lib. Dan.*, ed. Migne, col. 1454.
[7] *Comm. on Bk. of Dan.*, ed. Margoliouth, p. 34.
[8] *Bib. Sac.* iv, p. 309 a.   [9] *Bib. Sac., Proph. Omnes*, p. 73 b.
[10] *Exp. of Vis. of Proph. Dan.*, p. 29.   [11] *Das B. Dan erk.*, p. 104.
[12] *Das B. Dan. übers. u. erk.*, p. 191.   [13] *Dan. the Proph.*, 8th ed., p. 72.
[14] *The Bk. of Dan.*, ET, p. 224.   [15] *Das B. Dan. ausg.*, p. 297.
[16] *Crit. Comm. on Dan.*, p. 130.   [17] *Dan. and its Crit.*, p. 112.
[18] *Dan. u. die griech. Gef.*, p. 21.   [19] *Der Dan. der Römerz.*, pp. 31 f.
[20] *Comm. on Dan.*, p. 287.   [21] *Das B. Dan. übers. u. erk.*, p. 54.
[22] *Crit. Comm. on Dan.*, pp. 176 f. Cf. the *Westminster Assembly Ann.*, 2nd ed., on vii. 4: 'This hath not reference to Nebuchadnezzar'.
[23] *Proph. of OT*, ET v, pp. 169 ff., esp. p. 172.

though elsewhere in the book the editor recognized the Medo-Persian empire to be one. But there is no evidence whatever that the first kingdom was the Assyrian in any source our author used, and no evidence that Daniel lived in the Assyrian period, or that the work has been re-edited in the way supposed, and this very fanciful theory has secured little following. It is, however, found in the work of Bunsen,[1] Holtzmann,[2] and G. Jahn.[3] In any case Ewald agrees that in the present form of the book of Daniel the first kingdom is that of Nebuchadnezzar, and his theory concerns rather the alleged sources of our book than the book we have before us to-day.

That the author may have taken over the number of the world empires from some older source or tradition, in which the use was quite different from that he made of it, is not to be denied, though it cannot be positively proved. Meyer[4] and von Gall[5] think of a Persian origin, and Hommel[6] of a Babylonian, while Junker[7] holds the number to be schematic rather than historical.[8] All that is relevant here, however, is that from whatever source the writer of the book of Daniel derived the conception, we cannot define the significance it had in that source until we have it before us, while we can say with confidence that in the book of Daniel it refers to four successive historical kingdoms, of which the first was that ruled over by Nebuchadnezzar.

---

[1] *Gott in der Gesch.* i, pp. 514 ff.

[2] *Die jüng. Proph. u. die Schr.*, pp. 846 f.

[3] *Das B. Dan. nach der LXX herg.*, p. 67. König (NKZ xvi, 1905, p. 906) argues against Jahn that this view is ruled out by 'Thou art the head' in ii. 38. But on Jahn's view, as on Ewald's, the original meaning has been disguised by the present form. The real weakness of the view is that there is no evidence that the present form is not original.   [4] *Urspr. u. Anf.* ii, pp. 189 ff.

[5] ΒΑΣΙΛΕΙΑ ΤΟΥ ΘΕΟΥ, pp. 267 f.

[6] *Theol. Literaturbl.* xxiii, 1902, cols. 147 f. Hommel thinks the figures of chap. vii rest on Babylonian mythology, and that the origin of the ten horns is to be found in the ten prehistoric kings of Babylonian legend.

[7] *Unters. über lit. u. exeg. Prob. des B. Dan.*, p. 9.

[8] Cf. also Briggs, *Mess. Proph.*, p. 417: 'If the image and the beasts are symbols, so also are the numbers. The number four is usually symbolical of the wide extent of a thing.'

II. THE FOURTH KINGDOM IS THE GREEK

IT is here that the fundamental disagreement amongst expositors has always been found. For while the view that the fourth empire was the Roman long prevailed, it was by no means unchallenged, and in modern times a very large number of scholars have identified it with the Greek empire founded by Alexander, and reaching its climax, so far as the author of the book of Daniel was concerned, in the reign of Antiochus Epiphanes. Historically, indeed, this is an older view than the other, since it is found already in a passage in the *Sibylline Oracles*[1] which is commonly dated *circa* 140 B.C., but which I have shown reason to date a few years later.[2] Moreover, 4 Ezra (2 Esdras), which is our oldest witness to the Roman view, admits with clear reference to the Greek view that the Roman is not the original interpretation.[3] The Greek view is also represented in the Peshitta text of Daniel, where 'the kingdom of Greece' is prefixed to vii. 7 in the Syriac text, as printed in the Paris and London Polyglotts.[4] It is found besides, not only in the 'wicked Por-

---

[1] Book iii, line 397. The passage in which this reference occurs will be considered below.

[2] ZAW, New Series, iii, 1926, pp. 324–7.

[3] xii. 10–12: 'This is the interpretation of the vision which thou hast seen. The eagle which thou sawest come up from the sea is the fourth kingdom which appeared in vision to thy brother Daniel; but it was not interpreted unto him as I now interpret it unto thee' (ET of Box, in Charles's *Apoc. and Pseud.* ii, p. 613). Box (*The Ezra-Apoc.*, p. 268; cf. Oesterley, *II Esdras*, p. 139) says that Violet holds verse 12 to be an ancient gloss, and in accordance with this the verse is bracketed both in *Apoc. and Pseud.*, loc. cit., and in *The Ezra-Apoc.*, loc. cit. It is only the final words of the verse, however, 'or have interpreted it' (omitted above), which Violet regards as a gloss, since these are represented only in the Syriac and the Latin. The rest of the verse appears in all versions. Cf. Violet, *Die Esra-Apok.*, p. 346.

[4] The gloss is omitted in Lee's ed. It stands in the Ambrosian MS. (see Ceriani's photo-lithographic ed.), and it is probable that it stood in very early MSS. of the Peshitta. For Wyngarden has shown (*The Syr. Vers. of the Bk. of Dan.*, p. 34) that Ephraem Syrus used the Peshitta, and since he presents the Greek view of the fourth kingdom, which he is wholly unlikely to have invented, and since that view stands in surviving MSS. of the Peshitta, it is

phyry',[1] but in a long line of writers prior to the founding of
the modern critical school, including Ephraem Syrus, Polychronius, Cosmas Indicopleustes, an anonymous writer
quoted in Mai's *Scriptorum Veterum Nova Collectio*[2], Barhebraeus, Grotius, Junius, Broughton, Rollock, Polanus,
Willet, Piscator, l'Empereur, the Westminster Assembly's
Annotators, Lightfoot, Becmann, Calmet, and Venema.[3] To
these have been added a much greater number of more recent scholars, both within and without the critical school.
Nevertheless the Roman view still commands many adherents who hotly contest the case for the Greek view.

Wright imports prejudice into the question by saying:[4]
'The real objections of the modern school to the old
"Roman" interpretation arise from a determination to get
rid at all costs of the predictive element in prophecy, and
to reduce the prophecies of the Scriptures, Old and New, to
the position of being only guesses of the ancient seers, or
vaticinia post eventa.' That the Greek view commanded so
long and respectable an array of names amongst its suppor-
ters, prior to the establishment of the modern school, is a
sufficient refutation of this unworthy remark. That since
the establishment of the critical school, the Greek view has
continued to be held by scholars of unimpeachable orthodoxy, is ample proof that the case for that view rests on a far
more substantial basis than prejudice. J. Jahn[5], Rosenmüller, Zöckler, and Wescott,[6] to name no others, all of whom
accepted the traditional date and authorship of the book,

---

probable that it was already there in his time, and that it was from this source
that he took it. Wyngarden (ibid., p. 36) argues that the *terminus ad quem* for
the Peshiṭta Daniel is probably A.D. 200-50.

[1] *Apud* Jerome, on Dn vii. 7 (ed. Migne, col. 530).

[2] Of this writer Mai says: *Est homo antiquus et doctus, et ceterorum hujus
catenae participum societate dignus* (*Script. vet. nov. coll.* i, 1825 et 1831 ed.,
p. xxxiv).

[3] The references to the works of these writers will be given below.

[4] *Dan. and its Critics*, p. 128.

[5] Hengstenberg (*Gen. of Dan.*, ET, p. 8) calls Jahn the 'best defender' of
Daniel.

[6] The references to the works of these writers will be given below.

adopted the Greek view of the interpretation of the fourth kingdom, and it is particularly interesting to observe that a number of writers have based their adoption of the Greek view on the express claim that this alone allows due fulfilment to the predictions. They have argued that according to the dream of chapter ii the Messiah was to appear after the destruction of the fourth empire, and that in accordance with this Christ was born just at the commencement of the Roman Empire, while in the vision of chapter vii the fourth beast was destroyed just before the coming of the 'son of man'. This line of argument was followed by Cosmas Indicopleustes,[1] Polanus,[2] Willet,[3] Becmann,[4] Calmet,[5] and Stuart.[6] Similarly, in the Annotations published under the authority of the Westminster Assembly, we read: 'The truth is that the taking in the Romanes here is an errour hurtful to Daniels book and to all Christianity . . . and hath no colour of truth from Daniel.'[7]

Amongst those who identify the fourth kingdom with the Greek, culminating in the reign of Antiochus Epiphanes, there has been some disagreement, however, and Pusey[8] and d'Envieu[9] have tried to turn this against them, and to suggest that they may be allowed to answer one another. Their disagreement is as to the identity of the second and third kingdoms, and where so little information is given for their identification, no surprise can be occasioned by some disagreement. To suggest that difference on that point invalidates their agreement on the far more substantial question of the fourth kingdom, and in particular, of its climax, is wholly unwarranted. Three varieties of the Greek view have been advanced.[10] The most common view in

---

[1] *Top. Christ.* ii (146), (ed. Migne, col. 112; ET by McCrindle, p. 69).
[2] *In Dan. proph. comm.* i, pp. 104 f., or in Poole's *Synopsis*, iii, cols. 1419 f.
[3] *Hex. in Dan.*, p. 68.   [4] *Diss. de quarta mon.*, 4th ed., pp. 18 f.
[5] *Comm. litt. sur Dan.*, p. 583.   [6] *Comm. on Bk. of Dan.*, p. 189.
[7] *Assembly's Ann.*, 2nd ed., on ii. 40.
[8] *Dan. the Proph.*, 8th ed., pp. 103 f.
[9] *Le livre du proph. Dan.* ii, p. 641.
[10] The names of the principal adherents of each of these three views,

modern times is that the second kingdom is that of the Medes, the third that of the Persians, and the fourth that of Alexander and his successors. The second view is that the second kingdom is the Medo-Persian, the third the dominion of Alexander, and the fourth that of Alexander's successors. The third view is that the second kingdom is that of Belshazzar, the third the Medo-Persian, and the fourth that of Alexander and his successors.

But if these differences suffice to cast doubt on the Greek view, what shall be said of the Roman? For every age has brought its re-interpretation of this view, until they are found in bewildering profusion. There is no agreement whatever amongst its adherents as to how the Roman empire is to be defined, whether it has already ended or still continues under a fiction, or is suspended, whether the Little Horn is an individual or a succession, or whether the prophecy concerns the Papacy or the Mohammedan power. If solidarity on details is solemnly asked of the holders of the Greek view, the holders of the Roman view might surely be expected to set a better example. In fact, of course, the question cannot be decided by such means, but by the careful examination of the grounds on which the various views rest. And to these we must now address ourselves.

(a) *The Roman view is dictated by* a priori *considerations.*

The charge that the Greek view rests on an *a priori* disbelief in prophecy has been already denied and refuted. But that the Roman view rests on *a priori* considerations is sufficiently proved by its history. In the first place, it did not arise until after the Greek empire had passed away, its earliest appearance being found in 4 Ezra (2 Esdras),[1]

together with the references to their works, will be given below, when they are separately examined.

[1] xi. 1, xii. 10 ff. To the authors of the Apocalypse of Baruch xxxix and Rev. xiii, also, the fourth kingdom was to be identified with the Roman empire.

Josephus,[1] and the Epistle of Barnabas.[2] That the prophecy had had no literal fulfilment in relation to the Greek empire necessitated a reinterpretation by those who began with the assumption that it must be literally fulfilled. For the Greek empire had been succeeded by the Roman, and the Kingdom of God had not yet appeared to overthrow all earthly empires. To transfer the fulfilment to the termination of the Roman empire seemed a simple way out of the difficulty, and it was little wonder that the view became dominant in the Church,[3] being found in Irenaeus,[4] Hippolytus,[5]

[1] Charles (*Crit. Comm. on Dan.*, p. 169) claims that Josephus, in *Ant.* x. xi. 7 (x. 276) presents the Greek interpretation, since he states that the prophecies of Dn viii were fulfilled in Ant. Epiph. This, however, begs the question as to the identity of the fourth kingdom of chaps. ii and vii. Charles further says that the following sentence in Josephus, rendered by Whiston: 'In the very same manner Daniel also wrote concerning the Roman government, and that our country should be made desolate by them', is excised by Niese. I have not been able to find where Niese excises it, or on what grounds. In his six-volume ed. of Josephus' *Works*, he includes without comment the sentence τὸν αὐτὸν δὲ τρόπον ὁ Δανίηλος καὶ περὶ τῆς τῶν Ῥωμαίων ἡγεμονίας ἀνέγραψε, καὶ ὅτι ὑπ' αὐτῶν ἐρημωθήσεται (ii, p. 391), and in his *Flav. Jos. Ant. Epit.* he includes the same sentence, but with the substitution of χρόνον for τρόπον, and αἱρήσεται for ἐρημωθήσεται (p. 143). Furthermore, it has often been noted that in *Ant.* x. x. 4 (x. 210), after narrating the vision of chap. ii, Josephus says: 'Daniel did also declare the meaning of the stone to the king; but I do not think proper to relate it, since I have only undertaken to describe things past or things present, and not things that are future: yet if any one be so very desirous of knowing truth, as not to waive such points of curiosity, and cannot curb his inclination for understanding the uncertainties of futurity, and whether they will happen or not, let him be diligent in reading the book of Daniel, which he will find among the sacred writings' (ET of Whiston). It is hard to dispute that behind this cautious reserve lay the unwillingness to offend the authorities by presenting the Roman interpretation.

[2] *Ep. Barn.*, 4.

[3] For a catena of patristic citations, see Jan, *Ant. et pervulg. de quat. mon. sent. ass.*, chap. i. The ten horns of chap. vii were commonly reckoned to be ten future kings amongst whom the Roman empire should be divided, and the three uprooted horns were held to be Egypt, Libya, and Ethiopia (cf. Jerome, on vii. 8, ed. Migne, col. 531; Hippolytus, ed. Migne, cols. 644, 684, or ET in *Ante-Nic. Christ Lib.* vi, pp. 446, 474, ix, p. 108; Irenaeus, *Contra Haer.* v. xxvi. 1, ed. Massuet in Migne, col. 1192, or ed. Harvey, ii, p. 395, ET by Roberts and Rambaut, in *Ante-Nic. Christ. Lib.* ix, p. 125 f., or by Keble, p. 510; Petrus Comestor, *Hist. Lib. Dan.*, ed. Migne, col. 1454).

[4] Ibid.

[5] Cf. Bonwetsch, *Hippolyt's Komm. zum B. Dan.*, p. 196, or ed. Migne, cols. 644, 681, ET in *Ante-Nic. Christ. Lib.* ix, p. 108.

Origen,[1] Eusebius,[2] Aphraates,[3] Cyril of Jerusalem,[4] Chrysostom,[5] Jerome,[6] Theodoret,[7] Isidore of Pelusium,[8] Petrus Archidiaconus,[9] Petrus Comestor,[10] and Rupert of Deutz.[11] Jewish interpreters[12] were equally ready to adopt a Roman scheme, but whereas they looked for the fifth monarchy with the advent of the Messiah, Christian interpreters are divided as to whether the prophecies were fulfilled in the birth of Christ, or whether they are to be fulfilled in the Second Advent, the latter view being by far the more widely held.[13] Some have held that the prophecy of chapter ii began to be fulfilled in the birth of Christ,

---

[1] Cf. Migne, PG xii, col. 60.

[2] *Dem. Evang.*, Fragment of Bk. xv (ed. Migne, col. 793, ET by Ferrar, ii, p. 237).

[3] Homily v. 10 ff. (ed. Wright, pp. 89 ff., German tr. by Bert, pp. 78 ff., or ed. Parisot, in PS I. i, cols. 208 ff., ET by Gwynn, pp. 356 ff.—the reference in Parisot and Gwynn being v. 13 ff.). But Aphraates reckoned the successors of Alexander and the Romans as a single kingdom, the Greeks covering the first 269 years, and the Romans 293 years—to the death (A.D. 249) of Philip, reputed to have been the first Christian emperor (see note in Gwynn's ed., p. 359 n.). Aphraates also regards the ten horns as ten Greek kings who arose until Antiochus (v. 14, ed. Wright, p. 94, ed. Bert, p. 82, ed. Parisot, col. 220, ed. Gwynn, p. 359—v. 19 in the last two cases), he being the Little Horn.

[4] *Catech.* xv. xiii (ed. Migne, col. 888, ET in Pusey's *Lib. of Fath.*, p. 190, or by Gifford, p. 108).

[5] *Op. omn.*, ed. Montfaucon, vi, 1724, pp. 216, 237 f., or ed. Migne, PG lvi, cols. 208, 230.

[6] On Dn ii. 40 and vii. 7 (ed. Migne, cols. 504, 530).

[7] On Dn ii. 39 f. (ed. Schulze in Migne, PG lxxxi, col. 1304).

[8] *Epist. lib. quinque*, 1. ccxviii (ed. Possinus in Migne, col. 320).

[9] *Quaest. in Dan.*, ed. Migne, cols. 1347, 1352 f.

[10] *Hist. lib. Dan.*, ed. Migne, cols. 1449, 1453 f.

[11] *Op. omn.* i, pp. 615 a, 618 b, ii, pp. 540 a, 542 b; or ed. Migne, PL clxvii, cols. 1505, 1513, clxix, cols. 1345–1349 ff.

[12] Cf. *Midr. Lev. Rab.* xiii. 5, and *Gen. Rab.* xliv. 20. The Bab. Talmud (*Aboda Zara*, 2 b) states that Rabbi Johanan (died A.D. 279) held the Roman view. So, too, Rabbi Tanḥuma (cf. Buber, *Midr. Tanch.*, p. 91). Cf. too, Eisenmenger (*Entd. Jud.*, 1711 ed., i, p. 718, ii, 767, and Fischer, *Dan. u. seine drei Gef. in Talm. u. Midr.*, p. 50). For the idea of four world empires, culminating in the Roman—Babylonian, Median, Greek, and Roman—cf. also Targ. on Hab. iii. 17 (ed. Lagarde, p. 470).

[13] Henry (*Diff. crit. et hist. du livre de Dan.*, p. 152) observes: 'Faire dire au livre de Daniel que la destruction de l'Empire Romain doit être suivie de la seconde venue du Messie, c'est prêter à l'Ancien Testament une idée qu'il ne connaît pas, qu'il n'a jamais connue, et qu'il ne pouvait pas connaître'.

whose birth of a virgin is represented in the stone cut without hands, but that the consummation of the prophecies, and the final destruction of world empires and establishment of His abiding Kingdom, await the Second Advent. That many of the details of the vision fitted admirably with the Roman interpretation has often been claimed, though there has been little agreement as to the reference of these details. The duality of the legs of the image, or the iron and the clay, have often been held to foreshadow the division of the Roman empire between the Eastern and the Western emperors,[1] but Bullinger[2] found the reference to be to the older divisions between Marius and Sulla, Caesar and Pompey, Augustus and Antony. Others have thought the reference to be to the two consuls,[3] or the two sorts of government of the Roman empire, under the Republic and under the Emperors,[4] or to the ecclesiastical and the civil power of later days,[5] or to the Turkish and Christian powers of yet later days,[6] or to the conflict between

---

[1] So Nicolaus de Lyra (*Bib. Sac.* iv, p. 298 b), Pintus (*In Dan. comm.*, p. 44 c), Osiander (*Bib. Sac.*, *Proph. Omn.*, p. 70 a), Parker (*Vis. and Proph. of Dan.*, p. 5), Mencken (*Schriften*, vii, p. 150), Pusey (*Dan. the Proph.*, 8th ed., p. 68), Kliefoth (*Das B. Dan. übers. und erk.*, pp. 94 f., 206), Caspari (*Zur Einf. in das B. Dan.*, p. 118), Vigouroux (*Sainte Bib. Polygl.* vi, p. 273), Möller (*Einl. in d. AT*, p. 237). Pererius (*Comm. in Dan.*, pp. 122 f.) held the reference to be first to the Eastern and Western Roman empires, and then to the Turkish and Christian divisions of what had been the Roman empire. So, too, Graserus (*Hist. Ant.*, pp. 99 f.), and cf. Poole, below.

[2] *Dan. exp. hom. LXVI*, p. 19a. Cf. Rupert of Deutz (*Op. omn.* ii, p. 542b), Hugo of St. Chère (*Op. omn.* v, p. 148b), Huet (*Dem. Evang.*, p. 364), and Cornelius a Lapide (*Comm. in quat. proph. maj.*, 1727 ed., p. 1279). And cf. Poole (see below).

[3] So More (*Exp. of Vis. of Proph. Dan.*, p. 5). The iron and clay he held to be the secular and ecclesiastical power of later days (ibid., p. 6).

[4] So Prideaux (*O and NT Conn.* ii, p. 624), Poole (*Annotations*, on Dn ii. 41), Trochon (*Daniel*, p. 110). Poole held the division of the kingdom to refer to the Tyranny and the Aristocracy, and also to the Civil Wars of Sulla against Marius, and Caesar against Pompey, and the ten toes to represent the fissure of the Roman empire into ten kingdoms. The two legs he held to be the two consuls, and equally the Eastern and the Western emperors. He therefore combined many of the views that have been held.

[5] So Cocceius (*Op. omn.* iii, p. 325a).

[6] So Pererius and Graserus (see above); also Huit (*The Whole Proph. of Dan.*, pp. 59 ff.), who held the Turkish power to be the iron, hard to the Jews,

the Latin and the German and Slav races in modern
Europe.[1] The mingling of seed, referred to in ii.
43, has
been held to point to the fusion of races under the Roman
empire,[2] to marriage alliances contracted between Caesar
and Pompey, and between Augustus and Antony,[3] to the
association of Antony with Cleopatra, and of Titus with
Berenice,[4] to a series of marriages between the Roman
emperors,[5] or to the marriages of the German Otto II and
the Russian Vladimir with princesses of the Eastern empire
towards the close of the first Christian millennium.[6]

The disintegration of the Roman empire brought fresh
difficulties, which have been dealt with in the most varied of
ways. Some have maintained that the Roman empire was
prolonged in the states which were formed out of it, and
elaborate efforts have been made to identify ten such kingdoms with the ten horns of chapter vii. But even amongst
those who have taken this line no agreement has been
possible, and constantly fresh selections have been made. A
century ago Tyso collected[7] no less than twenty-nine different

and the Papacy to be the clay, flexible to the Jews. Jephet Ibn 'Ali, on the
contrary, held the iron to represent the Romans, and the clay the Arabs (see
Comm. on Dan., ed. Margoliouth, p. 13).

[1] So Auberlen (*Proph. of Dan. and Rev. of John*, ET, pp. 220 ff.). Cf.
Kliefoth (*Das B. Dan. übers. u. erk.*, p. 97. Gärtner (*Erk. des Proph. Dan. u.
der Off. Joh.*, p. 88) also interprets iron and clay as Latins (friends of Papacy)
and Germans (enemies of Papacy). Some recent writers have endeavoured to
bring the interpretation still more up to date by finding modern democracy
in the clay, or even Socialism. Cf. Stevens, *Bk. of Dan.*, p. 38 and Gaebelein,
The Proph. Dan., p. 31.

[2] So Sulpicius Severus (*Chron.* II. iii. 6, ed. Halm, p. 58, or ed. Migne,
cols. 129 f., ET by Roberts, p. 98). So, too, Knabenbauer (*Comm. in Dan.
Proph.*, p. 92), and Wright (*Dan. and its Crit.*, p. 48).

[3] So Huet (*Dem. Evang.*, p. 364).

[4] So Hertlein (*Der Dan. der Römerz.*, p. 28).

[5] Cf. Calovius (*Bib. Test. Vet. ill.* ii, p. 598) and Benzel (*Prob. hist. de quat.
orb. mon.*, pp. 37 ff.).

[6] So Hofmann (*Weiss. u. Erf.* i, p. 281). The first of these is noted by
Calovius (loc. cit.) as the fifteenth of his series of seventeen Roman inter-
marriages. Otto married Theophano in A.D. 972, and Vladimir married
Anna in A.D. 988.

[7] *Eluc. of Proph.*, pp. 100–10, 114. Mede's list may be quoted as an
example: Britons, Saxons, Franks, Burgundians, Visigoths, Suevians,
Vandals, Almanes, Ostrogoths, Greeks (see *Works*, p. 661). All such efforts

selections, from amongst a total of sixty-five names, that had been proposed prior to his day. Others have held the Roman empire to be prolonged, not through the states that sprang out of it, but by a legal fiction, through the Holy Roman empire.[1] That this came to an end in 1806 has not deterred some from finding a further continuation through a fresh fiction.[2] Thus Wright maintains[3] that it was continued under Napoleon, and revived by Napoleon III, and that it may be said still to exist.

Others, again, have held the ten horns of chapter vii to represent individuals, but there has been complete disagreement as to whether they are successive or contemporaneous.[4] The early Christian view was that they were the first ten Caesars,[5] and in modern times this view has been revived by Lagarde and Hertlein, who, however, locate the composition of the chapter *circa* A.D. 69.[6] Augustine, by a clear reinterpretation of this view to harmonize it with known history, held that the number 'ten' was indefinite,

---

are criticized by Venema (*Diss. ad Vat. Dan. emb.*, 2nd ed., pp. 170 ff.) and Tregelles (*Rem. on Proph. Vis. in Bk. of Dan.*, 5th ed., pp. 42, 68).

[1] Cf. Driver (*Bk. of Dan.*, p. 97) for a criticism of this view. Stokmann (*op. cit.*, pp. 49 f.) is the latest exponent of this interpretation. For an earlier presentation of a similar view, see Jan, *Diss. hist.-pol. de quat. mon.*, chap. i, and *Ant. et pervulg. de quat. mon. sent. ass.*, chap. v. Also, for an elaborate argument, unrelated to the Daniel passages, to prove that the Holy Roman Empire is the true heir and successor of the Roman empire, see Conring, *De Germ. Imp. Rom.*, in *Opera*, i, pp. 26–107. (Conring, however, held the Roman kingdom to be, not the fourth, but the fifth and enduring monarchy.)

[2] Mencken was bewildered by the rapid changes that took place between A.D. 1800 and 1809. He held that by the ten toes ten kingdoms were intended, but the turning of some of the states he had identified as amongst them into Republics caused him to revise his opinions, and to content himself with the assurance that the kingdoms would number ten at the time of the consummation (*Schriften*, vii, pp. 153 f.).

[3] *Dan. and its Crit.*, p. 127. Cf. also Boutflower, *In and Around the Bk. of Dan.*, p. 33.

[4] Pusey (*Dan. the Proph.*, 8th ed., p. 79), Keil (*The Bk. of Dan.*, ET, p. 240), and Stokmann (op. cit., p. 107) all insist that the horns are contemporaneous. So, earlier, Nicolaus de Lyra (*Bib. Sac.* iv, p. 310 a).

[5] This view is found in the Ep. of Barn. (cf. Lightfoot, *Apost. Fathers*, p. 240).

[6] Cf. Lagarde, in GGA, 1891, p. 509, and Hertlein, op. cit., p. 45. These both begin with Julius Caesar and Mark Antony.

equivalent to 'many', and that the 'ten horns' were to be identified with the entire succession of the monarchs of the Roman empire.[1] Others have followed him in holding the number to be indefinite,[2] and have interpreted even more vaguely, thus avoiding the necessity for any exact identification. Hengstenberg, on the other hand, dispenses with any attempt at identification by supposing that the number will be definite at the time of its final fulfilment,[3] and a similar view is taken by Reichel.[4]

Another factor was brought into the discussion by the Reformation, and it is not surprising that many Protestant scholars reinterpreted the prophecies to find the Papacy in them. They identified the Little Horn with the Papal power,[5] and found it to represent not an individual but a succession of persons. Naturally enough, this view found little favour with Roman Catholic writers,[6] though it has

---

[1] *De Civ. Dei*, xx. xxiii (ed. Migne, cols. 695 f., ET by Dods, ii, p. 394).

[2] So Calvin, who interprets (*Comm. on Bk. of Dan.*, ET by Myers, ii, p. 25) of the plurality of the provinces of the Roman empire, under the government of proconsuls or praetors, or, alternatively (p. 62) of the control of the Roman empire by the Senate, instead of by a single monarch. Wright, too, maintains (*Dan. and his Proph.*, p. 159) that the number is not specific, and again (*Dan. and its Crit.*, p. 127) that the horns are not particular kingdoms. Similarly Kliefoth (*op. cit.*, p. 94) and Briggs (*Mess. Proph.*, p. 418). D'Envieu (op. cit., ii, pp. 671 f.) holds the ten horns to represent a great many kings, while Trochon (*Daniel*, p. 177) holds the number to be symbolical of a definite and determined whole.   [3] Op. cit., ET, p. 171.

[4] TSK xli, 1848, p. 959: 'Jede Erklärung derselben durch die gegenwärtig bestehenden Staaten ist eine willkürliche; erst wenn die Zeit diesen letzten Weltreichs auch vorübergegangen, werden wir beurtheilen können, inwiefern die Theile dieses Reichs in der Zehn, als der Zahl der Vollendung, sich als die ein Ganzes bildenden darstellen.'

[5] Cf. Oecolampadius, *Comm. in Dan.*, pp. 89 ff.; Bullinger, *Dan. exp. hom. LXVI*, pp. 78 b f.; Abbot, *Ant. dem.*, passim; Parker, *Vis. and Proph. of Dan.*, passim; and More, *Exp. of Vis. of Proph. Dan.*, pp. 39 ff., 258 f. The view that the Papacy is to be identified with Antichrist is older, indeed, than the Reformation, and Zöckler (*Bk. of Dan.*, ET, p. 168) cites a study of Köhler's, in which many mediaeval writers who held this view are collected (see *Zeitsch. f. d. ges. luth. Theol. u. Kirche*, xxii, 1861, pp. 459 ff.). The Reformation gave the view fresh impetus, however. The oldest post-Reformation presentation of this view in English that I have been able to find is in Joye, *Exp. of Dan. the Proph.*, 1545, pp. 99 ff.

[6] Cf. Maldonatus, *Comm. in Dan.*, 1643 ed., p. 732; Bellarmine, *De Rom. Pont.* III. xxi, 1698 ed., in *Bibl. Max. Pont.* xviii, pp. 610 ff.; Cornelius a

had considerable vogue amongst Protestants, and especcially British Protestants,[1] and even yet survives.[2] Meanwhile Jewish scholars were bringing the Ottoman power into the prophecies, and were dividing the Roman empire into two parts, a Christian and a Mohammedan,[3] or were telescoping the Roman and the Greek empires into one with the argument that the Roman power sprang out of the Greek,[4] in the effort to identify the fourth kingdom, by a fresh reinterpretation, with the Ishmaelite empire.[5] Against

Lapide, *Comm. in quat. proph. maj.*, 1727 ed., pp. 1326, 1382; d'Envieu, op. cit. ii, pp. 696 ff.

[1] Not, however, exclusively amongst British Protestants. This view is found in Gärtner (*Erk. des Proph. Dan.*, pp. 104 ff.). In many English works it has been linked with the 'Year-Day theory' commonly associated with the name of Joseph Mede. Cf. Mede, *Works*, pp. 717 ff. (see also pp. 598 f.); Newton, *Observations upon Dan. and Apoc.*, pp. 74 ff., 90 ff., 123 (Whitla's ed., pp. 188 ff., 198 ff., 222, and cf. Whitla, ibid., pp. 101 ff.); Wintle, *Dan.*: *an imp. vers.*, pp. 107, 124 f., 211; Birks, *Four Proph. Emp.*, pp. 172 ff.; Rule, *Hist. Exp. of Bk. of Dan.*, pp. 197 ff. It is usual on this view to identify the three uprooted horns with the Exarchate of Ravenna, the kingdom of Lombardy, and the State of Rome. Cf. Mede, loc. cit., p. 661; Newton, op. cit., p. 75 (Whitla's ed., p. 189); Wintle, op. cit., p. 107. Parker, however, had more anciently identified them (op. cit., p. 17) with 'three Mahumetan Kings, one in Asia, the other in Syria, the third in Judaea, which were subdued by the Pope and his Western Armies, about the yeer 1099', while Rule has more recently identified them (op. cit., p. 203) with Rome, Apulia and Sicily. For criticisms of this whole viewpoint, cf. Tyso, *Eluc. of Proph.*, pp. 66 ff.; Lee, *Inquiry into . . . Prophecy*, pp. xii ff., and *Events and Times of Vis. of Dan. and St. John*, pp. xvii ff.; Tregelles, *Rem. on Proph. Vis. in Dan.*, 5th ed., pp. 42 f., 67 ff., 110–25; Cowles, *Ezek. and Dan.*, pp. 459 ff. Tyso observes (op. cit., p. 66) that 'all writers on chronological prophecy, who reckon a day for a year, have had their calculations falsified by time, whenever the predicted year has arrived, although they have fixed upon very different dates for the commencement of the prophetic periods'. Since his day a further century of failures has confirmed the criticism. (It should be noted that while the 'Year-day theory' is often associated with the name of Joseph Mede, Osiander anticipated him in taking the 1290 days of Dan. xii. 11 to mean 1290 years. See his *Bib. Sac., Proph. Omn.*, p. 76b.)

[2] Cf. Wright, *Dan. and his Proph.*, p. 166, and Boutflower, *In and Around Bk. of Dan.*, p. 33.

[3] So Ibn Yaḥya (cf. *Paraphrasis*, ed. l'Empereur, p. 51).

[4] So Ibn Ezra (cf. Gallé, *Dan. avec comm.*, pp. 73 ff.).

[5] Ibn Ezra identified the ten horns with ten Arab kingdoms—a view essentially similar to that of some of the Christian interpreters above referred to, but with the substitution of Arab for European kingdoms. Cf. Gallé, op. cit., p. 75, and Winter and Wünsche, *Gesch. d. rabb. Litt.* ii, p. 305 (where read Dan. vii. 4–8 for 5 Mose vii. 4–8).

such Jewish arguments Calvin fulminates,[1] but Oecolampadius is more accommodating, and holds that the Little
Horn means the Papacy and the successors of Mohammed
equally.[2] It is also to be noted that the Coptic version of
the book of Daniel contains a long additional chapter, in
which the four kingdoms are identified with the Persian, the
Roman, the Greek, and the Ishmaelite.[3]

To all of these the culmination of the prophecy was in the
future, and the establishment of the abiding kingdom had
not yet been achieved. There have not been wanting some,
however, who have held the founding of the fifth monarchy
to lie, not in the future, but in the past. Amongst these
was Calvin, who held[4] that there is no reference in the
prophecies to the Second Advent of Christ, and that the
enduring empire already exists. In his view the whole is to
be interpreted in relation to the life of Christ, and the
founding of the Christian Church. But the kingdom that
took its rise with the establishing of the Church was not a
world monarchy in the same sense as the others; nor could
it be said to have overthrown them. Hence Calvin did not
date its beginning from the birth of Christ, or from any
point in His ministry, but from the time when 'the Gospel
began to be promulgated and Christ became generally
known throughout the world'. He defined this as being
towards the end of the first century A.D., and as he agreed
that the Messiah's kingdom ought, by the prophecy, to
follow immediately on the end of the fourth world-empire,
he had to argue that the Roman empire came to an end at

[1] *Comm. on Bk. of Dan.*, ET by Myers, i, pp. 181 ff.
[2] *Comm. in Dan.*, pp. 89 ff. Osiander finds here only the Turk (*Bib. Sac.,
Proph. Omn.*, p. 73 b), following Luther, who says (*Der Proph. Dan. Deudsch*,
p. c i a) the Little Horn 'ist der Mahometh odder Türcke, der itzt Aegypten,
Asiam, und Greciam hat'. Similarly Huit (*Whole Proph. of Dan.*, pp. 187 ff.)
identified the Little Horn with the Turkish power, holding the three uprooted
horns to be Asia, Greece, and Syria.
[3] See Tattam, *Proph. Maj.* ii, pp. 386 ff. Note the transposition of the
Greek and Roman kingdoms here. And cf. Bevan (*Short Comm. on Dan.*,
p. 3) on this additional chapter.
[4] *Comm. on Bk. of Dan.*, ET by Myers, i, p. 186, ii, p. 37.

that time. He therefore presented the very artificial view that as from the time of Trajan the empire began to be transferred to foreigners, it may be said to have ended then.

Similarly Prideaux[1] held the fulfilment of the prophecy to be the founding of the Church, which, however, he dated from the Crucifixion. He therefore placed the decay of the Roman empire in the period beginning from the reign of Tiberius. Alcazar pushed back the fulfilment of the prophecy yet farther, holding[2] that the ten horns were the polyarchate, or Senate of Rome, and that the Little Horn was Julius Caesar. In this way he was able to find the climax of the vision and the termination of the four empires before the birth of Christ.[3]

Others have moved in the exactly opposite direction, and instead of finding that the prophecy concerns the past, including the founding of the fifth kingdom, have held that the ten horns represent ten kingdoms that have yet to be established.[4] In order to secure this they have been compelled to suppose that the prophecies leap over ages that they ignore.[5]

---

[1] *Op. cit.* ii, p. 624. [2] *In eas VT partes quas resp. Apoc.*, pp. 278 ff.

[3] The view of Auchincloss (*Bk. of Dan. Unlocked*, pp. 54 ff.) may here be noted, not for its intrinsic importance, but because it represents in the present century this Praeterist viewpoint, and finds the fulfilment of the prophecies in connexion with the first coming of Christ. The ten horns he holds to be the rulers that followed the Jugurthine War, with the family of the Caesars as the Little Horn, which in the person of its descendants should speak great words, and which made war with the saints in the Neronic persecution of the Christians.

[4] This view was common amongst the early Fathers. Cf. Irenaeus, *Contra Haer.* v. xxvi. 1 (ed. Massuet in Migne, col. 1192, ed. Harvey, ii, p. 395, ET by Roberts and Rambaut in *Ante-Nic. Christ. Lib.*, ix, pp. 125 f., or by Keble, p. 510); Lactantius, *Div. Inst.* vii. xvi (ed. Migne, col. 790, ET by Fletcher in *Ante-Nic. Christ. Lib.* xxi, p. 465, German tr. by Brandt in *Corp. script. ecc. lat.* xix, p. 638); Jerome, on vii. 8 (ed. Migne, col. 531); Petrus Archidiaconus (*Quaest. in Dan.*, ed. Migne, col. 1353). It is found also in Maldonatus (on vii. 7, *Comm. in Dan.*, 1643 ed., p. 732) and in Hengstenberg (op. cit., ET, p. 171), Tregelles (*Rem. on Proph. Vis. in Dan.*, p. 43), and Keil (op. cit., ET, p. 268).

[5] Hofmann (*Weiss. u. Erf.* i, p. 281) held that there is a gap of more than a millennium, and brought the culmination of the prophecy into the age in which he himself lived. The theory of breaks in prophecy is common to almost all holders of the Roman view of the fourth kingdom, the differences between them being as to where the breaks occur and the length of the

This theory reaches its extreme in the writings of Maitland,[1] Todd,[2] and Browne,[3] who, by following the principles of interpretation so widely adopted relentlessly to their logical conclusion, have demonstrated their absurdity. It will be convenient to note their views here, though they do not quite belong here, since they followed Lacunza (Julian Josafat Ben Ezra)[4] in making the Roman empire to be the *third*, and not the *fourth*, of the kingdoms. Unlike Lacunza,[5] however, they believed the fourth kingdom is still in the future. Todd observed[6] that the Roman view of the fourth kingdom involves more important errors now than it did when held by the ancients, and asked[7] in what sense the Roman empire can be said to owe its fall to Christianity? Similarly Maitland pointed out[8] that the Roman empire has long ceased to exist, but the fulfilment of vii. 22, 26f. has not yet come. Yet it ought to come under the fourth empire. He therefore built on the foundation assumption that the prophecy must be exactly fulfilled the conclusion that the fourth kingdom is still future. To provide for this desperate reinterpretation, these writers were

gaps. We shall have occasion below to note the various leaps that have been supposed to occur in chap. xi.

[1] *Proph. concerning Antichrist*, pp. 5 ff. Maitland held that the fourth kingdom of chap. vii is certainly the same as the fourth kingdom of chap. ii, but that possibly the four kingdoms of chap. vii are contemporary. This would be to thrust the whole of the vision of chap. vii into a time which is still future in our day, and to reach the climax of Futurism.

[2] *Discourses on Proph. rel. to Ant.*, pp. 55–90.

[3] *Ordo saec.*, pp. 675 ff.   [4] *Coming of Mess.*, ET, p. 140.

[5] Lacunza held the fourth kingdom of chap. ii to have begun to be formed from the fifth century of the Christian era, by the irruption of the barbarians, and to be a kingdom that lacks unity (p. 141). The four beasts of chap. vii he held to be explained differently, and to represent false religions—idolatry, Islam, false Christianity, and Deism or Antichristianity (pp. 162 ff.). For this latter view, cf. that presented in pseudo-Aquinas (*Exp. I super Apoc.*, in *Op. omn.*, Parma ed., xxiii, pp. 433 f.) that the four beasts of Dn vii are the Jews, Pagans, Arians, and Saracens. (On the wrong ascription of this treatise to Aquinas, cf. *Op. omn.*, Leonine ed., i, pp. cxxvi ff.).

[6] Op. cit., pp. 89 f.   [7] Ibid., p. 55.

[8] Op. cit., p. 6. Cf. Todd, op. cit., p. 69: 'To the reader of history no fact seems better attested or more certain, than that the Roman monarchy is extinct'.

compelled to assume that the first kingdom was the Chaldaeo-Medo-Persian,[1] and to make Alexander's empire the second, and to eliminate the manifestly impossible break between the fourth kingdom and the enduring kingdom by postulating a vast leap between the third kingdom and the fourth.

Between the 'Praeterist', the 'Futurist', and the 'Anti-papal' schools the warmest controversies have raged, and we need not here enter into all of their extravagances.[2] That they have been born of the *a priori* assumptions and preju-dices of their advocates has been clear to their opponents, even within the Roman school, and it is hardly to be disputed that we have a succession of reinterpretations in the light of history, as known to the date of the interpreter, to force into the prophecies each his own view of history.

It remains to note a further variety of the Roman view, to which reference has already been made, of a quite distinct character from those so far indicated. This is the view of Havet, Lagarde and Hertlein, that chapter vii dates from the first century A.D. and that it was therefore written by one who lived under the Roman Empire. Havet[3] locates the second half of the book of Daniel in Herodian times, while Lagarde[4] places chapters vii and ix–xii *circa* A.D. 69, and Hertlein[5] ascribes the composition of chapters i–vii to the

---

[1] Maitland, op. cit., p. 5; Browne, op. cit., p. 676; Todd, op. cit., pp. 78 ff. The last named, however, presents the alternative view that the Roman empire may be passed over entirely (pp. 80 ff.). For the view that the Chaldaean and the Medo-Persian empires are to be reckoned together as a single kingdom, these writers rest on Lacunza, op. cit., pp. 136 ff.

[2] A combination of the Praeterist and the anti-Papal views is found in Hawkins, *Treat. on Sec. Chap. of Dan.*, pp. 68 ff., where it is held that the Little Horn is the Papacy and the Khalifate, but that the fifth and enduring kingdom is that of Britain.

[3] *Le Christ. et ses orig.* iii, pp. 304 ff., and *Ét. sur la mod. des Proph.*, in *Rev. des Deux Mondes*, xciv, 1889, pp. 825–8.　　　[4] GGA, 1891, pp. 497–520.

[5] *Der Dan. der Römerzeit.* The linguistic data are a serious embarrassment to Hertlein's view. For while it is certain that the Aramaic of Daniel and Ezra is younger than the fifth cent. B.C., and probable that the Aramaic of Daniel is somewhat younger than that of Ezra, it is very improbable that the Aramaic of Daniel is of so late a date as the first century A.D., and strong reasons for so wide a separation of the Aramaic of Daniel from that of the Papyri and of Ezra would need to be presented. (Cf. Baumgartner, *Das Aram. im B. Dan.*,

first century A.D. Their agreement extends only to chapter vii, therefore. Lagarde and Hertlein hold the ten horns to be the line of the Roman emperors, beginning with Julius Caesar and Mark Antony, and the three uprooted horns to be Galba, Otho, and Vitellius, while Vespasian is held to be the Little Horn.[1] The Messianic expectations of the period are held to have inspired the author to look for the immediate advent of the kingdom of God.[2] Havet, on the other hand, thinks the ten horns are the Hasmonaeans.[3]

(b) *The Roman view does not fit the prophecies.*

This, as Driver observes,[4] is the fatal objection to the Roman view. For a theory which rests on the assumption

in ZAW, New Series, iv, 1927, pp. 81–133; Rowley, *Aram. of OT*; Charles, *Crit. Comm. on Dan.*, pp. lxxx ff.) Further, the fewness of Greek loan-words and the absence of Latin loan-words would call for some explanation in that age. I have argued (op. cit., pp. 147 ff.) that in the age of Antiochus Epiphanes, when Judaism was fighting against Greek culture even more than against Greek dominion, it was natural that Greek words should not be employed, save for special reasons. But in the days of Vespasian Judaism was not fighting against an alien culture so much as against an alien rule. This might, even so, prove a sufficient reason for the exclusion of Latinisms, but there would be no more reason to avoid Graecisms than Persian and Babylonian loan-words.

[1] Bernfeld (EJ v, col. 767) appears to follow Lagarde.

[2] This view finds it necessary to carry the sections of 1 Enoch and the Sib. Oracles, which contain allusions to the 'son of man' and the 'ten horns' into the first century A.D., and also to deny that the use of the term 'son of man', which the Gospels ascribe to Jesus, can have been really found on His lips. Hertlein is further compelled to place 1 Macc. also in the Christian era. Moreover, Dn vii seems to have belonged to the pre-Theodotionic version of the book of Daniel (cf. Swete, *Intro. to OT in Gk*, 2nd ed., pp. 47 f., 421 f.). The antiquity of this version is indicated by the fact that some NT quotations are made from it (ibid., p. 48), and we have no indication that Dn vii—or Dn i–vii, on Hertlein's view—forms an addition to that version. Further, Judaism and Christianity were already separating at the time of the alleged composition of Dn vii, and it is highly unlikely that a creation of that age would have secured acceptance by both Jews and Christians. The fact that the Christians made such immediate use of it as they are held to have made in the Gospels, would militate strongly against its acceptance as canonical by the Jews. The whole view must be regarded as one of the extravagances of criticism. (For further criticism of this view cf. Bertholet, DLZ xxxi, 1910, cols. 2062–4, 2523–5 and Marti, in HSAT, 3rd ed., ii, pp. 417 f., or 4th ed., ii, pp. 458 f.)

[3] *Le Christ. et ses orig.* iii, p. 308, and *Rev. des Deux Mondes*, xciv, 1889, p. 826.   [4] *Bk. of Dan.*, p. 97.

that the prophecies are a supernatural outlining of future events, yet which fails to establish the accordance of history with the prophecies, stands self-condemned.[1]

1. The claim that these prophecies have been already fulfilled, and that the ten horns and the Little Horn are creatures of the past, and that the fifth monarchy has been already established on the ruins of the Roman empire, breaks on the indisputable fact that world monarchies continue. Whether the fifth monarchy was to be the world dominion of the Messiah, as most hold, or whether it was to be a purely spiritual kingdom, as the Praeterist school holds, the prophecies clearly imply that all other world monarchies would end with its advent.[2] To this Calvin presents[3] the wholly unconvincing reply that as the prophecies were for encouragement, they ignored these further continuations of worldly power. That is to confess that their accord with history cannot be secured naturally.

Nor is this all. For both of the visions clearly contem-

---

[1] I do not wish to be understood to suggest that OT prophecy is without a supernatural content. There *is* a divine element, and there is *also* a human element in it. The prophet contemplated the conditions of his own day and generation in the light of what he saw of the heart of God, and by the divine illumination of his spirit penetrated the issue of the events he witnessed, and unfolded the end towards which men were pressing. His message came not by the suspension of his personality, but through the organ of his personality. And therefore his predictions were not inerrant—as the story of Jeremiah amply proves. But where the prophet is held to be predicting events that should take place centuries after his time, and to be unfolding a history that was wholly unrelated to the circumstances of his own day, his prophecy becomes entirely supernatural, and comes not through the organ of his personality, but by its suspension. On such a view, therefore, there is no room for error.

[2] Cosmas Indicopleustes, however, who held the Greek view of the fourth kingdom, and who found the stone cut without hands to refer to the Virgin Birth of Christ, held that the fifth and enduring kingdom was the Roman, which was established at the same time as Christ came (cf. *Topog. Christ.* ii. (146), ed. Migne, col. 112, ET by McCrindle, p. 69). Grotius, too (*Works*, i, pp. 457, 467) held the fifth kingdom to be *imperium Romanum quod sedes erit Ecclesiae*. Similarly, Conring (*Disc. ad Lamp. post.*, in *Opera*, ii, pp. 363 ff.), who also held the Greek view of the fourth kingdom, maintained the Roman to be the fifth kingdom, and held that, in its successor, the German empire, it was destined to endure for ever. Conring, however, differed from Cosmas in holding the stone cut without hands to stand for the Roman empire, as also did Amner (*Essay towards Interp. of Dan.*, pp. 219 ff.).

[3] *Comm. on Dan.*, ET by Myers, i, pp. 178, 187 f.

plate a catastrophic end of the world monarchies. In the one a stone smites the image and brings it down with a fall that shatters it to fragments, while in the other the fourth beast is slain and its body destroyed as the consequence of the great words which the Little Horn spake. Whatever significance this type of interpretation attaches to the Little Horn, it fails to relate its arrogance to a catastrophic end of the Roman empire. Yet that is required by the conditions.

Again, if the fourth beast is to be identified with Rome, its destruction should have preceded the establishment of the fifth kingdom. In both visions, indeed, is this clearly set forth. Yet it is impossible to pretend that the Roman empire terminated before the inauguration of the spiritual kingdom of Christ, whether the beginning of that kingdom be placed at the Nativity, the Crucifixion, the spread of the Gospel, or the age of Constantine. The supposition of Calvin that the Roman empire may be said to have ended at the time of Trajan, and the other similar suppositions that have been noted, are at once too artificial and too inappropriate to the conditions to be satisfying.

Further, we are told that when the fourth beast was destroyed, the other beasts were spared for a time, though denied any dominion.[1] But how can it be maintained that at any time contemplated by the various forms of this interpretation Babylon, Medo-Persia, and Greece enjoyed a measure of existence that was denied to Rome?

This last consideration is equally fatal to the view of Lagarde and Hertlein, that chapter vii was composed about A.D. 69. On their view it is not necessary to establish any exact accordance with history, so far as the culmination of the prophecies is concerned, since they find in that culmination

---

[1] The LXX has κύκλῳ αὐτοῦ for MT שאר חיותא, and Jahn (*Das B. Dan. nach der LXX herg.*, p. 70) holds this to be original. Bludau, however (*Die alex. Übers. des B. Dan.*, p. 41) takes it for a free rendering, and Charles (*Crit. Comm. on Dan.*, p. 186) traces it to a corruption of MT. Justin Martyr, who agrees in general with LXX in Dan., here agrees with MT and Theodotion against LXX (cf. Swete, *Intro. to OT in Gk.*, pp. 422 f.).

the author's expectation—not necessarily accurate—of the consummation of the events through which he was living. But it is wholly improbable that an author in that age would entertain the expectation that the Babylonian and Medo-Persian kingdoms, and the kingdom of Alexander, were about to be reconstituted, but without dominion. The collapse of the Roman empire would not automatically bring this about, and it is hard to see why any author in that age should expect it.[1]

2. But if the Praeterist view is unsatisfactory, not less so is the Futurist, in its varying forms and degrees of extravagance. For here the Little Horn is held to be a future Antichrist. But the eleventh horn arose before the destruction of the fourth beast, and clearly exercised the authority of the fourth kingdom, since it was owing to the insolence of the Little Horn that the fourth beast was destroyed. Yet the Roman empire has definitely passed away.[2]

The various shifts to which the interpreters are put to overcome the difficulty sufficiently testify to its reality. To try to prolong the Roman empire into the present by supposing its life to be continued in the states of modern Europe looks a simple enough expedient, but gives little help. For the bewildering variety of suggested identifications proves that there is no clear and exact accordance with history. It

---

[1] Wright (*Dan. and its Crit.*, p. 119) says that the meaning is not that the first three beasts shall survive the destruction of the fourth, but that the verse merely marks the contrast between the treatment that has been accorded the first three beasts, their kingdoms being successively incorporated in the kingdoms that followed, and that of the fourth beast, which should be utterly destroyed. But if they did not survive the fourth beast, then their utter destruction was involved in its destruction, and the point chosen to mark the *contrast* of treatment would be singularly ill-chosen, since it recorded the *community* of their disaster.

[2] Willet (*Hex. in Dan.*, p. 69): 'That fourth kingdome must continue vntill the coming of Christ, but if they vnderstand this prophesie of Christs second comming, the Romane Empire hath beene dissolued long since'. And cf. Henry, *Les diff. crit. et hist. de Dan.*, p. 152. Gaebelein tries to surmount this difficulty by the belief that the Roman empire is destined to be revived (op. cit., p. 82). But of the assumed gap in the history of the fourth empire the vision and its interpretation are alike silent.

is true that a measure of Roman culture and law is the common inheritance of the modern world, but to claim that this entitles us to say that the Roman empire still continues is entirely without warrant. For it could similarly be argued, as Ibn Ezra did argue, that the Roman empire was a continuation of the Greek, while the Seleucid empire could also lay good claim to be regarded as a continuation of the Babylonian.

The alternative expedient of finding the Roman empire continued to the present through the Holy Roman Empire fares no better. For that, too, has gone, and even Napoleon III is insufficient to carry it into a future we still await, or to avoid the inevitable gap between the Roman empire and a still awaited Antichrist. To contemplate a future in which the Roman empire shall be catastrophically destroyed is only possible if all historical realities are ignored.

Yet worse is the case of the thorough-going Futurist, who throws not only the Little Horn, but also the ten horns, into the future. For this makes still greater the gap between the Roman empire and the Little Horn, whose rule should precede its destruction, and Wright's judgement[1] that 'the Futurist exposition, with its idea of "breaks in prophecy", and its theory of long periods being passed over without mention . . . is, we maintain, a caricature of prophecy' is abundantly justified.

3. Nor can the view which identifies the eleventh horn with the Papacy command more confidence. For it is utterly unrelated to the conditions of the visions. For the eleventh, while it was diverse from the other horns, not merely sprang out of the fourth beast, but exercised the authority of the fourth beast, and it was owing to the arrogance of the Little Horn, as has already been insisted, that the fourth beast was destroyed. It is impossible to maintain that the Papacy exercises the *imperium Romanum*, or to suppose that the

[1] *Dan. and its Crit.*, p. 128. Cf. Kliefoth, op. cit., p. 96.

overthrow of that Roman empire that succeeded the Babylonian, Medo-Persian, and Greek empires awaits the consummation of Papal iniquity.

The Praeterist view is therefore under the necessity of
antedating the termination of the Roman empire, while the
other varieties of the Roman view are under the necessity of
prolonging by some fiction the life of that empire. They are
alike compelled to ignore the facts of history. Similarly, the
Praeterist view fails to show the required catastrophic end of
the Roman empire, while the alternatives look for a catastrophic end, but fail to find the empire that is to meet it.
That various dates may be assigned for the termination of
the Roman empire does not serve to argue its continued
existence. It does but show that its end was not catastrophic
and that therefore on any theory the Roman empire cannot
meet the conditions of the prophecies.

A further argument against the Roman theory was presented by Cowles, who appealed to geography. He pointed
out that Rome belonged to a wholly different geographical
theatre from the other empires—the Babylonian, the Medo-
Persian, and the Greek. These all, down to the Seleucid
kingdom, appeared on the same stage, but 'Rome never was
Asiatic, never was oriental; never therefore was a legitimate
successor of the first three of these great empires'.[1] The
same argument was offered much earlier by Polanus[2] and
Becmann,[3] and nearer to Cowles's day by Stuart,[4] and Bade,[5]
and it stands more recently in Zöckler.[6] Its relevance to the
vision of chapter ii is especially clear. For there it is implied
that the successive kingdoms incorporate their predecessors,
so that the impact of the stone upon the toes of the image

---

[1] *Ezek. and Dan.*, p. 355.
[2] *In Dan. proph. comm.* i, p. 106, or in Poole, *Synopsis*, iii, col. 1420.
[3] *Diss. de quarta mon.*, 4th ed., pp. 13 f.
[4] *Comm. on Bk. of Dan.*, p. 188.   [5] *Christ. des AT*, iii, Part 2, pp. 78 f.
[6] *Bk. of Dan.*, ET, p. 84 a: 'The four world-kingdoms are developed without exception on one and the same geographical stage, on the soil of the *Orbis
orientalis*, thus harmonizing with the Biblical representation under the symbol
of a *single* colossal human image.'

shatters not alone the fourth kingdom, but the whole image. But the Roman empire never has incorporated Babylonia and Medo-Persia, and at no time could its collapse be expected to cause them to break in pieces.

(c) *The Greek view does fit the prophecies.*

The difficulties attaching to the Roman view do not of themselves establish the Greek view, and it is therefore necessary to inquire whether this alternative is confronted with less serious difficulties, or can face them more successfully. All that concerns us at this point is to ask whether the identification of the fourth empire with the Greek, up to the time of Antiochus Epiphanes, and of the Little Horn with Antiochus, will harmonize with the conditions given in the visions. Most of those who in modern times hold the Greek view adopt the further view that the author—or the interpolator of these chapters[1]—lived in the time of Antiochus, and looked for an immediate catastrophic end of the Greek empire, which, however, failed to materialize. On this view, therefore, it is necessary to show, not exact accordance with the entire history of the period from the age in which the visions are laid to the age of their consummation, but accordance with the views of history which the author reveals elsewhere in his work, together with such accordance with the history of his own more immediate times as a person living in that age might be expected to know.

Not a few of the holders of the Greek view, however, have retained the traditional view of the date and authorship of the book. To them, therefore, the whole of the visions and their interpretation constitute true prophecies, and no parts can be treated as *vaticinia ex eventu*. Upon them, then, just as much as upon the holders of the Roman view of the fourth kingdom, is the duty incumbent of showing exact accordance between the prophecies and the history in which

---

[1] It has been observed above that a number of scholars, who hold that part of the book of Daniel is older than the Maccabean age, find Maccabean interpolations in the text of chapter ii, or of both chapters ii and vii.

they had their fulfilment. And as little are they able to do so. For the age of Antiochus Epiphanes was in no sense the prelude to the Messianic age, and there was no catastrophic end of the Greek empire in his day.

It has already been noted that some of those who adopt this form of the Greek view of the fourth empire point out that Christ was born at the beginning of the Roman empire, and therefore just after the termination of the Greek empire —which reached its final end with the annexation of the Ptolemaic kingdom. They hold that the fifth and enduring kingdom is the Kingdom of Christ, whom they find to be represented by the stone cut without hands out of the mountain. But while in chapter vii the 'son of man' first appears just after the destruction of the fourth beast, in chapter ii it is the impact of the stone upon the feet of the image that brings about its downfall. The birth of Christ can in no way be causally connected with the end of the Greek empire.

As little can the end of the Greek empire in the final swallowing up of Egypt be described as a catastrophic end of world empires, involving in its ruin the shattering of the incorporated Babylonian and Medo-Persian, or Median and Persian empires.

Nor can the insolent words of Antiochus Epiphanes, who is held to be the Little Horn, be related to the destruction of the Greek empire, or to the coming of Christ. It was because of the great words of the Little Horn that the doom was pronounced upon the fourth beast, and the enduring kingdom inaugurated.[1] Moreover the Little Horn made war upon the saints, but the victory was given unto them in the possession of the kingdom.[2] But the birth of Christ, and the establishment of His spiritual kingdom amongst men, can in no natural way be explained as the sequel of the acts or words of Antiochus Epiphanes, nor can His kingdom be supposed to have been given to any of the saints with whom Antiochus warred.

[1] Dn vii. 11, 25 f.   [2] Dn vii. 21 f., 25 ff.

Within the circle of those who hold the Greek view, therefore, there is a wide divergence at this point, and while up to the time of Antiochus Epiphanes their reading of history and of the visions runs concurrently, and they may be considered together, the only form of the Greek view which is here claimed to fit the prophecies is that which locates the composition of these chapters, at any rate in the form in which they now stand before us, in the Maccabean age. On this view the author was a man who was moved of the spirit of God to encourage his fellows to resist the attack of Antiochus Epiphanes upon the religion and culture of his race, and who rightly perceived that the victory must lie with them, if they were loyal unto their God, but whose message was coloured with Messianic hopes that were not to be fulfilled. The movement which he sought to further achieved an essential success, and the saints on whose side he was received the kingdom to the extent of the retention of their faith and the independence of their nation, but world empires were not toppled in the dust, nor was the Greek empire destroyed, nor did the stone, which he expected to fill the earth, grow until it did so. The author ceases, on this view, to be the impersonal mouthpiece of God, uttering an inerrant message, but he remains a man worthy to stand in the succession of the prophets, delivering a message as essentially right and worthy as theirs, yet dressed in hopes that transcended realities even as theirs. It is not, therefore, the desire to eliminate prediction from the page of Scripture which compels men to this view of the prophecies, but the belief that only so can we find the real greatness of the inspired personality of the author. A mere 'medium' who transmits the most wonderful message that bears no relation to his own personality and experience is far inferior to a prophet who out of the agony of his heart delivers a message that has come through the crucible of his own life and being. And the view of the author of Daniel which is here taken lifts him from being the former to be the latter. It is taken for no other reason than that it is demanded by the facts, and not the least at the point now under consideration. For this view, and no other, fits the conditions contained in chapters ii and vii of the book.

1. In chapter ii the fourth kingdom, which begins as an iron kingdom, becomes divided into iron and clay. The duality of the legs was imposed upon the author by the form of the vision, but it is probable that this suggested to him the Ptolemaic and Seleucid kingdoms. And then he wished to emphasize the duality of the nature of these two branches of the kingdom that had been Alexander's, and so employed the figure of iron and clay—the Seleucids of his day representing the iron and the Ptolemies the clay. But instead of depicting the iron as all in one foot and the clay as all in the other, he represents the iron and clay as mixed, and speaks of the mingling of themselves together with the seed of men. Nor are we at a loss to explain what marriage alliances between the Seleucids and the Ptolemies he can have had in mind.

Shortly before the death of Ptolemy Philadelphus in 247–246 B.C., that monarch made peace with Antiochus Theos, and sealed the peace by giving his daughter Berenice in marriage to Antiochus. On the death of Ptolemy, however, Antiochus returned to Laodice, the wife he had divorced in favour of Berenice, and when he died under somewhat suspicious circumstances, war broke out between Laodice and Berenice.[1] Here then is one intermarriage between the Lagid and the Seleucid houses, which proved to be a mingling of iron and clay, yielding no true cohesion. Torrey believes that this is the whole reference of the passage, and he bases his dating of the whole of the first part of the book of Daniel on this ground.[2] More generally,

[1] Cf. Bevan, HS i, pp. 179 ff.; Bouché-Leclercq. *Hist. des Lag.* i, pp. 210 f., and *Hist. des Sél.* i, pp. 89 ff.; Tarn, CAH vii, pp. 715 ff.

[2] TCA xv, pp. 245 f. On Torrey's view the Ptolemies are the iron and the Seleucids the clay. Torrey's dating of the first part of the book was antici-

however, a second intermarriage is held to be referred to. For after the battle of Paneion, in 198 B.C., the victorious Antiochus the Great betrothed his daughter Cleopatra to Ptolemy Epiphanes, and a year or two later, in the winter of 193–192 B.C., they were married.[1] But again intermarriage did not herald a lasting agreement between the two houses, and the results of the marriage were disappointing to Antiochus.

Nor is this all mere groundless conjecture, of exactly the same kind as the variety of explanations that have been noted above as offered by the adherents of the Roman view, extending to marriages that took place as late as the end of the first millennium of the Christian era. For in chapter xi we find clear references to both of these intermarriages, and the principle above enunciated that we should look for accordance with the views of history revealed by the author elsewhere in his work will therefore allow our interpretation here. For in xi. 6 the daughter of the king of the south who comes to the king of the north is clearly Berenice, and the ineffectiveness of the marriage is also set forth, while in xi. 17 the marriage of Cleopatra is indicated, together with the fact that she failed to be a bond of cohesion between the two kingdoms. In these two intermarriages, therefore, we have the material that is required to explain the transfer of some of the clay to mingle with the iron, and some of the iron to mingle with the clay.

But, it may be asked, why should but two divisions of the Greek empire be referred to? The author certainly knew of other divisions. For in viii. 8, where he is admittedly speaking of the Greek empire, he tells how the Great Horn—which clearly means Alexander—was broken, and how in its place sprang up four horns. This is generally held to refer to the four Greek kingdoms which were established

---

pated, so far as chapter ii is concerned, by Bertholdt, who assigned it to the period of Ant. Theos and Ptol. Philad. (*Dan. neu übers. u. erk.*, p. 62).

[1] Cf. Bevan, HS ii, pp. 38, 57; Bouché-Leclercq, *Hist. des Lag.* i, pp. 336, 387. Holleaux (CAH viii, p. 199), puts the marriage in 194–193 B.C.

as the result of the general scramble for power that followed the death of Alexander.[1] If, then, the author knew of other divisions, why should he refer to but two here?

To this question the answer is not difficult. The author was primarily interested in the Jewish people, and he therefore ignored those parts of the Greek empire which had no relation to Palestinian affairs, especially since the human form of the image, by the natural duality of its legs, helped to impose this limitation. And again when we look to chapter xi to learn the mind of the author, we find that, after noting that the kingdom of Alexander should be divided towards the four winds of heaven, he immediately limits himself to the kings of the south and the kings of the north, i.e. to the Ptolemaic and Seleucid kingdoms. Similarly in chapter viii, after the breaking of the Great Horn and the springing up of the four horns, he immediately comes to the Little Horn that waxed great towards 'the glorious land'— i.e. Palestine—and ignores all that does not concern his own people. It is therefore precisely the same mentality and outlook that we find in chapter ii, when we see in it a concentrating of interest in the fourth empire in the Seleucid and Ptolemaic kingdoms.

Nor is the more specific reference to the immediate circumstances of the Maccabean age wanting. It has been observed that Torrey, on the basis of ii. 40-43, dates the entire first half of the book of Daniel *circa* 245 B.C. But he has adduced no evidence to show that at that time there was a hope of the immediate foundation of an abiding kingdom on the ruins of the Greek, nor is there anything in the situation at that time to warrant any Jewish expectation that

---

[1] Jerome (on viii. 5 ff., xi. 4, ed. Migne, cols. 536, 539) held these to be Ptolemy Lagi (Egypt), Philip Arrhidaeus (Macedonia), Seleucus (Syria and Babylonia), and Antigonus (Asia Minor). Many writers have thought of a somewhat later time, after the elimination of Philip (317 B.C.), and have, therefore, favoured the substitution of Cassander (Macedonia and Greece) for him. Others have thought of a yet later time, following the battle of Ipsus (301 B.C.), which eliminated Antigonus, and so have further substituted Lysimachus (Thrace) for him.

an independent theocratic state was about to be established. An author of that day might have known, as Torrey argues, that the Greek empire was not holding together, and the failure of the first of the two above noted intermarriages between the Seleucid and Lagid houses might have been familiar to him. He might have dreamed of the collapse of the Greek empire through the mutual jealousies and divisions of the houses between which it was divided. But that was not the consummation he looked for. He looked for a stone cut without hands to smite the divided kingdom. And it is just here that the weakness of Torrey's case lies. For there was nothing in the circumstances of that day to warrant such an expectation. But in the days of Antiochus Epiphanes, when the destructive nature of the fourth kingdom, as described in ii. 40, reached its climax in the wanton measures of Antiochus against the Jews,[1] the movement headed by Judas Maccabaeus provided the occasion for the hopes here proclaimed. The spontaneous outburst in which the Maccabean revolt began might fittingly be indicated under the figure of a stone cut without hands. The smallness of its beginnings needs no demonstration, and the success that befel its impact on the Seleucid power, and the growth of its own power that followed, might well encourage the hope that by this movement the Messianic kingdom would be inaugurated. That it was of God who could doubt? And so our author could write of the kingdom that the God of heaven should set up.

[1] Moore (*Judaism*, i, pp. 50 ff.) well traces the interaction of different factors that led to the fact and the form of Antiochus' persecution, and shows that Ant. had no thought of an attack on Judaism as such, as witnessed by the fact that there is no evidence that Jews in Syria and Babylonia were molested in the observance of their religion. Seleucid rule was at first welcomed by the Jews, but heavy taxation produced disillusionment, to which was added the policy of hellenization adopted by Ant. Epiph. This aroused a religious opposition, which inevitably fed disaffection to the Seleucids, and encouraged a reaction to Ptolemaic sympathies. Hence, when Ant. returned from Egypt, after being foiled by Rome, he was inevitably driven still further into his mistaken policy. To abandon the hellenizing party in Jerusalem would be to desert the only friends he had, and to yield before the opposition might well but serve to feed it. Hence, to meet an opposition whose political importance

H

2. Not less appropriate to the conditions of that age is chapter vii. Here we find that after noting the destructive ǁ character of the fourth beast, the writer immediately comes to its ten horns, which are mentioned only to bring him to the Little Horn. But the Little Horn vitally concerns Jewish interests, and figures here on that account. Once again, therefore, we have an exclusively Jewish point of view. The ten horns are declared to be ten kings, but the only thing recorded about them is that the Little Horn came up in their midst and three of them were plucked up before it. They appear merely because of their relation to the Little Horn, and to relate that horn to the fourth beast.

(*a*) As to the identification of the ten horns, there has been much divergence of opinion amongst the holders of the Greek view, and Pusey has argued[1] that the uncertainty of their identification throws doubt on the Greek view of the fourth kingdom. This, however, by no means follows. For we have already seen that the Roman view has led to no more agreement as to the identification of the horns, but rather less. Indeed, the disagreement amongst the holders of the Greek view is mainly confined to narrow limits, and is due to the very scanty information we are given about these horns. We must, however, at this point examine with some care the identifications that have been proposed, before we can establish the claim that the probable interpretation is one that could reasonably have entered into the mind of a Maccabean author.

We may at the outset dismiss the view commonly associated with Bleek's name. He believed[2] that the ten horns represented ten divisions of the empire of Alexander, or the commanders who held them. The ten he selected were (1) Craterus (Macedonia), (2) Antipater (Greece),

---

was its chief offence to him, he redoubled his attack on the religious root out of which it sprang. Cf. Oesterley and Robinson, *Intro. to OT*, pp. 333 f.

[1] *Dan. the Proph.*, 8th ed., p. 155: 'Schemes so various and so contradictory could not leave an easy conscience.'

[2] Cf. *Jahrbücher für deutsche Theol.* v, 1860, pp. 60 ff., 68 n.

(3) Lysimachus (Thrace), (4) Leonnatus (Lesser Phrygia), (5) Antigonus (Greater Phrygia), (6) Cassander (Caria), (7) Eumenes (Cappadocia), (8) Laomedon (Syria), (9) Pithon (Media), (10) Ptolemy Lagi (Egypt). He then identified the Little Horn with Seleucus Nicator and the Syrian kingdom, the three horns that went down before it being Antigonus, Ptolemy Lagi, and Lysimachus. Seleucus Nicator must then be equated with the Seleucid dynasty, which is further equated with Antiochus Epiphanes, the representative of the house in whom the author's interest culminates. Critics have not been slow to point to the arbitrariness of the choice of ten, and to show how incomplete is the list of the commanders,[1] and the artificiality of the view has been generally recognized. It is also to be noted that while the number of the divisions of Alexander's empire was constantly varying until three stable houses—the Seleucid, the Lagid, and the Antigonid—were established, with an ever varying number of smaller independent, or semi-independent, states on the fringes of their domains, the author of the book of Daniel elsewhere refers to four divisions of the kingdom. If, then, his purpose here had been to crystallize numerically the division of Alexander's empire, it is much more likely that he would have adopted the same figure as he elsewhere uses for this purpose. One follower has been found for Bleek in this view, in the person of Davidson.[2] It does not, however, seem to be generally recognized that he had also a predecessor. For a view fundamentally the same, though with a different selection of commanders, was found much earlier than the days of Bleek in the work of Venema,[3] while

[1] Cf. Zündel, *Krit. Unters.*, pp. 110 f.; Pusey, op. cit., pp. 156 ff.; Kliefoth, op. cit., p. 237; Keil, op. cit., ET, pp. 255 f.; Wright, *Dan. and his Proph.*, p. 162.   [2] *Intro. to OT* iii, p. 210.

[3] Op. cit., pp. 192, 246 ff. Venema's choice consisted of: (1) Antigonus and (2) Demetrius (Asia), (3) Lysimachus (Thrace), (4) Cassander (Macedonia), (5) Ptolemy Lagi (Egypt), (6) Philetaerus (Pergamene Asia), (7) Bas or Ziboetes (Bithynia), (8) Mithridates (Pontus), (9) Ariarathes (Cappadocia), (10) Atropates (Media Atropatia). He held that Seleucus Nicator was the Little Horn, and Antigonus, Demetrius, and Lysimachus the three uprooted horns.

the oldest anticipation of it stands in the work of Cosmas Indicopleustes,[1] who identified the horns with those amongst whom Alexander's empire was divided after his death, but without closer specification. This whole view-point is very similar to that of those who on the Roman view seek to identify ten kingdoms which have sprung out of the Roman empire, but whereas it has been a very popular viewpoint amongst the members of the Roman school, the holders of the Greek view of the fourth kingdom have with almost complete unanimity rejected such an interpretation.

Again, there have not been wanting some to suggest on the Greek view, as on the Roman, that the number is indefinite, and that there is no need for exact identification,[2] Most, however, are of the opinion that the number is a precise one, and that the author had in mind ten definite persons. Many attempts have been made, therefore, to identify them with ten successive kings. Against this opponents of the Greek view have argued[3] that the ten horns were seen simultaneously, while the eleventh horn came up subsequently, and that therefore the ten horns cannot be successive kings, but must represent either individuals or states that were contemporaneous. The hollowness of this argument needs little demonstration. In chapter ii we are told that Nebuchadnezzar saw an image, whereof the four parts are specifically declared to represent four successive monarchies. The simultaneity of their appearance in the vision is not fatal to their succession in interpretation. Similarly, in the visions of the butler and the baker in Gen. xl, the three branches and the three baskets, which were seen simultaneously, represent three successive days. Again, in Pharaoh's vision in Gen. xli, the seven fat kine, representing seven successive years, are seen together, and

---

[1] *Topog. Christ.* ii (145), ed. Migne, col. 109, ET by McCrindle, p. 68. Behrmann's view (*Das B. Dan. übers. u. erk.*, p. 46) closely agrees with this.
[2] So Zöckler, *Bk. of Dan.*, ET, pp. 153 b, 165 b; Behrmann, op. cit., p. 46; Montgomery, *Comm. on Dan.*, p. 293 n.; Rigaux, *L'Antéchrist*, p. 165.
[3] So, e.g., Keil, op. cit., ET, p. 255; Wright, *Dan. and its Crit.*, p. 107.

continue in the vision until the seven lean kine, representing seven later years, appear. It is clear, therefore, that no legitimate objection can be made here against the identification of the horns with successive kings.

Various principles for their identification have been adopted. Some have tried to find ten kings, all of whom came into direct relationship with Palestine. Thus Porphyry believed[1] that they were Macedonian, Egyptian, and Syrian kings of outstanding cruelty, though his actual identifications have not come down to us, save for the three uprooted horns, which will be noted below. Rosenmüller, who follows Porphyry in the identification of these three uprooted horns, holds them to be outside the number of the ten, which he identifies[2] as follows: (1) Antigonus, (2) Demetrius Poliorcetes, (3) Ptolemy Soter, (4) Ptolemy Philadelphus, (5) Ptolemy Euergetes, (6) Ptolemy Philopator, (7) Ptolemy Epiphanes, (8) Ptolemy Philometor, (9) Antiochus Magnus, (10) Seleucus Philopator. Rosenmüller's view was anticipated by Becmann,[3] save that the latter omitted Ptolemy Philometor, but added at the end Antiochus Epiphanes, whom he held to be the tenth and Little Horn. Grotius,[4] too, held that the Little Horn was not an eleventh, but the tenth, and favoured a mixed list of the horns, including both Seleucids and Lagids. His identifications were (1) Ptolemy Lagi, (2) Seleucus Nicator, (3) Ptolemy Eupator,[5] (4) Ptolemy Euergetes, (5) Seleucus Callinicus, (6) Antiochus Magnus, (7) Ptolemy Philopator, (8) Ptolemy Epiphanes,

---

[1] *Apud* Jerome, on vii. 7 (ed. Migne, col. 530): *decem reges enumerat, qui fuerunt saevissimi: ipsosque reges non unius ponit regni, verbi gratia, Macedoniae, Syriae, Asiae et Aegypti, sed de diversis regnis unum efficit regnum ordinem.*

[2] *Schol. in VT*, Part x, p. 237.   [3] *Diss. de quarta mon.*, 4th ed., pp. 21 ff.

[4] *Op. omn. theol.*, 1732 ed., i, p. 466.

[5] Pusey (op. cit., p. 150 n.) says that Eupator is an apocryphal king. Mahaffy, however, argued (*Emp. Ptol.*, p. 329 f.) that there was such a king, though somewhat later than Grotius placed him. Mahaffy put him after Ptol. Epiph., and regarded him as a brother of Ptol. Philom., who died early. This view is now found to be untenable. Cf. the full note, with reference to all the literature, in Bouché-Leclercq, *Hist. des Lag.* ii, p. 56 n.; also Bevan, *Hist. of Egypt under Ptol. Dyn.*, p. 282 n.

(9) Seleucus Philopator, (10) Antiochus Epiphanes. Both in making the Little Horn to be the tenth, and in his identifications, Grotius was followed by Broughton,[1] save that the latter substituted Antiochus Theos for Ptolemy Eupator, and Broughton was followed by Amner,[2] who, however, modified his list by introducing Ptolemy Philadelphus before Antiochus Theos, in order to make Antiochus Epiphanes the eleventh, instead of the tenth horn. A somewhat similar list is presented by Cowles,[3] who identified the ten horns with the kings mentioned in chapter xi. In this he thought he was adopting a wholly new principle,[4] but in the discussion of the book of Daniel originality is hard, and Grotius,[5] Broughton,[6] and Amner,[7] had all anticipated him in the principle,[8] though their identifications were slightly different from his. For Cowles found five kings of the south—Ptolemy Lagi, Ptolemy Philadelphus, Ptolemy Euergetes, Ptolemy Philopator, Ptolemy Philometor—and five kings of the north—Seleucus Nicator, Antiochus Theos, Seleucus Callinicus, Antiochus Magnus, Seleucus Philopator—and, unlike Grotius and Broughton, found the uprooted horns amongst the ten.[9] It remains to be noted that the latest commentator on the book of Daniel, Obbink,[10] adopts a similar view that the ten horns contain both

---

[1] *Works*, 1662 ed., pp. 212–18.

[2] *Essay towards Int. of Dan.*, p. 161.   [3] *Ezek. and Dan.*, p. 360.

[4] Ibid., p. 359: 'No commentator within my knowledge seems to have counted them (i.e. the kings of chap. xi), or to have noticed that the kings of any prominence in this narrative are ten. But such is the fact.'

[5] Cf. *Op. omn. theol.*, loc. cit.

[6] Broughton's identifications of the horns are set forth in his exposition of chap. xi.   [7] Loc. cit.

[8] It may be noted, too, that Bosanquet (*Mess. the Prince*, pp. 115 ff.) found the key to the ten horns in chap. xi, but held the verses which contain the key there to be glosses. Gunkel also (*Schöpf. u. Chaos*, p. 326 n.) believed that the ten horns could only be explained in connexion with chap. xi, though he did not specify his identifications.

[9] Desprez (*Dan., or the Apoc. of OT*, p. 109) adopted a similar principle to that of Cowles, but identified with Ptol. Philad. (xi. 5), Ant. Theos (xi. 6), Ptol. Euerg. (xi. 7), Sel. Call. (xi. 8), Ptol. Philop. (xi. 9), Ant. Magn. (xi. 11, 13, 15), Ptol. Epiph. (xi. 14), Sel. Philop. (xi. 20), Demetr. (xi. 22) and Ptol. Philom. (xi. 25, 40).   [10] *Daniël*, p. 106.

Seleucids and Lagids, but unlike all the interpreters so far noted, he precedes them with Alexander the Great. For the first eight of the horns he favours the following list: (1) Alexander Magnus, (2) Ptolemy Soter, (3) Ptolemy Philadelphus, (4) Ptolemy Euergetes, (5) Ptolemy Philopator, (6) Ptolemy Epiphanes, (7) Antiochus Magnus, (8) Seleucus Philopator.

Common to all these suggestions is the persuasion that all of the horns must in some way be brought into relationship with the Jews, either as the sovereigns of Palestinian territory, or as claimants to its possession. The schemes which make some or all of the uprooted horns to be outside the number of the ten would seem to be definitely unable to satisfy the conditions, and equally so those which bring the Little Horn into the number of ten, in disregard of the statement that it sprang up amongst the already noted ten. The principle enunciated above, that we should seek accordance with the views of history which our author reveals elsewhere, might seem to favour the very acute scheme of Cowles, were it not that he is compelled to ignore Seleucus Ceraunus, who is certainly referred to in Dn. xi. 10, and Ptolemy Epiphanes, who is in all probability to be found in xi. 14. It is improbable, therefore, that this view is a relevant application of this principle. Of all the arrangements so far noted, that of Obbink has the greatest probability. Nevertheless, it too, in common with all of these views, breaks on the fact that in a passage in the Sibylline Oracles, which will be considered below—a passage dating almost certainly from the second century B.C.—we find a reference to 'ten horns' in a context which would seem to define it as having a Seleucid, rather than a mixed, meaning. And since the term there is almost certainly derived from its use in the book of Daniel, it is probable that here, too, it should be given a Seleucid interpretation, rather than taken to include both Lagids and Seleucids.

Nor is it necessary to bring all of the horns into relation

with Palestine. The author's primary interest was in his
own people, but every detail of the vision need not be
related to them. It suffices if every detail is related to what
is related to them, and if it serves a purpose germane to the
fundamental purpose which is found in the vision. And
since, on the view which is here taken, the vision, though
ostensibly located in the period of the Neo-Babylonian
empire, was written in the period of the Greek dominion,
the author could lightly bridge the interval with the four
empires, and then concentrate on that element of the fourth
empire which would bring him to the climax in which his
real interest lay. It is probable, therefore, that he discarded
all else in the fourth empire save that line of kings which
would bring him to Antiochus Epiphanes, viz. the Seleucid
line.[1] And immediately the fourth empire became for him
identified with the Seleucid line. For the Jew of the
Maccabean age the *imperium Graecum* was exercised by
Antiochus Epiphanes,[2] and hence the Syrian kingdom[3]
could be so identified in the thought of our author with the
fourth kingdom that its destruction could be thought of as
the destruction of the Greek empire. To us the fluidity of
thought that can pass from the Greek empire to the Syrian
part of it, and then treat the part as a whole, is unnatural,
but as Oesterley says in writing of another Jewish apocalypse:[4] 'there is sometimes a danger of looking at these

---

[1] Junker protests (op. cit., p. 44) that the Ptolemies also belonged to the
Greek empire, and should equally be reckoned. But they could not be
reckoned in the same succession as the Seleucids, and could only have been
indicated beside them in some other feature of the beast. They are not thus
indicated because immaterial to the author's present purpose.

[2] Cf. Cowles, op. cit., p. 352: 'So far as it (i.e. the fourth kingdom) affected
the Jews, it was chiefly embodied in Antiochus Epiphanes'.

[3] Bevan (*Jer. under High Priests*, pp. 23 f.) warns us against the use of this
common, but misleading, phrase, since it is apt to obscure the fact that the
Seleucid realm was a wide and cumbrous one, with more than one capital, and
that it was never a Syrian kingdom in the sense that its authority was exercised
by persons of Syrian race. Its use may perhaps be allowed in virtue of its
established currency, especially where, as here, the reader is not likely to
forget that its dominion was essentially a Greek, or Macedonian, dominion.

[4] *II Esdras*, p. xii.

ancient writings from too "Western" a point of view; incongruities, and even contradictions, were not such dreadful things to the Oriental mind of long ago as they are to the Occidental modern. The Apocalyptists, especially, were not exact thinkers.' We have to remember, too, that there was a certain fluidity in the whole conception of the Macedonian empire, which, despite its actual divisions, was treated as ideally one,[1] making it easy to treat the part theoretically as the whole. And especially easy was it to do so at the time with which we are dealing. For apart from the Seleucid power there was little of the empire of Alexander left. The Macedonian kingdom had now been annexed by Rome, and even the Seleucid power had been shorn, while the Ptolemaic kingdom had sunk to be of such negligible strength that it had surrendered to Roman protection. The Seleucid power had but to crack and naught would be left. Hence there is nothing inappropriate to the circumstances of the time in the representation of the Seleucid monarch as exercising in that day whatever authority the fourth beast retained, and nothing improbable in the view that the author merely used the device of the ten horns to carry him from the establishment of the empire to its climax in his own day.

If, then, we identify the ten horns in some way with the Seleucid kingdom, we recognize that they are mentioned, not because of their individual relation to the Jews, but because of their relation to Antiochus Epiphanes,[2] in whom all the nameless horror of the fourth beast came to a head. Most, indeed, of the adherents of the Greek view of the fourth kingdom believe that the reference is to the Seleucid

---

[1] Cf. Niese, *Gesch. der griech. u. mak. Staaten*, ii, p. 123: 'Das Reich Alexanders ist trotz den Teilungen immer noch als ein Ganzes anzusehen, zusammengehalten durch die gleiche Nationalität und Verwandtschaft der herrschenden Völker, der Makedonier und Hellenen, die in allen Teilen angesiedelt waren. . . . Jeder der neuen Könige hielt sich berechtigt, nach Vermögen und Gelegenheit seinen Teil zu vergrössern, ja selbst das Ganze in Anspruch zu nehmen.'

[2] Cf. Bevan, *Short Comm. on Dan.*, p. 116 : 'The ten kings are mentioned, not on their own account, but because they lead up to the eleventh.'

dynasty.[1] There is some disagreement, however, as to whether Alexander the Great is to be counted amongst them, or whether they begin with Seleucus Nicator,[2] and a greater disagreement as to the identification of the last three horns. Leaving for the moment the latter difficulty, we may note that Calmet,[3] Eichhorn,[4] Bertholdt,[5] Dereser,[6] von Lengerke,[7] Maurer,[8] Stuart,[9] Bade,[10] Merx,[11] Ewald,[12] Strong,[13] Delitzsch,[14] Vatke,[15] Meinhold,[16] Farrar,[17] and Lagrange[18] all began with Seleucus Nicator, and made the first seven horns to be (1) Seleucus Nicator, (2) Antiochus Soter, (3) Antiochus Theos, (4) Seleucus Callinicus, (5) Seleucus Ceraunus, (6) Antiochus Magnus, (7) Seleucus

---

[1] Rollock (*In lib. Dan. proph.*, p. 261) and Willet (*Hex. in Dan.*, pp. 212, 215), following Junius (*Op. omn. theol.* i, col. 1255) and Polanus (*In Dan. proph. Comm.* ii, p. 43) identified the ten horns with (1) Sel. Nic., (2) Ant. Sot., (3) Ant. Theos, (4) Sel. Call., (5) Ptol. Euerg., (6) Sel. Cer., (7) Ant. Magn., (8) Ptol. Philop., (9) Sel. Philop., (10) Ant. Epiph. So, too, Piscator (*In Dan. Comm.*, p. 66). The two Ptolemies are here included on the ground that they held Syria for a time by right of conquest, and are therefore to be reckoned in the line of the Syrian kings. But Ptol. Philop. did not occupy Syria—an idea based, perhaps, on Jerome's comment on xi. 10 ff. (ed. Migne, col. 561), where, however, Syria stands for Coele-Syria—and there is no evidence that Ptol. Euerg. assumed the Syrian diadem (cf. Bevan, *Hist. of Egypt under Ptol. Dyn.*, pp. 195 ff.), while even if he had, he could only be regarded as a break in the Seleucid line, and not a member of it. Further, the making of the tenth horn to be the Little Horn does not accord with the statements of the chapter, as has been already noted.

[2] An anonymous writer, quoted in Mai's *Script. vet. nov. coll.* i, 1825 et 1831, p. 47 (= 1825 ed., p. 203), precedes the first seven Seleucid kings with Alexander, Antigonus, and Demetrius, and so obtains ten. A similar view is taken by Turmel (*Annales de phil. chrét.*, 3rd series, i, 1902–3, p. 13), who holds that the ten horns were the seven predecessors of Antiochus Epiphanes, and three generals who preceded them. On this view the uprooted horns are outside the number of the ten.

[3] *Comm. litt. sur Dan.*, p. 653 n. [4] *Heb. Proph.* iii, p. 442.
[5] *Dan. neu übers. u. erk.*, p. 432. [6] *Ezech. u. Dan.*, 2nd ed., p. 357.
[7] *Das B. Dan. verd. u. ausg.*, p. 320.
[8] *Comm. gramm. crit. in VT*, ii, p. 130.
[9] *Comm. on Dan.*, p. 208. [10] *Christ. des AT*, iii, Part 2, p. 89.
[11] *Cur in lib. Dan.*, p. 21. [12] *Proph. of OT*, ET v, p. 248.
[13] In Zöckler, *Bk. of Dan.*, ET by Strong, pp. 44, 46 (Table quoted from M'Clintock and Strong's *Cyclopaedia*, s.v. Daniel).
[14] In PRE, 2nd ed., iii, p. 476.
[15] *Hist.-krit. Einl. in das AT*, ed. Preiss, p. 653.
[16] *Das B. Dan. ausg.*, p. 299. [17] *Bk. of Dan.*, p. 241.
[18] RB, New Series, i, 1904, p. 504.

Philopator; while Hitzig,[1] Kamphausen,[2] Bevan,[3] von Gall,[4] Prince,[5] Marti,[6] Steuernagel,[7] Charles,[8] Andrews,[9] and Bewer,[10] precede these with Alexander, to provide the first eight of the ten horns. It seems to me highly improbable that Alexander would be counted in the succession of the Seleucid kings. For while the Greek empire was reckoned as one, despite its territorial division,[11] and was treated as a continuation of the empire of Alexander, it must be remembered that the Seleucid era dated from Seleucus Nicator. Clearly, therefore, to members of the Seleucid house, Alexander did not belong to their succession, and the dynasty was regarded as a separate unit within the Greek kingdom. Further, it is to be noted that in chapter viii Alexander is represented by the Great Horn. When this horn was broken four horns came up in its stead, and by these four horns, as has already been said, the author probably intended the four main kingdoms which sprang out of Alexander's dominions.[12] If, then, in chapter viii, one of the four horns represented the Seleucid line, Alexander was not reckoned in that line there, and it is

[1] *Das B. Dan. erk.*, p. 121.   [2] *Dan.* (in Bunsen's *Bibelwerk*), p. 661.
[3] *Short Comm. on Dan.*, p. 116.   [4] *Die Einheitl. des B. Dan.*, pp. 95 f.
[5] *Crit. Comm. on Dan.*, p. 133.
[6] *Das B. Dan. erk.*, p. 51, and HSAT, 4th ed., ii, p. 477 note d.
[7] *Lehrb. der Einl. in das AT*, p. 655.
[8] *Book of Dan.* (Cent. Bib.), p. 71, and *Crit. Comm. on Dan.*, p. 172.
[9] In *Peake's Commentary*, p. 528.   [10] *Lit. of OT in Hist. Dev.*, p. 413.
[11] Cf. Bevan, HS i, pp. 57 f.: 'We may pause to note that the name of king had no *territorial* reference. These kings are never officially styled kings *of Egypt* or *of Asia*. If they are so called by historians, it is merely for the purpose of convenient distinction. It connoted rather a personal relation to the Macedonian people. *Ideally* there was one Macedonian Empire as in the Middle Ages there was one Roman Empire. But the dignity of Macedonian King was borne conjointly or concurrently by several chieftains, just as the dignity of Roman Emperor was borne concurrently by the Western and the Byzantine prince.'
[12] However these four are identified—and it has been noted above that different views have been held—it must not be supposed that there were four enduring kingdoms. Cf. Bevan, *Jer. under High Priests*, p. 21: 'Thirty years after Alexander's death, the five who were still carrying on the contest all assumed the title of kings, and when we look on still another thirty years we find that it has come to the formation of three kingdoms, which are to be ruled by the descendants of the most fortunate three out of those five.'

unlikely, therefore, that the author reckoned him with the Seleucids here. I therefore believe that the first seven horns were the first seven Seleucid kings, from Seleucus Nicator to Seleucus Philopator.

(b) As to the identification of the three uprooted horns, it has been already said that there is a very wide divergence of opinion. Rosenmüller,[1] following Porphyry,[2] held them to be (1) Ptolemy Philometor, (2) Ptolemy Physcon (Euergetes II), and (3) Artaxias of Armenia. But it has been pointed out in reply[3] that none of these can be said to have been uprooted before Antiochus Epiphanes. For though the latter invaded Egypt, so far from either of the Ptolemies being uprooted, the final issue was that the Egyptians, who had made Ptolemy Physcon their king in place of the captive Ptolemy Philometor, acknowledged them both as joint kings,[4] while after his defeat of Artaxias, Antiochus left him in the occupation of his throne.[5] Moreover, even if Antiochus had uprooted them from Egypt or from Armenia, these events would still have been irrelevant here. For they could not on this ground be brought into any succession of ten that included Antiochus.[6] Rosenmüller, indeed, puts them definitely outside the ten, and his view has been criticized above on this ground, as also has that of Grotius, who held[7] the three uprooted horns to be (1) Seleucus Philopator, (2) Demetrius, and (3) Ptolemy Philopator, of whom one stood outside the number of the ten, according to his identification.[8]

---

[1] *Schol. in VT*, Part x, p. 238.

[2] *Apud* Jerome, on vii. 8 (ed. Migne, col. 531). Jerome strangely says: *quorum priores* (i.e. the two Ptolemies) *multo antequam Antiochus nasceretur, mortui sunt*. Pintus follows Jerome with the remark (*In Dan. comm.*, p. 140 b): *Sed deceptus est (Porphyrius) ob historiarum ignorationem: nam duo illi Ptolemaei priusquam ipse nasceretur, mortui sunt*. In fact, of course, both survived Antiochus.

[3] Cf. Pusey, op. cit., pp. 152, 154.

[4] Cf. Bevan, HS ii, p. 142.   [5] Ibid., p. 158.

[6] It will be seen below, however, that there is reason to connect Ptol. Philom. with an uprooting from Syria, and thus to bring him into relevant connexion with the Seleucid line.   [7] *Op. omn. theol.* i, p. 466.

[8] Cf. Broughton (*Works*, 1662 ed., p. 218), who differed slightly from

L'Empereur[1] found the same three as Grotius, but it is difficult to see how Ptolemy Philopator, who died long before Antiochus Epiphanes figured as a candidate for the Syrian throne, can be said to have been uprooted before him.[2]

Cowles, in accordance with his principle that the clue to the identification of the horns is found in chapter xi, holds[3] the three uprooted horns to be (1) Antiochus Magnus, (2) Seleucus Philopator, and (3) Ptolemy Philometor,[4] and compares the verses in that chapter that record their end.[5] Thus in xi. 19 we read of Antiochus Magnus: 'he shall stumble and fall, and shall not be found'; in xi. 20, of Seleucus Philopator: 'he shall be destroyed, neither in anger, nor in battle': and in xi. 25, of Ptolemy Philometor: 'he shall not stand, for they shall devise devices against him'. This is certainly very ingenious, but there is nothing in chapter xi to connect the failure or end of these kings, save for the last, with Antiochus Epiphanes, whereas vii. 24 says that the Little Horn shall put down the three kings

Grotius here in making the three uprooted horns to be (1) Sel. Philop., (2) Demetr., and (3) Ptol. Philom., of whom two stood outside his own list of ten horns. Cf. *Assembly's Ann.*, 2nd ed., on vii. 24, where the same identifications as Broughton's are made.

[1] Cf. *Paraph. Ios. Iach. in Dan.*, pp. 133 f.

[2] Ptol. Philop. has been included by some others also. Thus Willet (*Hex. in Dan.*, pp. 212, 218), who follows Junius (*Op. omn. theol.*, 1613 ed., i, col. 1255) in including him, says he was expelled from Syria, after his alleged temporary occupation of the kingdom, by Antiochus the Great and his son Epiphanes. But the statement is unsubstantiated, and there is no evidence that Philopator made any pretensions to the Syrian throne, or that he was ever expelled from Syria by the Antiochi. Junius makes the other two uprooted horns to be Sel. Philop. and Demetrius, in agreement with Grotius, while Willet makes them to be Antiochus Magnus and Sel. Philop. On the view of Junius, Demetrius stood outside the number of the ten, but on Willet's view all the uprooted horns belonged to the ten.

[3] *Ezek. and Dan.*, p. 361.

[4] Piscator made the same identifications (cf. *In proph. Dan. comm.*, p. 66). Rigaux, who regards the number of the horns as a round one, and who therefore does not attempt to identify all of them, suggests that the three uprooted horns are (1) Ant. Magn. (2) Sel. Philop., (3) Demetrius (see *L'Antéchrist*, p. 165).

[5] Desprez (*Dan., or the Apoc. of OT*, p. 109) by means of a similar principle to that of Cowles, identifies the three uprooted horns with Sel. Philop., Demetrius, and Ptol. Philom.

represented by the three uprooted horns. It is difficult to see how the end of Antiochus the Great can be said to have been brought about either at the instigation of, or in the interests of, Antiochus Epiphanes.

Most of the scholars who hold the ten horns to be the Seleucid line, together with Alexander, and who thus find Seleucus Philopator to be the eighth horn, regard the latter as one of the uprooted horns. That monarch was murdered by his minister Heliodorus, and though the murder was perpetrated in no sense in the interests of Antiochus, but in those of Heliodorus himself, it is certainly true that it opened the way to the throne for Antiochus.[1] The remaining two horns they hold to be Heliodorus himself, who aspired to the control of the kingdom, but who failed to establish himself when Antiochus appeared to claim the throne, and Demetrius, the rightful heir, who was a hostage at Rome, and whose claim was passed over. This is the view of Calmet,[2] Hitzig,[3] Kamphausen,[4] von Gall,[5] Buhl,[6] Prince,[7] Marti,[8] Steuernagel,[9] Charles,[10] Andrews,[11] and Bewer;[12] it

[1] There could be no objection to holding the terms of vii. 8—'before which three of the first horns were plucked up by the roots'—to include Philopator. But it is more difficult to see how vii. 24—'he shall put down three kings'—would allow his inclusion.

[2] *Comm. litt. sur Dan.*, p. 655. Calmet does not, however, include Alexander amongst the horns. He would appear to complete the number by including Ptol. Philom., though not counting him one of the three uprooted horns. He also presents an alternative view that the three uprooted horns are Egypt, Armenia, and Palestine, bringing vii. 8 into connexion with viii. 9. With this latter view, cf. Polychronius (in Mai, *Script. vet. nov. coll.* i, 1825 et 1831, p. 11), who identified them with the Persians, the Egyptians, and the Jews, and Barhebraeus (*Schol. zum B. Dan.*, ed. Freimann, p. 9), who holds them to stand for Persia, Egypt, and Asia Minor.

[3] *Das B. Dan. erk.*, p. 121.   [4] *Daniel* (in Bunsen's *Bibelwerk*), p. 661.
[5] *Die Einheitl. des B. Dan.*, p. 96.
[6] PRE, 3rd ed., iv, p. 453.   [7] *Crit. Comm. on Dan.*, p. 134.
[8] *Das B. Dan. erk.*, p. 51, and HSAT, 4th ed., ii, p. 477, note d. In the latter passage, Marti leaves it open whether the final horn of the ten is Demetrius or his brother, on whom see below.
[9] *Lehrb. der Einl. in das AT*, p. 655.
[10] *Bk. of Dan.* (Cent. Bib.), p. 71, and *Crit. Comm. on Dan.*, p. 172.
[11] In *Peake's Commentary*, p. 528. He adds that the evidence is not conclusive in the case of Demetrius. (Note that Demetrius is not one of the ten horns on Andrews's reckoning.)   [12] *Lit. of OT in Hist. Dev.*, p. 413.

is also the view of Amner,[1] who held the ten horns to comprise both Lagids and Seleucids.

To some, however, it has not commended itself as wholly satisfactory, on the ground that Demetrius was not actually king, but only heir. They have therefore preferred to substitute in his place a brother of his, who is said in a fragment of John of Antioch's[2] to have been put to death by Antiochus Epiphanes. This brother, indeed, appears to have been actually proclaimed king, after the murder of Seleucus Philopator,[3] and E. R. Bevan believes that coins were struck in his name.[4] This view was first suggested by von Gutschmid,[5] and it has been adopted by Hilgenfeld,[6] A. A. Bevan,[7] and Niese.[8]

But what claim has Heliodorus to a place in the Seleucid line? There is no evidence that he actually took the title of king, and as E. R. Bevan points out,[9] he would doubtless have weakened his position by so doing. And if he did not take the title of king, he would be less likely to be included than Demetrius, who was at least the rightful heir. Obbink therefore holds[10] the three uprooted horns to be (1) Seleucus Philopator, (2) his murdered son, and (3) Demetrius.

Those scholars who regard the ten horns as beginning with Seleucus Nicator, and who therefore find Seleucus

---

[1] *Essay towards Int. of Dan.*, p. 162. On Amner's view, only Seleucus Philopator was one of the ten horns.

[2] Cf. Müller, FHG iv, p. 558, No. 58: Ὅτι Ἀντίοχος (sc. ὁ Ἐπιφανής), ὁ τῆς Συρίας βασιλεύς, τοῦ Σελεύκου (sc. τοῦ Φιλοπάτορος) τοῦ ἀδελφοῦ παῖδα ὑποτοπήσας διέφθειρεν· ἑτέροις τὸν τούτου φόνον ἐπανεγκών, οὓς δὴ καὶ διὰ φόβον διεχρήσατο.

[3] Cf. Bevan, HS ii, p. 126. See further, id., CAH viii, pp. 498, 713 f., where the view is taken that Epiphanes did not at first displace his nephew, but occupied the throne jointly with him.

[4] HS ii, p. 126 n. In that case his name was Antiochus. See also Otto, in PW viii, col. 14.

[5] *Rhein. Mus. für Phil.*, New Series, xv, 1860, pp. 316–18, reprinted in *Kl. Schriften*, ii, pp. 175-9.   [6] *Esr. u. Dan. u. ihre neu. Bearb.*, p. 82 n.

[7] *Short Comm. on Dan.*, p. 118.

[8] *Gesch. der griech. u. mak. Staaten*, iii, pp. 92 f.

[9] HS ii, p. 126. In a foot-note he adds that if he had assumed the diadem, he would doubtless have put the son of Seleucus to death. Cf. also id., CAH viii, p. 497, and Bouché-Leclercq, *Hist. des Sél.* i, p. 240: 'Mais prendre lui-même le diadème eût été une folie.'   [10] *Daniël*, p. 106.

Philopator to be the seventh horn, are compelled to seek three persons, excluding Seleucus himself, who were uprooted before Antiochus Epiphanes. It is usual to find them in (1) Heliodorus, (2) Demetrius, and (3) Ptolemy Philometor.[1] This is the view of Bertholdt,[2] Bade,[3] Eichhorn,[4] Dereser,[5] von Lengerke,[6] Maurer,[7] Stuart,[8] Ewald,[9] Strong,[10] Delitzsch,[11] Vatke,[12] Meinhold,[13] Farrar,[14] and Lagrange.[15] The title of Ptolemy Philometor to a place in the Seleucid line is denied by the critics of this view, and it has been already agreed that Antiochus' attempt to annex Egypt cannot be held to be an uprooting of Philometor, appropriate to the conditions here, since it was not an uprooting of him from the Seleucid line. It is to be remembered, however, that Philometor was a Seleucid on his mother's side, since he was the son of Cleopatra, the sister of the murdered Seleucus Philopator. It has been thought that Cleopatra perhaps claimed the throne for her son, and several writers have definitely stated that she did so,[16] but Pusey rightly says[17] that of this there is no vestige in history. But Jerome, while not mentioning Cleopatra, refers to the views of those who say that an effort was made to seize the throne for Ptolemy Philometor by a party in Syria that favoured him.[18]

---

[1] Turmel, who holds the uprooted horns to be outside the number of the ten, similarly identifies them with Demetrius, Theodore (= Heliodorus) and Ptol. Philom. (*Annales de phil. chrét.* 3rd Series, i, 1902-3, pp. 13 f.).

[2] *Dan. neu übers. u. erk.*, p. 433.   [3] *Die hebr. Proph.* iii, p. 442.

[4] *Ezech. u. Dan.*, 2nd ed., p. 357.

[5] *Das B. Dan. verd. u. ausg.*, pp. 320 f.

[6] *Comm. gramm. crit. in VT*, ii, p. 130.   [7] *Comm. on Dan.*, pp. 208 f.

[8] *Christ. des AT*, iii, Part 2, p. 89.   [9] *Proph. of OT*, ET v, p. 248.

[10] In Zöckler, *Bk. of Dan.*, ET by Strong, p. 46 (table quoted from M'Clintock and Strong's *Cyclopaedia*, s.v. Daniel).

[11] PRE, 2nd ed., iii, p. 476.

[12] *Hist.-krit. Einl. in das AT*, ed. Preiss, p. 653.

[13] *Das B. Dan. ausg.*, p. 299.   [14] *Bk. of Dan.*, p. 241.

[15] RB, New Series, i, 1904, p. 504.

[16] So Bertholdt, loc. cit.; Eichhorn, op. cit., iii, p. 443; von Lengerke, op. cit., p. 321; Stuart, op. cit., p. 209.

[17] Op. cit., p. 152 n. So, too, Hitzig, *Das B. Dan. erk.*, p. 122.

[18] On xi. 21 (ed. Migne, col. 566): *stabit in loco Seleuci frater ejus Antiochus Epiphanes, cui primum ab his qui in Syria Ptolemaeo favebant non dabatur honor*

Bevan[1] believes this is merely a deduction of Porphyry's,[2] resting on no sound historical basis. It cannot be denied, however, that Porphyry had access to sources now lost, and we cannot rule out the possibility that the tradition is sound, and that there were some who advocated the claims of Ptolemy Philometor, when Heliodorus murdered Seleucus Philopator.[3] And certainly if any claim at all had been made on behalf of Philometor, however slender it might be in fact, it is easily to be understood that a Jewish writer, looking back on that claim after some experience of the rule of Antiochus Epiphanes, would recognize its validity in comparison with that of Antiochus. I therefore hold that Ptolemy Philometor is rightly to be identified with one of the uprooted horns.

I disagree with the aforementioned scholars, however, who hold the other two to be Heliodorus and Demetrius. That Heliodorus, who appears neither to have been proclaimed king, nor to have been even an aspirant to the title of king, but rather to have been satisfied with the exercise of the reality of power[4], and who was certainly not in any sense a Seleucid, should be included amongst the ten horns, appears to me to be wholly improbable. On the other hand,

regius, sed postea simulatione clementiae obtinuit regnum Syriae. In view of the fact, however, that Jerome sometimes uses Syria for Coele-Syria, we cannot be certain that the reference is not to a *Palestinian* party that favoured the restoration of Ptolemaic rule there. Bouché-Leclercq accepts the tradition that there was a Syrian party favourable to the claims of Ptolemy to the throne. See *Hist. des Lag.* i, p. 241.

[1] *Short Comm. on Dan.*, p. 117. Cf. Wilcken in PW i, col. 2471.

[2] Jerome does not explicitly say this is Porphyry's view, but the context clearly implies it.

[3] It is to be observed that when war broke out between Philometor and Antiochus, after the death of Cleopatra, the regents who governed Egypt in the name of Philometor announced to the Alexandrian populace, on their setting out with the young king to invade Coele-Syria, that they would bring the Syrian kingdom under the Ptolemaic crown (cf. Bevan, HS ii, p. 135). This would seem to imply a pretension to the Syrian throne at that time, which might well be a revival of one unsuccessfully advanced a few years earlier.

[4] Appian's reference to Heliodorus as ἐς τὴν ἀρχὴν βιαζόμενον (*Syr.* 45, ed. Mendelssohn, i, p. 416) does not involve the conclusion that he had made an open claim to the title of king. Cf. White's translation (ii, p. 191): 'when Heliodorus sought to possess himself of the government.'

I

it is in every way probable that the brother of Demetrius, if he was actually proclaimed king, should be included. As for Demetrius, it is to be observed that Bevan, though he eliminates his name, agrees that his inclusion would not be unlikely[1]. It is true that he lived to come to the throne later, and that Antiochus but postponed his reign, but a writer during the reign of Antiochus Epiphanes could not know that Demetrius would ultimately come to the throne, and to such a writer it would seem that Demetrius had been definitely robbed of the throne he could rightly claim. I therefore hold the three uprooted horns to be (1) Demetrius (2) his murdered brother, Antiochus, and (3) Ptolemy Philometor.

Wright criticizes the various identifications that have been made by saying[2] that it is absurd to think that persons who never sat on the Syrian throne could be represented as horns of the beast. This argument fails in the case of the murdered son of Seleucus, while Demetrius could not be referred to as one who never sat on the Syrian throne. It is even recorded that Ptolemy Philometor later occupied the Syrian throne for a brief moment. Our authorities for this are a reference in Polybius[3], and a statement in 1 Maccabees[4] and in Josephus[5]. Mahaffy claims that the tradition is attested by coins[6], which represent him with his diadem as king, not of Egypt, but of Syria, but Bevan says that though he was invited to assume the Syrian diadem, he prudently resisted the offer[7]. In any case there was no effective occupation of the Syrian throne, for the tradition merely tells us that he was persuaded to put on two diadems,

---

[1] *Short Comm. on Dan.*, p. 118.

[2] *Dan. and his Proph.*, p. 162. Cf. Hengstenberg, op. cit., ET, p. 168: 'Not a single one of these three pretenders to the crown (i.e. Heliodorus, Philometor and Demetrius) is produced by any historian in the list of Syrian kings.'

[3] xxxix. 7 (xl. 12): Πτολεμαῖος ὁ τῆς Συρίας βασιλεύς (Loeb ed., vi, p. 450).

[4] 1 Macc. xi. 13.

[5] *Ant.* XIII. iv. 7 (XIII. 113 f., ed. Niese, iii, p. 171).

[6] *Emp. Ptol.*, p. 366.

[7] HS ii, pp. 220 f., and *Hist. of Egypt under Ptol. Dyn.*, p. 304.

but immediately relinquished the Syrian, through unwillingness to antagonize the Romans[1]. But since neither Demetrius nor Ptolemy occupied the Syrian throne until later than the date to which the composition of the book of Daniel is ascribed, the essential contention of Wright is not met by these events. But it can scarcely be denied that an author who regarded the title of Antiochus to the Seleucid throne as inferior to that of these three, might without any absurdity include them amongst the ten horns. They were not, save for the brother of Demetrius, *de facto* kings who preceded Antiochus on the throne, but *de jure* they were before him in this writer's view, and were uprooted to make way for him.

(c) But whatever the details of the ten horns may have been, we have early testimony to the substantial point at issue, which is that somehow they pointed to the Seleucid line. This early testimony has been already referred to. It is found in the Sibylline Oracles, iii. 388-400. The passage reads[2]:

> ἥξει καὶ ποτ' ἄπιστος[3] ἐς 'Ασίδος ὄλβιον οὖδας
> ἀνὴρ πορφυρέην λώπην ἐπιειμένος ὤμοις
> 390 ἄγριος ἀλλοδίκης φλογόεις· ἤγειρε γὰρ αὐτοῦ[4]
> πρόσθε κεραυνὸς φῶτα·[5] κακὸν δ' 'Ασίη ζυγὸν ἕξει
> πᾶσα, πολὺν δὲ χθὼν πίεται φόνον ὀμβρηθεῖσα.
> ἀλλὰ καὶ ὡς πανάϊστον ἅπαντ'[6] 'Αΐδης θεραπεύσει·[7]
> ὧν δή περ γενεὴν αὐτὸς θέλει ἐξαπολέσσαι,
> 395 ἐκ τῶν δὴ γενεῆς κείνου γένος ἐξαπολεῖται·
> ῥίζαν ἴαν γε διδούς,[8] ἣν καὶ[9] κόψει βροτολοιγός

---

[1] Bouché-Leclercq accepts this tradition that he did for a moment wear the two crowns, but that when the excitement subsided he relinquished the Syrian. See *Hist. des Lag.* ii, p. 52, and *Hist. des Sél.* i, p. 343.

[2] The text quoted is from the edition of Geffcken, *Die Or. Sib.*, 1902. The variations in the texts of Alexandre (ΧΡΗΣΜΟΙ ΣΙΒΥΛΛΙΑΚΟΙ, 1st ed., 1841, 2nd ed., 1869) and Rzach (*Or. Sib.*, 1891) are indicated in the following notes.

[3] Rzach reads ἄπυστος and Alexandre ἄπυστ' [εἰς] 'Ασσίδος. Alexandre notes (1869 ed., p. 104): *Codd. omnes ἄπιστ' pro ἄπυστα ac deinde ἐξ ἀσσίδος*.

[4] Alex. reads αὐτὸν and Rz. ἤγειρε δὲ τοῦτον.

[5] Rz. reads κεραύνιος ἄνδρα.

[6] Rz. reads ἄνακτ'

[7] Rz. reads ὀλοθρεύσει.

[8] Rz. reads ἀναδούς for γε διδούς.

[9] Rz. reads περ.

ἐκ δέκα δὴ¹ κεράτων, *παρὰ δὴ² φυτὸν ἄλλο φυτεύσει,*
κόψει πορφυρέης γενεῆς³ γενετῆρα μαχητήν
καὐτὸς ὑφ'⁴ *υἱῶν ὧν ἐς ὁμόφρονα αἴσιον ἄρρης⁵*
400 φθεῖται· καὶ τότε δὴ παραφυόμενον κέρας ἄρξει.⁶

Lanchester's translation of this passage is as follows:⁷

One day there shall come unexpectedly to Asia's wealthy land
A man clad with a purple cloak upon his shoulders,
390 Savage, a stranger from justice, fiery: for he hath exalted himself
Even against the thunder, a mortal as he is. And all Asia shall
    have an evil yoke,
And the drenched earth shall drink large draughts of blood.
But even so Hades shall attend him utterly destroyed
By the race of those whose family he wishes to destroy
395 By them shall his own family be destroyed.
Yet after leaving one root, which the Destroyer shall cut off
From among ten horns, he shall put forth a side-shoot⁸.
He shall cut down the warrior parent of the purple race,

---

¹ Rz. reads μέν.
² Alex. reads δέ. Cf. Rzach, Denkschr. der kais. Akad. der Wiss. (phil.-hist. Cl.), xxxviii, 1890, IV Abhand., p. 31.
³ Rz. reads πορφύρεος γενέτης. Cf. ibid.   ⁴ Alex. reads ἀφ'.
⁵ This line is certainly corrupt. Ewald notes (Abhand. über Entst. Inh. u. Werth der Sib. Bücher, p. 14 n.) that some MSS. read "Αρης, and says this should be read, or the word understood in this sense. Alex. (1869 ed., p. 104) says: 'Codd. in fine ἄρης vel ἄρρης, sine sensu, pro quo nos ἀρχῆς suspiciamur; nihil tamen definimus. Est enim versus omnino corruptus et desperatus, eratque jam talis saeculo III desinente uti patebit ex ultimis Sibyllinis libris. Sensus velle videtur ἀφ' υἱῶν ὧν ἐς ὁμόφρονα δέξεται ἀρχήν seu simile quid. Legerat Sibyllista libri xi ἀφ' υἱωνῶν, et de Judaeis intellexerat. Cf. xi. 48, 56, 100.' Rzach proposes to read ὑφ' υἱωνοῦ ὀλοόφρων δῆμος "Αρης (for discussion of the passage, cf. Denkschr. der kais. Akad., loc. cit.), while Geffcken suggests (Komp. u. Entst. der Or. Sib., pp. 10 f.) ὑφ' υἱωνῶν ἐν ὁμοφροσύνῃσιν "Αρηος. Lanchester (in Charles's Apoc. and Pseud. ii, p. 386) follows the reading ὑφ' υἱωνῶν καθ' ὁμόφρονα αἶσαν "Αρηος.
⁶ Both Rzach and Geffcken note the verbal parallel between the closing lines and Sib. Or. xi. 250 ff.:

κόψει πορφύρεος γενέτης γενετῆρα μαχητήν
καὐτὸς ἀφ' [Rzach ὑφ'] υἱῆος, πρὶν δὴ φυτὸν ἄλλο φυτεύσει
ἐκλείψει· ῥίζῃ δ' ἀναθηλήσει μετέπειτα
αὐτοφυής· τοῦ δὴ παραφυόμενον γένος ἔσται [Alex. ἐστίν].

⁷ In Charles's Apoc. and Pseud. ii, pp. 385 f.
⁸ The rendering of this line is given as corrected by Charles, ibid., p. xii. Bate (Sib. Or., Bks. III–V) renders: 'from among ten heads, before it genders another shoot', following the reading of xi. 251. So Geffcken (Komp. u. Entst. der Or. Sib., p. 10).

‡And he himself at the hand of his grandsons shall perish in a like fate of war‡ :[1]
400 And then a parasite horn shall have dominion.

The emendation and rendering of Lanchester are open to the objection, as he himself admits, that the passage becomes out of accord with the historical facts with which his interpretation connects it. For he takes it to mean that Alexander Balas should perish at the hands of the grandsons of Demetrius. To import the reference to grandsons into the text under such circumstances is hardly to present a likely emendation. Geffcken's emendation is open to a similar objection. For he connects the passage with the struggles of Antiochus Cyzicenus against his half-brother Antiochus Grypus and the latter's sons. He takes it to mean that Cyzicenus would destroy the family of him whose sons are destined to destroy his own. He should, however, put out one shoot, Antiochus Eusebes, whom Philip, the descendant of ten kings, should strike down before Cyzicenus should plant another; and though he should strike down Grypus, he himself should be the victim of Grypus' sons, his own nephews. Here again Geffcken admits the difficulties, which are that υἰωνὸς does not mean *nephew*, but *grandson*, and that Eusebes was not struck down by Philip[2].

Where corruption is admitted, and no convincing emendation has been found, a further effort may be pardoned, and I have elsewhere[3] suggested the reading:

καὐτὸς ἀφ' υἱῶν, ὧν ἐς ὁμόφρονα αἴσιμον ῎Αρης
φθέρσει·

---

[1] This rendering follows the emendation noted above as Lanchester's. Bate (op. cit.) renders: 'and perish himself at the hands of his grandsons †joined in a compact of war†', while Bouché-Leclercq (*Revue de l'hist. des Relig.* ix, p. 222) has: 'Il frappera le père belliqueux de la race de pourpre et périra lui-même sous les coups des fils, auxquels la concorde assurera le succès: alors enfin règnera la corne engendrée à côté.'

[2] Bevan (HS ii, p. 263 n.) observes that the end of Eusebes is variously reported. Three accounts are preserved, of which none connects his end with Philip. Josephus (*Ant.* XIII. xiii. 4 (XIII. 368, ed. Niese, iii, p. 219)) says he died fighting against the Parthians. Cf. Bouché-Leclercq, *Hist. des Sél.* ii, pp. 605 ff.   [3] ZAW, New Series, iii, 1926, pp. 324–7.

and the rendering:

> And he himself (shall be cut off) to make way for his sons, whom
>   Ares on a like fated (day)
> Shall destroy.

This yields a meaning in agreement with the historical facts with which the passage is commonly connected, and is not open to serious grammatical objection[1].

As to the interpretation of the passage, and its historical references, there has been much disagreement. Alexandre held[2] the passage to date from the second century A.D., and the reference of the phrase 'the conqueror of Asia' to be to Hadrian. Bousset, on the other hand, holds[3] the material to be ancient, and the reference to have been originally to Alexander the Great, the 'one root' being Roxana's son[4]. But he thinks the passage has been altered to make it applicable to a Seleucid king[5]. In this view he is followed by Bate[6].

More generally the 'man clad with the purple cloak' is taken to be Antiochus Epiphanes. This interpretation was first proposed by Hilgenfeld[7], and it has been followed by Ewald[8], Schürer[9], Driver[10], Lanchester[11], and Charles[12]. Its

---

[1] The two uncommon grammatical features of the text, as thus read and interpreted, are the meaning attached to the preposition ἀπό, and the supplying of a passive verb 'shall be cut off' from an active. Of the former I adduced some clear parallels from the Septuagint, but of the latter, owing to my residence in China at the time, and the consequent absence of reference facilities, I was able to adduce no parallel. I can now add that Jelf (*Gramm. of Gk. Lang.* 5th ed., ii, p. 636) quotes passages from Thucydides and Sophocles, where a passive verb has to be supplied from an active, and Kühner (*Ausf. Gramm. der griech. Spr.* II. ii, p. 565) adds a further example from Xenophon. Jelf (loc. cit.) also notes an example in NT Greek, in Rom. ii. 8.

[2] ΧΡΗΣΜΟΙ ΣΙΒΥΛΛΙΑΚΟΙ, 2nd ed., pp. xvi f.; cf. 1st ed., ii, pp. 367 ff.

[3] ZNW iii, 1902, pp. 34 f.

[4] So, too, Henry (op. cit., p. 99 n.) holds the man clothed in purple to be Alexander, and the ten horns to represent the division of his empire, while the side-shoot stands for the Seleucids.

[5] Pusey (op. cit., p. 368 n.) interpreted the passage of Alexander, his infant son being the one root. But he admitted the impossibility of attaching any historical meaning to the rest of the details.

[6] *Sib. Or., Bks. III–V*, p. 22.   [7] *Die jüd. Apok.*, pp. 68 ff.

[8] *Abhand. über Entst. Inh. u. Werth der Sib. Bücher*, pp. 13 ff.

[9] GJV, 4th ed., iii, pp. 575 f. (ET II. iii, pp. 281 f.).

[10] *Bk. of Dan.*, p. 98 n.   [11] Loc. cit.   [12] *Crit. Comm. on Dan.*, p. 168.

appropriateness to the historical circumstances of the second century B.C. only failed at the admittedly corrupt line 399, but if the emendation and rendering I have proposed are adopted, the correspondence is complete. The family Antiochus wished to destroy was that of Seleucus Philopator; the root that was cut off was Antiochus Eupator, the son.and successor of Epiphanes; the destroyer was Demetrius Soter, son of Philopator; the side-shoot was Alexander Balas, who 'cut down the warrior parent of the purple race', i.e. Demetrius Soter, but was himself treacherously murdered when fleeing from Ptolemy Philometor. The sons for whom this murder made way were Demetrius Nicator and Antiochus Sidetes, the sons of Demetrius Soter, who ascended the throne in 144–143 and 138–137 B.C. respectively[1]. The parasite horn was Alexander Zabinas, who claimed to be the son of Sidetes.

The 'ten horns' of this passage would therefore seem to stand for the Seleucid line of kings, from which Eupator was cut off, and Zabinas is called a parasite horn because he claimed to be a Seleucid, though in reality he was not. The expression 'ten horns' is commonly held to be a definite allusion to Dn vii. 7, and it would therefore seem to indicate that at the time this passage was written, it was understood to refer to the Seleucid dynasty. That it here includes Antiochus Epiphanes is doubtless due to the fact that it had acquired associations and had come to be a synonym for the Seleucids. The date of this Sibylline passage is generally given as *circa* 140 B.C., but it is more probable that it should be dated slightly later—between 129 B.C. and 122 B.C.[2] We may therefore say that at this time the fourth

---

[1] These are the dates arrived at by Kolbe (cf. *Beitr. zur syr. u. jüd. Gesch.*, p. 61). Bevan (HS ii, pp. 221 f., 237) gives 145 B.C. and 138 B.C., and Oesterley (*Hist. of Isr.* ii, pp. 466 f.) 145 B.C. and 139–138 B.C., while Bouché-Leclercq (*Hist. des Sél.*, i, pp. 347 ff.) gives 145 B.C. and 139 B.C. With the last named agrees Cary (*Hist. of Gk. World from 323 to 146 B.C.*, p. 415).

[2] See ZAW, New Series, iii, 1926, p. 326. This date is in close agreement with that suggested by Ewald, who dated Sib. Or. III 98–828 *circa* 124 B.C. (see *Abhand. über Entst. Inh. u. Werth der Sib. Bücher*, pp. 9 ff.). Alexandre

beast was held to refer to the Greek empire, and the ten
horns to the Seleucid line. And this is our earliest witness
to the interpretation of the passage.

(d) If there is uncertainty as to the precise identification
of all the ten horns, there is no uncertainty as to the aptness
of the identification of the Little Horn with Antiochus
Epiphanes. The Roman school can agree as little here as
in the matter of the ten horns, and within its ranks the most
varied suggestions have been made, ranging from Julius
Caesar through Nero and Vespasian and Trajan to the Papacy
and the Khalifate and a future Antichrist. But within the
Greek school there is unanimity on the identification with
Antiochus Epiphanes[1].

The Little Horn is said to be 'diverse from his fellows';
Bevan writes[2] of Epiphanes: 'No other king of his house
had been such as he', and describes at length his unique-
ness. The Little Horn 'put down three kings'; Epiphanes
brushed aside, as has been above said, Demetrius, his
brother, and Ptolemy Philometor. The Little Horn had
'a mouth speaking great things'; the author of 1 Maccabees
says[3] of Antiochus Epiphanes that 'he spake very presump-
tuously'. The interpretation of the vision says of the Little
Horn that 'he made war with the saints, and prevailed

(op. cit., 2nd ed., pp. xiii ff.) contests this view. Cf. also Larocque (RArch
New Series, xx, 1869, pp. 261 ff.) and Hilgenfeld (*Zeitsch. für wiss. Theol.* iii,
1860, pp. 313 ff., and xiv, 1871, pp. 32 ff.).

[1] Bleek's view that the Little Horn was primarily Seleucus Nicator and the
Seleucid dynasty has been noted above. So far as the present point is concerned, his view is not seriously different from that of other scholars, since he
too brings the climax and termination of the Little Horn into the reign of
Antiochus Epiphanes. (Cf. his earlier *Über Verf. u. Zweck des B. Dan.*,
p. 236: 'Bei allen Weissagungen im Buche Daniel geht die Bestimmtheit der
Vorhersagung und ihr genaues Zusammentreffen mit der Geschichte immer
nur bis auf die Zeit der Tyrannei des Antiochus Epiphanes oder bis auf
dessen Tod.') So, too, Henry (op. cit., p. 99 n.), who holds that a horn must
stand for a dynasty and not for an individual, finds that the eyes and the
mouth of the Little Horn represent Antiochus Epiphanes, and so brings the
climax to the same age. The inappropriateness of Henry's view needs little
demonstration, however. For if the horn stood for a dynasty, two different
parts of it would hardly stand for a single individual.

[2] HS ii, p. 128.   [3] 1 Macc. i. 24.

against them', and that 'he shall speak words against the Most High, and shall wear out the saints of the Most High: and shall think to change times and the law'; of Antiochus Epiphanes the author of 1 Maccabees says[1]: 'And King Antiochus wrote to his whole kingdom, that all should be one people, and that each should forsake his own laws. . . . And the king sent letters . . . unto Jerusalem and the cities of Judah, that they should follow laws strange to the land, and should forbid whole burnt offerings and sacrifice and drink-offerings in the sanctuary; and should profane the sabbaths and feasts, and pollute the sanctuary and them that were holy; . . . so that they might forget the law and change all the ordinances. . . . And they made Israel to hide themselves in every place of refuge which they had.' Of the Little Horn it is said: 'They shall be given into his hand until a time and times and half a time'; of Antiochus we are told that he interrupted the daily sacrifices in the Temple for three and a half years.[2]

If Antiochus is regarded as the Little Horn, it is easy to

---

[1] 1 Macc. i. 41 ff.

[2] Cf. Josephus, *Wars*, I. i. 1 (I. 32, ed. Niese, vi, p. 10, or Loeb ed., ii, pp. 18 f.). Kahrstedt discusses this at length and says: 'Das Datum Daniels ist völlig unmöglich.' He argues that Antiochus could not have arrived in Palestine before the middle of August 168 B.C., and that the setting up of the idol-altar probably took place in December, making three years and not three and a half between the suspension of sacrifice and its resumption (*Syr. Terr. in hell. Zeit*, p. 129 f.). This is in agreement with 1 Macc. i. 59, iv. 52, according to which it was three years from the sacrificing on the idol-altar to the restoration of sacrifice according to the Jewish law. Kahrstedt explains the three and a half years of Daniel by the change from the Seleucid era in the Spring of 166 B.C. to a Jewish reckoning from Nisan, giving a short 'year' for 167–166 B.C. In view of the exact reckoning by days given in the book of Daniel, however, this does not seem a very probable explanation. It is more likely that the cessation of sacrifice according to the Jewish law took place some time before the commencement of the idol sacrifices in the Temple, and it may well have antedated the actual arrival of Antiochus in Palestine. Cf. Bleek, *Über Verf. u. Zweck des B. Dan.*, p. 289: 'Die 3½ Zeiten oder 7 halbe Jahre sind wohl wahrscheinlich nicht, wie Berthold meint, von dem Tage, wo der heidnische Opferdienst in Jerusalem eingerichtet wurde, sondern von dem etwas früheren Zeitpunkte an zu rechnen, wo die Stadt Jerusalem durch den Apollonius, den Feldherrn des Antiochus, hinterlistigerweise eingenommen wurde.'

see how the author could identify him in thought with the fourth beast. It is true that Antiochus did not exercise all the authority of the Greek empire as Alexander left it, but at the time of the Maccabean revolt he exercised all the effective authority that remained. For it has been observed that the Macedonian kingdom had been annexed by Rome, and that Ptolemy had placed himself under the protection of Rome. Further, from the point of view of the Jews, the authority of the Greek empire was vested in him, and since the empire was ideally one, even though Egypt had not appeared so helpless, it would have been simple to regard him as the representative of the entire beast, especially as he so notably exemplified the destructive and devouring nature ascribed to the beast. The extent of his empire was less than that of Alexander, but the destructive character of the Greek kingdom reached its climax in him. How fully he manifested the nature of the beast that 'devoured and brake in pieces and stamped the residue with its feet' needs no demonstration here. In *Sib. Or.* iii. 613, in a passage that would seem to refer to Antiochus Epiphanes, we read: 'He shall break up everything, and fill everything with miseries',[1] while 1 Macc. i. 16–39 gives a vivid description of the devastation he spread.

It does not seem to have been noticed that on this view alone can the fate of the four beasts find a simple and natural explanation. The fourth beast 'was slain, and his body destroyed, and he was given to be burned with fire', but 'as for the rest of the beasts[2], their dominion was taken away: yet their lives were prolonged for a season and a time'. It has been already noted that on the Roman view it is impossible to suppose that on the destruction of the Roman

[1] Πάντα δὲ συγκόψει καὶ πάντα κακῶν ἀναπλήσει. The translation is that of Lanchester, in Charles, *Apoc. and Pseud.* ii, p. 389.

[2] Behrmann (*Das B. Dan. übers. u. erk.*, p. 47) holds that these are really the first seven horns, which have here become beasts. This is in accordance with his view that the horns are not a succession of kings, but the parts of the Greek empire. It is much more natural, however, to regard the beasts of vii. 11 f. as the same as the already mentioned four beasts.

empire, whether that event is dated in the past or in the future, a measure of life denied to Rome was, or shall be, continued to Babylon, Medo-Persia, and Greece. But the kingdom ruled over by Antiochus Epiphanes comprised Palestine, Syria, Mesopotamia and Babylonia, and a remnant of title to the more remote east. Asia Minor had been lost by Antiochus the Great beyond recovery, but while Seleucid power in the east had considerably crumbled, the east was still reckoned part of their dominions, and it was in an effort to re-establish the reality of power there that Antiochus Epiphanes ultimately met his end. An author in 165 B.C., who looked for the collapse of the Seleucid house, might well anticipate the disintegration of its kingdom. He might look for Media and Persia and Babylonia to become independent states for a time—though not exercising any imperial sway over other states—until the Messianic kingdom which was to be established in Palestine should spread to include them and fill the earth. On the other hand, with the collapse of the Seleucid rule and the dissolution of the kingdom, the Macedonian empire would come to a total end throughout the realm of the Seleucids. For the Macedonian empire was diverse from the Babylonian, Median, and Persian empires in that its fount lay outside its dominions, so far at any rate as the Seleucid kingdom was concerned. It was not a Syrian sway that the Seleucids exercised, but a Greek sway[1], and the breaking up of their kingdom would restore racial kingdoms throughout the area they controlled, but amongst those racial kingdoms there would be no Greek or Macedonian state. While, therefore, the Seleucid kingdom would lose not only its dominion but its very being, Babylonia, Media, and Persia would continue to exist temporarily as separate states until

---

[1] Cf. Cary (op. cit., p. 246): 'In all the new Greek monarchies of the Near East the status of Greeks and Orientals was kept distinct. The Oriental stood under a different law from the Greek.' And below, on the same page: 'The governing classes in the succession-states of Alexander's empire always remained Hellenic.'

the kingdom of the saints, symbolized by the 'son of man', absorbed them.[1]

On this view it becomes clear how the collapse of the entire image could be regarded as a single catastrophic event in chapter ii, and yet the destruction of the four beasts in chapter vii be not simultaneous. For since the empires represented by the parts of the image were territorially incorporated in the succeeding empires, the collapse of the image which resulted in its being shattered could well represent the expected break-up of the loosely compacted Selucid empire into its component fragments[2], while it has been just shown that such a splitting asunder of the empire would automatically involve the disappearance of a Seleucid unit.

(d) *The Greek view is supported by the other visions*

In chapter viii we have the vision of the ram and the goat, where the goat is explicitly stated to represent Greece. On the head of the goat is a 'notable horn', which is stated to be the first king, i.e. Alexander. When this horn is broken four notable horns arise in its place, and these are said to be four kingdoms which shall arise. Out of one of these horns there came a Little Horn, which is declared to represent a

---

[1] Nestle (*Marg. u. Mat.*, pp. 39 f.) suggested that the *great sea* of vii. 2 is the Mediterranean, and that the purview of the vision of chap. vii was limited to the shores of the Mediterranean. He then identified the four beasts with the four kingdoms of the Diadochoi recognized elsewhere in the book of Dan.—Egypt, Macedonia, Asia Minor, and Syria, with Antiochus IV as the Little Horn. On this view he supposed that vii. 12 was intelligible. But this seems less reasonable than the view taken above. For it is more likely that the prolongation of life, but without dominion, meant independence, but without empire, than that it meant subjection to a foreign power. But in the time of Antiochus, Macedonia and Asia Minor had already been swallowed up by Rome, and Egypt appeared on the point of extinction. The collapse of the Syrian kingdom could not be expected to restore them to independence, or in any way to affect their destiny.

[2] Cf. Bevan (*Jer. under High Priests*, pp. 23 f.): 'It is difficult to say at first what we are to consider the centre of this unwieldly kingdom. If by centre we mean the residence of the king and his court, it was rather a moving camp than a fixed city. But there were capitals for the different parts of the kingdom ... and the king was sometimes in one, sometimes in another, according to the need of the moment.'

king of fierce countenance. It is admitted by all schools[1]
that this Little Horn represents Antiochus Epiphanes. It
is, however, denied by many opponents of the Greek view
of the fourth empire that the Little Horn of chapter viii is
the same as the Little Horn of chapter vii.

The phrase is, indeed, not identical. In vii. 8, which is
in the Aramaic part of the book, we have קֶרֶן אָחֳרִי זְעֵירָה,
while in viii. 9, which is in the Hebrew part of the book,
we have קֶרֶן־אַחַת מִצְּעִירָה. But this difference does not
demand that the reference must be different. For in viii.
13 we find the expression הַפֶּשַׁע שֹׁמֵם, in ix. 27 שִׁקּוּצִים מְשֹׁמֵם,
in xi. 31 הַשִּׁקּוּץ מְשֹׁמֵם, and in xii. 11 שִׁקּוּץ שֹׁמֵם. But
although no two of these expressions are identical, most
scholars allow that at least two of them have the same
reference, while many hold that they all have the same reference. But if even two of these slightly different expressions
may have the same reference, it can scarcely be denied that
the slightly different terms used for the Little Horns of
chapters vii and viii may denote the same person.

Efforts have been made, however, to distinguish between
the horns of chapters vii and viii on other grounds. It has
been pointed out by many writers[2] that the fourth beast of
chapter vii had ten horns, while the he-goat of chapter viii
had four horns, and further that the Little Horn of chapter
vii appeared amongst the horns, while that of chapter viii
appeared as an off-shoot from one of the horns. But this is
all beside the issue. No one has maintained that all the
details of the visions in chapters vii and viii are identical.

[1] Or nearly all. For the Futurist writers of the more extreme wing have
supposed that there is an 'immense interval' in chap. viii, and have maintained that there is a leap after vv. 8 and 22 into times yet to be. See
Tregelles, *Rem. on Proph. Vis. in Dan.*, pp. 132 f; and cf. Newton, *Obs.
upon Dan. and Apoc.*, pp. 119 ff. (Whitla's ed., pp. 220 ff.), and Tyso, *Eluc.
of Proph.*, p. 47.

[2] Cf. Pusey, op. cit., p. 91; Volck, *Vind. Dan.*, pp. 10 f.; Kliefoth, op. cit.,
pp. 229 f.; Keil, op. cit., ET, pp. 253, 258; Deane, op. cit., p. 134; Wright,
Dan. and his Proph., p. 163; Hertlein, op. cit., pp. 40 f.; Boutflower, *In and
Around Bk. of Dan.*, p. 15.

Had they been there would have been no need to repeat the chapter. Chapters ii and vii by general agreement refer to the same four world-empires, but the details are determined in part by the forms into which the visions are cast. So, here, our author limits himself in chapter viii to the Medo-Persian and Greek empires, and is therefore content with two beasts instead of four. He therefore chooses a fresh way of indicating, by means of features of the he-goat, characteristic features of the empire it represents. What has to be asked is not whether they are precisely the same features as were noted in chapter vii, but whether the features of chapters vii and viii equally fit the same empire. The ten horns of chapter vii are stated to be ten kings, and have been interpreted above of the Seleucid line, including the three whose claims were passed over in favour of Antiochus Epiphanes. In that connexion Antiochus is appropriately represented as having arisen amongst the horns. But in chapter viii the horns are stated to represent the divisions of Alexander's empire. One of these horns therefore represents the Seleucid line, and is to be equated with the whole series of ten horns of the previous chapter. To have mentioned another horn arising among the four horns of chapter viii would have implied a fifth division of the empire. But Antiochus Epiphanes, who could rightly be described as an eleventh horn in the succession of the Seleucid house, could not be described as a fifth power alongside the other four, since the power he represented was one of the four. He is therefore here appropriately indicated under the figure of an off-shoot from one of the four horns, viz. the Seleucid horn. That the two visions are not co-extensive does not forbid their climax and termination to coincide. But the details of each had to be determined by its own form and range.

The real case for the identification of the Little Horns of chapters vii and viii, however, does not rest on the similarity of the terms, but on the indications of the character and deeds of the person each stands for. The Little Horn of

chapter viii was 'a king of fierce countenance', who 'waxed
exceeding great toward the south and toward the east and
toward the glorious land'; the Little Horn of chapter vii
had 'a look more stout than his fellows' and 'a mouth
speaking great things'. The Little Horn of chapter viii was
one who should 'destroy the mighty ones and the holy
people', and should 'prosper and do his pleasure'; the
Little Horn of chapter vii was one who 'made war with the
saints and prevailed against them'. The Little Horn of
chapter viii 'waxed great even to the host of heaven', and
'magnified itself even to the prince of the host'; the Little
Horn of chapter vii was one who should 'speak words
against the Most High'. The Little Horn of chapter viii
was one who 'took away the continual burnt offering', and
through whom 'the place of the sanctuary was cast down';
the Little Horn of chapter vii was one who should 'think
to change times and the law'. The period of the Little
Horn's exercise of unlicensed power is defined in chapter
viii as two thousand three hundred evenings and mornings,
and in chapter vii as a time and times and half a time.
It would carry us too far to traverse the various meanings,
that have been assigned to these periods of time, and
would open up the entire question of the chronological data
of the visions; but the view that the former expression
means eleven hundred and fifty days, and therefore something over three years, and that the latter means three and
a half years, brings these into close connexion, the one being
a specific reckoning, however, and the other being a more
general definition of the period. The Little Horn of
chapter viii is to be 'broken without hand'; the Little Horn
of chapter vii has his dominion taken away, and is consumed
and destroyed by the judgement of the 'ancient of days'.

It cannot be denied that there is much similarity in all
this. Indeed, Keil admits[1] that 'there is more plausibility

---

[1] Op. cit., ET, p. 258. Cf. Deane, op. cit., p. 134. The extreme Futurist
school recognizes this similarity, but unnaturally makes a leap in the middle

in criticism which gives prominence to the resemblance in the description of the two violent persecutors of the people of God who arise out of the Javanic and the fourth world-kingdom, and are represented in chapter viii as well as in chapter vii under the figure of a little horn'.

So again in chapter xi, though there is no figure of a Little Horn, there is sufficient indication that the Seleucid king in whom the vision reaches its climax is to be identified with the Little Horn of chapter vii. It is admitted by writers of all schools, save the more extreme sections of the Futurist[1], that xi. 21 refers to Antiochus Epiphanes, and to the plain reader the king of that verse continues throughout the rest of the chapter. Concerning him we are told that he 'shall have indignation against the holy covenant and shall do his pleasure', that he shall 'profane the sanctuary' and 'take away the continual burnt offering', that he 'shall exalt himself and magnify himself above every god, and shall speak marvellous things against the God of gods'. Through his persecution of the people that know their God, we are told that 'some shall fall by the sword and by flame, by captivity and by spoil', and in the sequel to the vision, that stands in chapter xii, we learn that the result of this persecution shall be the 'breaking in pieces of the power of the holy people'. The period of the persecutor's unchecked power is there given as 'for a time, times, and an half'. In the midst of his evil fury we are told that 'he shall come to his end', but no human means of his destruction are indicated. Instead, we are told that at that time Michael

---

of chap. viii, in order to identify the Little Horn of that chap. with the future Antichrist it desiderates in chap. vii. So, too, Captain Maitland (*Brief and Conn. View of Proph.*, pp. 40 ff.) recognized the similarity, and so, by a *tour de force*, argued that while the he-goat of chap. viii is the Macedonian empire, the Little Horn of that chap. represents Rome, which then becomes the Papacy!

[1] It will be seen below that this school springs from Alexander the Great, in xi. 4, right across the ages to still unreached time. It thus eliminates Antiochus Epiphanes altogether from the chapter. Todd goes even farther, and eliminates Alexander from the chapter (cf. *Disc. on Proph. rel. to Ant.*, pp. 170 ff.).

shall stand up and the dead shall be raised. Not only so, but a judgement is clearly implied, since we learn that the raised should be appointed 'some to everlasting life and some to shame and everlasting contempt'. Here the connexions with both chapter viii and chapter vii are manifest, but it is only the latter that concern us here. The king who exalts himself and speaks marvellous things against the God of gods recalls the Little Horn that had a mouth speaking great things, and that spoke words against the Most High; the king who breaks in pieces the power of the holy people recalls the Little Horn that made war with the saints and prevailed against them; the period of the persecution carried through by the wilful king in the one chapter recalls the similar period of the persecution carried through by the Little Horn in the other; the overthrow of the kingdom that is in the one chapter so clearly the end of all earthly monarchies that it is followed by the resurrection of the dead to final and everlasting judgement, recalls the overthrow of the Little Horn, which inaugurates the eternal kingdom of the saints, and is itself also associated with a great judgement scene.

Some of those who deny the Greek view of the fourth empire recognize the similarities between the climaxes of chapters vii and xi, and therefore maintain that there is a break in the latter chapter. They cannot deny that the chapter opens with an account of the establishment of the Greek empire, but the necessity of their theory that it should end in the yet unreached future requires them to make a sudden leap somewhere in the chapter, and to maintain that there is no logical or historical connexion between the one part and the other. But there is no agreement amongst the holders of this view as to where this yawning chasm occurs. The extreme Futurist school makes the break after xi. 4[1], and by this means eliminates

---

[1] Cf. Tyso, *Eluc. of Proph.*, p. 47; Tregelles, *Rem. on Proph. Vis. in Bk. of Dan.*, pp. 132 f. Even more extreme is Todd, who does not even find

K

Antiochus Epiphanes and all his predecessors from the chapter, which is made to leap from Alexander the Great over all the history of the Macedonian and Roman empires, and all the history of modern Europe, into time yet to be. Wright's characterization of such views as a mere caricature of prophecy has already been quoted, and it will be agreed that it requires no little hardihood to deny that the history of the Seleucids and Lagids lies plainly in the chapter. Some, however, have affirmed that the chapter breaks away from that history at xi. 21, from which point it deals with a future Antichrist. This is the view that stands in Hippolytus[1] and Jerome[2]. That it requires us to read the chapter in an unnatural way is clear, and Wright justly says[3] that it is absurd so to interpret. Not less so are the views that the break is to be found at xi. 26[4], or at xi. 31[5], and Westcott's opinion that such views are 'wholly unfounded and arbitrary'[6] is fully warranted. Much more popular has been the view that the chapter passes from Seleucid history to still future time at xi. 36. This view is an ancient one, referred to already in Jerome[7], and it has reappeared in Alexander in this chapter. He holds that it deals with a single king of the north and a single king of the south, both of whom are still future. See op. cit., pp. 170 ff., 186 f.

[1] Cf. Bonwetsch, *Hippolyt's Komm. zum B. Dan.*, p. 310, or ed. Migne, cols. 664 f.; ET by Salmond, in *Ante-Nic. Christ. Lib.* vi, p. 460.

[2] On xi. 21, ed. Migne, col. 565. Jerome claims that this is in accordance with Scriptural method in general, and with our author's method in particular, instancing his leap from the fourth Persian king in xi. 2 to Alexander in xi. 3. That passage will be dealt with below, but assuming here with Jerome that the leap is from Xerxes to Alexander, there is a real historical and logical connexion there that is entirely lacking here. For in xi. 2 the reader is carried to the period of the clash between Persia and Greece, and in xi. 3 to the final issue of that clash in the emergence of Alexander as the conqueror of Asia. Cf. Pusey (op. cit., p. 139): 'His (i.e. Xerxes') invasion and failure were the far distant causes of the expedition of Alexander.' But between Seleucus Philopator and an Antichrist who is to appear *in consummatione mundi* there is no conceivable causal link.

[3] *Dan. and his Proph.*, p. 279. Cf. Cowles, *Ezek. and Dan.*, pp. 444 f.

[4] So Hugo of St. Chère, *Op. omn.* v, p. 162 b.

[5] So Wintle, *Dan.: An. imp. vers. att.*, p. 187. Cowles (op. cit., p. 442) says: 'Such interpretation is simply monstrous.'

[6] See Smith's *Dict. of Bib.*, 2nd ed., I. i, p. 711 a b. Cf. Hoffmann, *Ant. IV Epiph.*, pp. 93 f.

[7] On xi. 36, ed. Migne, col. 570.

many authors, including Luther[1], Oecolampadius[2], Pintus[3], Osiander[4], Graserus[5], Huit[6], More[7], Geier[8], Birks[9], Pusey[10], Gärtner[11], Kelly[12], Kliefoth[13], Füller[14], Rohling[15], and Düsterwald[16]. Moreover, Jewish interpreters have found a break here, though they have not coincided with Christian scholars in their ideas of the length of the leap. For Rashi[17] found the succeeding verses to refer to the Roman empire, and Ibn Ezra, Ibn Yaḥya, and Abravanel found Constantine the Great in them[18]. Strangely enough, Calvin, whose wrath so often boils over at the views of Jewish scholars, agrees here with Rashi. He declares that there is no soundness in the conclusion of those who find Antichrist here, but himself leaps from Antiochus to the Roman empire[19]. Wright, however, says[20] of verses 36–40: 'It is impossible that the section can refer to any other than Antiochus Epiphanes.' No less unnatural, however, is Wright's own view, for he makes a similar leap, though at a slightly later point. For he holds that the prophecy originally existed as a pre-Maccabean document, containing a general prophecy of the Greek empire to its close, but that

[1] Cf. *Ausl. des eilften Cap. Dan.*, in *Sämtliche Schriften*, ed. Walch, vi, pp. 1457 ff. In his earlier work (*Der Proph. Dan. Deudsch*, p. e i b) he had rather implied that he made the break at the end of chap. xi, saying: 'Das zwellft Capitel, wie es alle Lerer eintrechtig auslegen gebet ganz und gar unter Antiochus namen auff den Endechrist und auf diese letzte zeit da wir ynnen leben.'   [2] *Comm. in Dan. lib. duo*, pp. 155 f.
[3] *In div. vat. Dan. comm.*, p. 200 b.   [4] *Bib. Sacr., Proph. Omn.*, p. 76 a.
[5] *Hist. Ant.*—an exposition of xi. 36–45.
[6] *Whole Proph. of Dan. exp.*, pp. 319 ff.
[7] *Exp. of Vis. of Proph. Dan.*, p. 201.
[8] *Prael. Acad. in Dan.*, p. 319.   [9] *Two Later Vis. of Dan.*, pp. 255 ff.
[10] *Op. cit.*, pp. 97 f.   [11] *Erk. des Proph. Dan. u. der Off. Joh.*, pp. 174 ff.
[12] *Notes on Bk. of Dan.*, p. 191.   [13] *Op. cit.*, pp. 461 ff.
[14] *Der Prof. Dan. erk.*, pp. 318 f.   [15] *Das B. Dan. übers. u. erk.*, p. 333.
[16] *Die Weltr. und das Gottesr.*, p. 166. This view still flourishes indeed. Cf. Gaebelein, *The Proph. Dan.*, p. 179, and Stevens, *Bk. of Dan.*, pp. 204 f.
[17] Cf. Breithaupt, *Jarchi comm. in proph. maj.*, p. 793; or Gallé, *Dan. avec comm.*, pp. 143 f.
[18] Cf. Gallé, ibid.; l'Empereur, *Paraphr. Ios. Iach. in Dan.*, p. 244; Hulsius, ריב יהוה עם יהודה, pp. 562 f.
[19] *Comm. on Bk. of Dan.*, ET ii, pp. 338 ff.
[20] *Dan. and his Proph.*, p. 298.

from xi. 40 it sprang away to the Messianic deliverance[1]. This general prophecy he holds to have been overlaid with glosses, down to xi. 39, believing that these were added in the Maccabean age, and that they gave the chapter its present links with Antiochus Epiphanes[2]. But no evidence is forthcoming that the alleged glosses are not original to the chapter, and it is no more likely that a glossator should introduce exact history to the Maccabean days and leave general hopes for the future, than that the original author should have done this in a composition of that age. That Wright so clearly finds the stamp of the days of Antiochus Epiphanes in the chapter as it now stands is valuable testimony to its present character, and is not, in itself, evidence that that character is unoriginal. It remains to notice that d'Envieu, who rejects all these treatments of the chapter[3], holds that the break occurs at xi. 45, and that chapter xii is independent of chapter xi[4].

But none of these ways, unsatisfactory as they are in themselves, can solve the real difficulties. To interpret the fourth empire of chapter vii as the Roman, and to deny that chapter xi originally, or in its present climax, refers to Antiochus Epiphanes, may seem to explain the similarities between chapters vii and xi. But the connexions between chapters xi and viii are equally striking. In chapter xi we read: 'And arms shall stand on his part, and they shall profane the sanctuary . . . . and shall take away the continual burnt offering, and they shall set up the abomination that maketh desolate'; and in chapter viii 'and it (i.e. the Little Horn) took away from him the continual burnt

---

[1] Ibid., pp. 310 ff. The view that there is a break at xi. 40 is not a new one. It is found in Poole (*Ann. upon Bib.* ii, ad loc.), and is criticized by Cowles (*Ezek. and Dan.*, p. 444). It is also criticized recently by Rigaux (*L'Anté-christ*, p. 161).

[2] Other views that find Maccabean glosses in this chap., presented by Lange, Bosanquet, Zöckler, and Küper, have been already noted.

[3] *Le livre du proph. Dan.* ii, pp. 1435 ff.

[4] Ibid., pp. 1441. So, too, Vigouroux, *Sainte Bib. Polyg.* vi, p. 363; and so, earlier, Trochon, *Daniel*, p. 249.

offering, and the place of his sanctuary was cast down', with a further reference to 'the continual burnt offering and the transgression that maketh desolate'; in chapter xi we read: 'and he shall exalt himself and magnify himself above every god, and shall speak marvellous things against the God of gods', and in chapter viii: 'and it waxed great, even to the host of heaven; and some of the host and of the stars it cast down to the ground, and trampled upon them. Yea, it magnified itself, even to the prince of the host'; in chapter xi the saints 'fall by the sword and by flame, by captivity and by spoil', while the king continues to 'do according to his will', and in chapter viii we are told that 'he shall destroy wonderfully, and shall prosper and do his pleasure; he shall destroy the mighty ones and the holy people'[1]. It is therefore the case that chapters vii and viii have close links with one another, and that chapter xi has links with both, and the attempt to cut chapter xi loose, in its present form, from the reference to the Maccabean age, though it may seem to account for the similarity with chapter vii, does not account for the equally striking similarity with chapter viii, while the view that chapter xi has been glossed in the Maccabean age can present no more than *a priori* arguments in its favour, and fails to account for that close similarity between the climax in the Messianic age and the climax in the Maccabean age, which made possible the glossing of an account of the one that should convert it into an account of the other.

[1] Boutflower (*In and Around Bk. of Dan.*, pp. 224 f.) gives a fuller table, showing the marked similarities between chaps. viii and xi. Where some holders of the Roman view of the fourth empire so emphasize the links between chaps. viii and xi, and others so emphasize the links between chaps. vii and xi, there would seem to be every justification for recognizing the links between chap. xi and both of these earlier chaps., especially when the Futurist wing of the Roman school agrees that there are strong links between chaps. vii and viii. Rigaux (*L'Antéchrist*, pp. 167 f., n.) gives a table of parallels between the four visions of Daniel and passages in the books of Maccabees, showing how closely the visions are linked together, and how they are linked also with the events of Maccabean days. For the connexions between chaps. vii, viii, ix, and xi, cf. also Desprez, *Dan., or the Apoc. of OT*, pp. 114 ff.

But so far we have ignored chapter ix. In the climax of that vision we read that 'the people of the prince that shall come shall destroy the city and the sanctuary', where the city is defined in the context as Jerusalem. We further read that for the half of a week 'he shall cause the sacrifice and the oblation to cease', while the clause that follows is of obscure significance, but contains a phrase which appears to be intimately connected with the ones rendered 'abomination that maketh desolate' in xi. 31 and xii. 11. It would carry us far from our present subject to discuss the various meanings put upon chapter ix by those who deny that this chapter also refers to the period of Antiochus Epiphanes. We should but find ourselves in what Montgomery has called[1] the 'Dismal Swamp of Old Testament criticism'. We may, however, note some links between that chapter and the other chapters we are considering. In chapter viii the Little Horn waxed great against 'the glorious land', i.e. Palestine, and in chapter xi the last and infamous king enters 'the glorious land', and here again in chapter ix the prince's people come to Jerusalem. Again we find destruction of the city and the sanctuary, closely parallel to the war on the saints in chapter vii, the destroying of the holy people and the casting down of the sanctuary in chapter viii, and the massacre of the people and profanation of the sanctuary in chapter xi. Again we have interference with the sacrifices, as in chapters viii and xi, recalling too the interference with the law in chapter vii. And again the period of the distresses is said to be half a week, or three and a half days, a period that once more recalls the time and times and half a time of chapter vii, and the time, times and a half of chapter xii. And if the day and time of these expressions is rightly equated with a year, the two thousand three hundred evenings and mornings, or three years odd, of chapter viii is also recalled.

How are all of these striking similarities to be accounted

---

[1] *Comm. on Dan.*, p. 400.

for, if the reference is not the same in all of these cases? That an author should single out from some millennia yet future in his day some crises in history, all of which could be described in terms that clearly suggest common features, would be surprising enough. But on the traditional view of the passages, he was singularly lacking in balance and proportion. If the first vision looked for the establishment of a universal and everlasting kingdom, in an age still future in our day, its climax is cut adrift from both the age and the world of the author, and concerns a vaster world than he can have conceived. Yet the second vision deals with the temporary overrunning of Palestine by Antiochus Epiphanes, and his profanation of the Temple for some three years or so. This is scarcely comparable in significance with the first vision. For a Jew of the second century B.C. it would be of enormous significance, and if he looked for this to be the prelude to the establishment of the Messianic kingdom, it would be of universal significance, and the two things would be linked in importance for him. But to one writing some centuries earlier, with a vision that spanned ages reaching into time to which we still look forward, it would be surprising to single out this incident of temporary and local significance, and set it alongside the other of vastly wider and more enduring significance. The third vision, as traditionally interpreted, finds its climax in the birth of Christ, or the Crucifixion, or the destruction of Jerusalem[1]. As to whether this primarily concerns the Jewish nation, or has a far wider significance, opinions differ according to the particular interpretation adopted, but on any of these identifications it would be a far more

---

[1] Tyso (op. cit., p. 38) gives a table of twenty-three different reckonings of the beginning and ending of the seventy weeks, in which the beginning varies from 1589 B.C. to 356 B.C., and the end from 163 B.C. to A.D. 1841. Of these twenty-three Newton and Calmet make the period to terminate at the birth of Christ (2 and 1 B.C. respectively), several (notably Julius Africanus, A.D. 30, and Prideaux, A.D. 33) at the Crucifixion, and several (notably Polanus, A.D. 68, Joseph Mede, A.D. 69, and Clemens Alexandrinus, Rashi, and Ibn Ezra, all A.D. 70) at the destruction of Jerusalem.

epoch-marking event than the profanation of the Temple by Antiochus Epiphanes. The fourth vision, again, deals with the end of the age, and the resurrection of the just and the unjust, and the abolition of death for the righteous. Here again, therefore, the climax is of universal significance Yet somehow the author has muddled it up with material which deals with Antiochus Epiphanes once more, and in such a way that it is impossible to secure any agreement as to where he leaps from one to the other, or what conceivable connexion there can be between them. Or, if Wright's view be adopted[1], he has muddled his climax with material that dealt with the Greek kingdom of Alexander, which has long since passed away, and with which it stands in no recognizably intimate connexion. How was it that the author was so unable to differentiate, on his own spacious canvas, the things of really big and enduring significance from the things of local and temporary significance? In the vast range of his perspective, things should have assumed their true historical importance.

The extremer wing of the Futurist school sees this perfectly clearly, and therefore cuts every prophecy adrift from Antiochus Epiphanes, and finds no reference to him even in chapters viii and xi. It is thus able frankly to recognize the links between all of these chapters, and to interpret them all as of comparably important issues. But the price it is forced to pay is an impossibly high one. For it has to assume those fantastic breaks in all the prophecies of which the prophecies themselves give no hint, and to postulate a fundamental irrationality in the prophecies, since their opening is held to be completely irrelevant to their conclusion.

The favourite alternative of the other schools, from the days of Jerome[2], has been to maintain that Antiochus

---

[1] Ignoring, therefore, the material which Wright supposes to have been later imported into the chapter.

[2] Cf. Jerome on xi. 21 (ed. Migne, cols. 565 f.): *cumque multa quae postea lecturi et exposituri sumus, super Antiochi persona conveniant, typum eum volunt*

Epiphanes deserves a place in these visions that stretch to the end of the age, since he was a type of Antichrist. But the rich variety of persons who have been successively identified as Antichrist himself would suggest that many even more suitable types might have been chosen by one whose vision was so far ranging. What led him to select Antiochus? And what led him to conceal the fact that Antiochus was but a type? And what led him to pass from his type to the Antichrist he typified in such a subtle way that no ordinary reader of chapter xi would suspect such a transition, and no agreement as to where the transition took place is possible even amongst those who maintain there was one?[1]

Far more reasonable, therefore, does it seem to hold that the similarities in the climaxes of these chapters are due to their identity, and to believe that the clear references to Antiochus Epiphanes in some of the visions locate that climax. On this view the author had an exaggerated sense of the significance of contemporary events, just as so many of his interpreters, who have believed the climax of the prophecies was about to be reached in their own day, have had an exaggerated sense of the significance of the events of their times. Recognizing the seriousness of the attack on his faith that Antiochus was making, and rightly inspiring his contemporaries to battle for their faith, he mistakenly thought the victory would be final and would inaugurate the kingdom that has no end.

Antichristi habere: et quae in illo ex parte praecesserint, in Antichristo ex toto esse complenda . . . Antichristus pessimum regem Antiochum, qui sanctos persecutus est, templumque violavit, recte typum sui habuisse credendus est. Cf. also Nicolaus de Lyra, *Bib. Sacr.* iv, p. 324 a, and many others.

[1] Cf. Driver (LOT, 9th ed., p. 497): 'Whatever typical significance may attach to the *whole* character of Antiochus, it can hardly be legitimate, in a *continuous* description, with no apparent change of subject, to refer part to the type and part to the antitype.' Cf., too, Wright (*Dan. and his Proph.*, p. 280): 'Nor is the theory of a double interpretation of prophecy satisfactory. It is incongruous to regard a prophecy first as predicting in detail events which were to occur prior to the beginning of Messianic days, and then as predicting a second set of events to take place at the end of the world. Such a theory may have been excusable in the loose interpretations of bygone days; it is indefensible in the present age of critical interpretation.'

III. THE SECOND AND THIRD KINGDOMS ARE THE MEDIAN AND THE PERSIAN RESPECTIVELY

THE traditional identification of the second and third empires, that has accompanied the Roman view of the fourth, has been with the Medo-Persian and the Greek empires respectively[1]. But with the establishment of the fourth empire as the Greek, that view of the middle two empires falls to the ground. Amongst the holders of the Greek view of the fourth empire, however, there has been some difference of opinion as to the identification of these two[2].

[1] The curious view of Auchincloss (*Bk. of Dan. Unlocked*, pp. 53 ff.) may here be recorded. For chap. ii he adopts the traditional view, but for chap. vii he holds the kingdoms to be (1) Medo-Persian, (2) Greek, from the Battle of Marathon to Philip of Macedon, (3) Macedonian, (4) Roman. The artificial date for the termination of the Medo-Persian empire would alone invalidate the scheme, and equally so the introduction of the Greek, as distinct from, and prior to, Alexander. For that was in a different geographical world, and did not touch the things in which our author's interest lay. In chap. viii Auchincloss finds the he-goat with the Great Horn to be the Greek power that prevailed at Marathon, Salamis, and Plataea, and that continued its conquests in Alexander. It will be argued below that the combining of the Median and Persian empires in a single animal in chap. viii does not involve their combination in chap. vii, since even in chap. viii they are clearly differentiated within the one beast. But on the view of Auchincloss, chap. viii presents as entirely identical two of the kingdoms which he wishes to separate in chap. vii. It is gratuitous to attribute to the author two essentially different views of history.

[2] Wilson (*Princeton Theol. Rev.* xxii, 1924, p. 377) says: 'The assumption that Alexander and his successors, especially the kingdom of the Seleucids, represent the fourth kingdom of Daniel, depends on the further assumption that the second kingdom was Median.' That it depends on no such assumption is clearly demonstrated in the foregoing pages, where no assumptions as to the second empire have been made. It is also clearly demonstrated by the fact, of which Wilson would seem to have been unaware, that a long line of scholars, as will be shown in the following sections, have found the fourth kingdom to be the Seleucid, though they have *not* held the second empire to be Median. Wilson therefore commits a complete *ignoratio elenchi* when he heads the section of his article *The Fourth Kingdom*, and confines his discussion entirely to the attempt to prove that the *second* kingdom is not the Median.

(a) *The identification with the Medo-Persian empire and the rule of Alexander is improbable*

This view agrees with the traditional view in the identification of the second empire, but by separating the kingdom of Alexander from that of his successors secures the necessary number[1]. It has enjoyed much greater popularity than is sometimes supposed[2], and the majority of its adherents have held firmly to the view that the book of Daniel is the composition of one who lived at the Babylonian court in the sixth century B.C. The oldest advocate of this view of whom we have any knowledge is Porphyry[3]. It next appears in the work of Polychronius[4], after which it seems to have been forgotten until Grotius[5] revived it. Then it had considerable vogue, being adopted by Junius[6], Broughton[7], Rollock[8], Polanus[9], Willet[10], Piscator[11], l'Empereur[12], the Westminster Assembly's annotators[13], Lightfoot[14], Becmann[15], Calmet[16], Amner[17], J. Jahn[18],

[1] Conring (*Disc. ad Lamp. post.*, p. 365), in his interpretation of chap. vii, also separated the kingdom of Alexander from that of his successors, though in other respects he differed from the view now under examination. He identified the four kingdoms of that vision with the Median, the Persian, Alexander's, and that of his successors.

[2] Keil, e.g., states (op. cit., ET, p. 245 n.) that this view found no favour until the end of the eighteenth century. He refers to it as the view of Polychronius and Grotius, and adds that it 'has found only one weak advocate in J. C. Becmann'. How thoroughly inaccurate this statement is will appear from the list of advocates of this view given below.

[3] *Apud* Jerome, on vii. 7 (ed. Migne, col. 530).

[4] In Mai, *Script. vet. nov. coll.* i, 1825 et 1831, p. 4. Polychronius so interprets chap. ii, but in chap. vii he finds the second beast to represent the Median kingdom of Darius, the third the Persian kingdom of Cyrus, and the fourth the Greek kingdom of Alexander. Cf. ibid., p. 11.

[5] *Op. omn. theol.* i, pp. 456, 466.

[6] *Op. omn. theol.* i, cols. 1181 ff., 1240 ff.

[7] *Works*, pp. 180, 188.   [8] *In lib. Dan. proph.*, pp. 46 ff., 240 ff.

[9] *In Dan. proph. comm.* i, pp. 102 ff., ii, pp. 12 ff., or in Poole, *Synopsis*, iii, cols. 1419 f., 1473.   [10] *Hex. in Dan.*, pp. 208, 211.

[11] *In Dan. comm.*, p. 17.   [12] *Paraph. Ios. Iach. in Dan.*, note on pp. 52 f.

[13] *Assembly's Ann.*, 2nd ed., on ii. 39 f., vii. 5 ff.

[14] *Works*, i, p. 134.   [15] *Diss. de quarta mon.*, *passim*.

[16] *Comm. litt. sur Dan.*, pp. 582 f., 650 f.

[17] *Essay towards Int. of Dan.*, pp. 141 ff., 219 ff.

[18] *Einl. in die göttl. Bücher des AB*, II. ii, pp. 614 ff. (ET, p. 408). Jahn

Bertholdt[1], Rosenmüller[2], Herzfeld[3], Stuart[4], Desprez[5], Merx[6], Cowles[7] and Zöckler[8], while in recent years it has been adopted or championed by Turmel[9], Lagrange[10], and Buzy[11].

Its division of the kingdom of Alexander from that of his successors has been criticized by several writers[12], and it has been pointed out[13] that in viii. 21 it is said that the he-goat represents the king (= kingdom) of Greece, where this single description clearly includes the Great Horn (i.e. Alexander) and the four horns (i.e. the principal divisions of his kingdom). To this it may be replied that the details of one vision do not bind the interpretation of another, and that just as some hold that two of the kingdoms of chapters ii and vii are combined in the two-horned ram of chapter viii, so it is equally legitimate to find in the he-goat two of these kingdoms. But the two cases are not quite on all fours. For when viii. 21 tells us that the Great Horn was the first king of the kingdom represented by the he-goat, it is implied that the succeeding

holds this view for chap. vii only. For chap. ii he holds them to be the Median and the Persian kingdoms.

[1] *Dan. neu übers. u. erk.*, pp. 216 ff., 425 f.

[2] *Schol. in VT*, Part x, pp. 108 f., 220, 224, 237.

[3] *Gesch. des Volkes Isr.* i, p. 423.   [4] *Comm. on Dan.*, pp. 176 ff.

[5] The second and third kingdoms of chap. vii Desprez quite definitely identified with the Medo-Persian kingdom and the Greek kingdom of Alexander and his four potent successors (*Dan., or the Apoc. of OT*, pp. 93 ff.), but he is uncertain whether the second and third kingdoms of chap. ii are the Median and the Persian kingdoms, or the Medo-Persian kingdom and that of Alexander (ibid., pp. 89 f.).

[6] Merx identified the second and third kingdoms of chap. vii with the Persian kingdom and that of Alexander (*Cur in lib. Dan.*, p. 21), but in chap. ii found the kingdoms represented by the breast and belly to be the Median kingdom of Darius and the Persian kingdom of Cyrus (ibid., pp. 19 f.).

[7] *Ezek. and Dan.*, pp. 307 ff.   [8] *Bk. of Dan.*, ET, pp. 85 f.

[9] *Annales de Phil. Chrét.*, 3rd Series, i, 1902–3, p. 14.

[10] RB, New Series, i, 1904, p. 503.

[11] RB, New Series, xv, 1918, pp. 413 ff., and *Les Symb. de l'AT*, pp. 267, 282.

[12] Cf. Parker, *Vis. and Proph. of Dan.*, pp. 1 ff., 8 ff.; Hengstenberg, op. cit., ET, pp. 164 ff.; Hitzig, *Das B. Dan. erk.*, pp. 36 f., 121; Pusey, op. cit. pp. 139 ff.; Kliefoth, op. cit., p. 102; Stokmann, op. cit., p. 49 n.

[13] Hitzig, op. cit., p. 36.

horns belonged to the same kingdom. Moreover, a racial distinction can be found between the Medes and the Persians, whereas there was no racial difference between Alexander's empire and that of his successors, yet it is clearly implied in the visions of the book of Daniel that the successive kingdoms were racially distinct from one another[1].

Again, it has been noted[2] that on this view it would be very hard to explain why we should be told that the fourth kingdom was diverse from all its predecessors. For the succession states were ideally a single empire, which continued the empire of Alexander. Further, these states did not come into being by the conquest or overthrow of Alexander's empire, as the latter did by the overthrow of the Persian, or the Persian by the overthrow of its predecessors, but as a development out of it.

The four heads of the third beast provide another difficulty for this interpretation. Willet tried to meet the case by holding[3] that the four heads are the captains of Alexander who governed the kingdom as regents, but who afterwards constituted the fourth kingdom. This fourth kingdom thus had its beginning under the third, but its succession and continuance make the fourth. This only serves to expose the embarrassment of the case for this view, for it acknowledges the intimate connexion between its third and its fourth kingdoms, and the essential impossibility of any real severance between them. Bertholdt, however, held[4] that the four heads merely indicate that Alexander's rule would reach out in all directions. There is nothing peculiar to Alexander's empire in this symbolism, though it will be agreed below that it is possible that no fuller significance is to be attached to the heads.

Finally, if the third kingdom is that of Alexander and the fourth that of his successors, it is impossible to see how the

---

[1] Cf. Hengstenberg, op. cit., p. 166. [2] Cf. Hitzig., op. cit., pp. 36 f.
[3] *Hex. in Dan.*, pp. 208, 211. [4] Op. cit., p. 427.

author could contemplate the prolonging of the life of the
third, though without its dominion, after the destruction
of the fourth.

(b) *The identification with the reign of Belshazzar and the Medo-Persian empire is improbable*

This is a view which has commanded little support. In
the nineteenth century it was held by Hitzig[1], who, however, limited it to the vision in chapter ii, holding that in
chapter vii the four kingdoms were to be identified with the
reign of Belshazzar, the Median empire, the Persian empire,
and the Greek empire[2]. Hitzig found a solitary follower in
Redepenning[3], but the view seemed unlikely to attract any
further adherents. Within the present century, however,
it has been revived by Van Hoonacker[4], who carries it also
into chapter vii, and who has been more recently followed
by Goettsberger[5]. Once more, however, we find that the
view is older than is commonly supposed, for it already
appears nearly two centuries before the time of Hitzig in
the work of Conring[6]. The latter, like Hitzig, confined this
interpretation to chapter ii, where he held the four parts
of the image to represent Nebuchadnezzar, the successors
of Nebuchadnezzar, the Persian empire, and the Greek
empire. In chapter vii he identified the four empires with
the Median, the Persian, Alexander's, and that of Alexander's successors. The agreement between Hitzig and
Conring extends only to chapter ii, therefore, and even here
Hitzig does not follow Conring in all details. For the latter
believed the stone cut without hands to be the Roman
empire.

In the form in which Conring and Hitzig presented the
view there was little to be said for it. For it is wholly

---

[1] *Heidelb. Jahrb. der Lit.* xxv, 1832, pp. 131 f., and *Das B. Dan. erk.*, p. 37.
[2] Ibid., p. 99.   [3] TSK vi, 1833, p. 863.
[4] ET xiii, 1901–2, pp. 420 ff., and *Le Muséon*, xliv, 1931, pp. 169 ff.
[5] *Das B. Dan. übers. u. erk.*, pp. 25, 54.
[6] *Disc. ad Lamp. post.*, pp. 363 ff.

improbable that the four kingdoms of chapter ii are different from those of chapter vii, and especially unlikely that two of the kingdoms are the same in both visions, but separated in the one vision by one world-monarchy only, and in the other by two, or that in the one vision the Medo-Persian and the Greek should each be conceived as a single kingdom and in the other vision they should each be regarded as two separate kingdoms. For these interpretations involve discrepant views of the course of history, that could only be found here after it was first proved that the chapters issued from different hands. It has been above urged that the details of one vision do not bind the interpretation of the details of others, but interpretations which find the same philosophy of history in the different visions are to that extent more probable than those which do not. From this weakness the theory is delivered in the hands of Van Hoonacker and Goettsberger. But even here it can claim only the most superficial case.

All adherents of this view lay great stress on the pronoun 'thou' in ii. 37 f: 'Thou, O king, art king of kings . . . thou art the head of gold.' They therefore identify the first kingdom with the personal rule of Nebuchadnezzar. Some bridge is then needed to get from this to the kingdom of the Medes and Persians, which is held to be the third kingdom, and the book of Daniel offers the obvious means of supplying the need in the person of Belshazzar. Van Hoonacker reinforces this by pointing out that in chapter vii the second beast is addressed in the words: 'Arise, devour much flesh.' He holds this to be a reference to the feast of Belshazzar, recorded in chapter v. In chapter ii, moreover, all that is said about the second kingdom is that it is inferior to the first, and it is claimed that this well suits the comparison between the reign of Nebuchadnezzar and that of Belshazzar.

But these arguments are altogether insufficient to commend the theory, and offer no defence against the obvious criticisms. For the book of Daniel presents Belshazzar as the son and successor of Nebuchadnezzar, as Junker has pointed out in criticism of this view[1], and the author clearly did not conceive of Belshazzar as ruling over a different kingdom. Certainly he did not think of any racial distinction between the empire of Nebuchadnezzar and that of Belshazzar, such as distinguished the other kingdoms of these visions. Further, the introduction of vii. 5 does not seem particularly apt. For in chapter v Belshazzar is not pilloried for his gluttony, but for his profanity in using the sacred vessels. Fatal, too, to this view is the consideration we have found to be fatal to others. For it can offer no intelligible interpretation of vii. 12. It is inconceivable that the kingdom of Nebuchadnezzar and that of Belshazzar should be represented as surviving the destruction of the fourth empire, alongside one another, as two distinct yet contemporaneous kingdoms. For territorially the seat of authority in the two empires was the same.

(c) *The identification with the Median and the Persian empires is in every way probable*

The upholders of the traditional view of the authorship of the book of Daniel are fond of associating modern critical views with the name of 'wicked Porphyry', and enlisting the aid of prejudice for their discredit. The identification of the second and third empires with those of the Medes and the Persians does not appear in Porphyry, however, whose views at this point coincide, as has been noted above, with those of many ardent upholders of the traditional view of the origin of the book. Instead, this identification is found in the Peshitta version of the book of Daniel[2], in Ephraem

---

[1] *Unters. über lit. u. exeg. Prob. des B. Dan.*, p. 8.

[2] This version prefixes to vii. 5 'the kingdom of the Medes', and to vii. 6 'the kingdom of the Persians'. These glosses are omitted in Lee's ed., but stand in the Paris and London Polyglotts. They are found in the Ambrosian MS. (see Ceriani's ed.).

Syrus[1] and in Cosmas Indicopleustes[2]. It also stands in an anonymous commentator whose work is published in Mai's *Scriptorum Veterum Nova Collectio*[3]. For many centuries it lay forgotten, and save that it stands in the work of Barhebraeus[4], it was not until the eighteenth century that it was revived. It has been seen above that in the meantime the Greek view of the fourth empire had flourished, but it had been coupled with the view of the second and third empires that has been examined under (a) above. In the eighteenth century, however, the view now under examination was revived by Venema[5], and in the nineteenth century it grew steadily in favour, until it has become by far the most widely held form of the Greek view. It has counted among its adherents Eichhorn[6], de Wette[7], Dereser[8], von Lengerke[9], Maurer[10], Bade[11], Hilgenfeld[12], Bleek[13], Westcott[14] Davidson[15], Kamphausen[16], Kranichfeld[17], Graf[18], Delitzsch[19], Kuenen[20], Reuss[21] and Vatke[22], amongst older scholars, and

---

[1] *Op. omn.*, Syriac and Latin, ii, pp. 205, 214.

[2] *Top. Christ.* ii (145), ed. Migne, col. 109, ET, p. 68.

[3] i, 1825 et 1831, pp. 34 f., 47 (1825 ed., pp. 176, 203). In the former passage he identifies the second kingdom of chap. ii with that of the Medes, and in the latter passage he identifies the fourth kingdom of chap. vii with the Greek kingdom of Alexander and his successors. It remains to be inferred that the third kingdom is that of the Persians.

[4] See *Schol. zum B. Dan.*, ed. Freimann, pp. 5, 8.

[5] *Diss. ad Vat. Dan. emb.*, pp. 47 ff., 110 ff.

[6] *Einl. in das AT*, 4th ed., iv, pp. 483 ff., and *Die heb. Proph.* iii, pp. 430, 438 ff.

[7] *Lehrb. der hist.-krit. Einl. in die Bib.* i, 1817, p. 277 (6th ed., pp. 381 f.; ET ii, p. 487 n.).

[8] *Die Proph. Ezech. u. Dan.*, 2nd ed., by Scholz, pp. 317, 352 ff.

[9] *Das B. Dan. verd. u. ausg.*, pp. 89 ff.

[10] *Comm. gram. crit. in VT*, ii, pp. 92 f.

[11] *Christ. des AT*, iii, Part 2, p. 79.   [12] *Die jüd. Apok.*, p. 26.

[13] *Jahrb. für deutsche Theol.* v, 1860, pp. 65 f.

[14] In Smith's *Dict. of Bib.*, 1st ed., i, p. 395 a (2nd ed., I. i, p. 711 b).

[15] *Intro. to OT*, iii, p. 207.

[16] *Dan.* (in Bunsen's *Bibelwerk*), pp. 644, 660 f.; *Das B. Dan. u. die neu. Geschichtsf.*, p. 11; EB i, col. 1006.   [17] *Das B. Dan. erk.*, pp. 120 ff.

[18] In Schenkel's *Bibel-lex.* i, p. 567.   [19] In PRE, 2nd ed., iii, p. 475.

[20] *Prophets and Prophecy*, ET, pp. 141 ff.

[21] *Litt. pol. et pol.*, pp. 219, 254, and *Die Gesch. der HSAT*, p. 601.

[22] *Hist.-krit. Einl. in das AT*, ed. Preiss, p. 653.

Schürer[1], Meinhold[2], Bevan[3], Behrmann[4], von Gall[5], Curtis[6], Buhl[7], Prince[8], Driver[9], Marti[10], Bertholet[11], Steuernagel[12], Andrews[13], Haller[14], Baumgartner[15], Montgomery[16], Charles[17], Willet[18], Obbink[19], and Eissfeldt[20], amongst more recent scholars.

In its favour are the considerations that the book of Daniel represents a Median king as having held rule after the overthrow of the kingdom of Belshazzar and before the reign of Cyrus, and that it repeatedly emphasizes a racial distinction between Darius the Mede and Cyrus the Persian. Here, then, in the Babylonian, Median, Persian, and Greek kingdoms are four distinct kingdoms, all of which figure in the book of Daniel, and which are racially and historically separate. To these four kingdoms there are specific references in the book, so that on the basis of the contents of the book itself, if it is the production of a single writer, we can affirm that in the author's view of history there were four successive kingdoms, counting from the Babylonian to the Greek. To the Roman kingdom, however, there is no open and specific reference, and it has only been found in the book by conjectural and disputed interpretation. Where four successive, racially different, kingdoms are explicitly referred to in the book, the natural interpretation of the four kingdoms of these visions is that these are they.

---

[1] GJV, 4th ed., iii, p. 265; ET by Taylor and Christie, HJP ii. iii, p. 52.
[2] *Das B. Dan. ausg.*, p. 274. Meinhold holds this view of chap. ii only. Cf. his view of chap. vii, ibid., p. 306.   [3] *Short Comm. on Dan.*, pp. 66 f., 115.
[4] *Das B. Dan. übers. u. erk.*, pp. 16, 45.
[5] *Die Einheitl. des B. Dan.*, pp. 94 f., 105 ff.
[6] In DB i, p. 555.   [7] In PRE, 3rd ed., iv, p. 452.
[8] *Crit. Comm. on Dan.*, pp. 70 f.   [9] *Bk. of Dan.*, pp. 99 f.
[10] *Das B. Dan. erk.*, pp. 15 f., 48, and HSAT, 4th ed., ii, pp. 463, 476.
[11] *Dan. u. die griech. Gef.*, p. 21, and RGG, 1st ed., i, col. 1962.
[12] *Lehrb. der Einl. in das AT*, p. 654.
[13] In *Peake's Comm.*, pp. 526, 528.   [14] *Das Judentum*, 2nd ed., p. 298.
[15] *Das B. Dan.*, pp. 16 ff., and RGG, 2nd ed., i, col. 1780.
[16] *Comm. on Dan.*, p. 61.   [17] *Crit. Comm. on Dan.*, pp. 167 ff.
[18] In *Abingdon Comm.*, pp. 750, 754.   [19] *Daniël*, p. 76.
[20] *Einl. in das AT*, p. 575.

Further, it has been already noted that these four empires all held sway in the geographical region to which the author of Daniel is limited in his outlook and interest, but that the Greek empire, alone of them, had no racial home and fount within that region. Hence its life could not be thought of as surviving its imperial collapse, whereas the life of the other three could be thought of as so surviving.

The repeated criticisms that have been launched against this view by the adherents of the Roman view of the fourth kingdom appear to be mainly beside the point. Thus, it is argued[1] that it is an historical error to suppose that a Median kingdom intervened between the fall of Babylon and the reign of Cyrus, and that we have no right to father on to the author of the book of Daniel so grave an error in the interests of our theory. That it is an historical error is undoubtedly true, and the foregoing pages have amply established this, but the point at issue is whether this historical error belonged to the thought of our author, and his completely unhistorical account of Darius the Mede sufficiently proves his ignorance of the facts. It is he who states that Darius the Mede succeeded Belshazzar, and who elsewhere speaks of 'Darius the son of Ahasuerus, of the seed of the Medes, which was made king over the realm of the Chaldaeans'. It is he who says that Daniel prospered 'in the reign of Darius, and in the reign of Cyrus the Persian'. It is he who represents one as coming to Daniel in a vision which he saw in the third year of Cyrus, king of Persia, and speaking to him retrospectively of the first year of Darius the Mede. It is therefore he who distinguishes between the race of Darius and that of Cyrus, and who sets a Median control of Babylon between Belshazzar and the Persian rule, and the principle that the visions are to be interpreted by the view of the course of history which the

---

[1] Cf. Auberlen, *Proph. of Dan. and Rev. of St. John*, ET, p. 187; Pusey, op. cit., p. 123; Keil, op. cit., ET, p. 249.

author reveals elsewhere in his book leads unmistakably to the identification of the second empire with the Median.

To this it is replied[1] that the author of Daniel does not distinguish between the Medes and the Persians. He refers to the laws of the Medes and Persians as binding on Darius; he tells how Daniel interpreted to Belshazzar the writing on the wall as meaning that the Babylonian kingdom should be taken, not by the Medes, but by the Medes and Persians. Further, in chapter viii he represents the Medo-Persian kingdom under the figure of a single animal. What clearer evidence, it is asked, could he give that he knew that the Babylonian empire fell to a combined Medo-Persian power, and that Cyrus was the real conqueror and Darius the Mede a subordinate ruler in the Medo-Persian empire? Against this, however, it is to be noted that in v. 28 it is said that the Babylonian kingdom shall be *divided*, and given to the Medes and Persians. Clearly, therefore, the author supposed that just as on the fall of Nineveh the Assyrian dominions were divided between the Medes and the Chaldaeans, so the Babylonian empire was now divided, and part of it fell to the Medes and part to the Persians, as two separate but allied powers. He was aware of some connexion between them, and so could speak of them as under a common legal code. But that does not entail the supposition that he was unable to distinguish between them. Nor does chapter viii, to which appeal is so often made. For while the ram does certainly stand for the Medo-Persian empire, a distinction is made within its history of two headships, which are by general consent identified with a Median and a Persian, and of these it is said that the one preceded the other, but was in some unspecified respect not the equal of the other. The lesser horn, whether inferior in power or in persistence, is clearly the Median.

[1] Cf. Hengstenberg, op. cit., ET, pp. 162 f.; Pusey, op. cit., pp. 131 ff.; Keil, op. cit., ET, pp. 249 ff.; Jahn, *Das B. Dan. nach der LXX herg.*, p. 67; Wright, *Dan. and his Proph.*, p. 153; Boutflower, op. cit., p. 15; Hertlein, op. cit., pp. 15 f.

Manifestly, then, our author did distinguish between the Medes and Persians[1], though he also recognized that there was a closer connexion between them than between the Babylonians and either, or the Greeks and either. He treats them as allied powers under a Median hegemony at the time of the fall of Babylon, changing over before long to a Persian hegemony, which lasted until the conflict with Alexander. And because he recognized a racial distinction between them, he could represent in the visions of chapters ii and vii a succession of four different races which had exercised world dominion within the world of his purview.

Wright has remarked[2], somewhat contemptuously: 'Porphyry did not, however, dream of the modern invention of a Median empire.' It is difficult to see what he can have meant by so loose a sentence. The view that the Median empire is the second of the four empires of these visions is no modern invention. A view which is found in manuscripts of the Peshitta version of Daniel, and in the writings of Ephraem Syrus and Cosmas Indicopleustes can scarcely be called a modern invention[3]. Nor did any of these invent the Median empire. That belongs to well-authenticated history. For there was a Median empire of no little power, which allied itself with the Babylonian state when the latter was struggling for independence under Nabopolassar, and which attacked and conquered Nineveh and Assyria, a Median empire to which Persia belonged before Cyrus revolted against Astyages and converted it into a Persian empire. A Median empire is in no sense an invention, and

---

[1] Cf. Reuss (*Litt. pol. et pol.*, p. 219): 'Notre auteur distingue partout les Mèdes et les Perses', and von Gall (*Die Einheitl. des B. Dan.*, p. 106): 'Im ganzen Danielbuch wird das persische Reich scharf von dem medischen unterschieden.'   [2] *Dan. and his Proph.*, p. 154.

[3] It may also be noted that Conring (*Disc. ad Lamp. post.*, p. 365) found the Median empire as distinct from the Persian in the vision of chap. vii. But as he held the Median to be the first there, his view involved no conflict with history. In chap. ii he held (ibid.) the parts of the image to stand for Nebuchadnezzar, his successors, the Persian empire, and the Greek. He found no place for the Median empire in that vision therefore.

the error which our author displays is not in supposing there was a Median empire before there was a Persian, but in supposing it stood between the Babylonian and the Persian, instead of being contemporary with the Babylonian, and ending somewhat before it.

It is often pointed out by adherents of the view which is here taken that an author with few trustworthy historical sources open to him, but with the Old Testament in his hand, might easily have been led to suppose that Babylon fell to the Medes by reading Jeremiah's prophecies that the Medes should take the city[1]. In that prophet's day the Persians had not yet loomed on the horizon as an independent power, whereas the conquerors of Nineveh could not fail to be known and dreaded, and it was natural to expect that any peril to Babylon would be from them. But a later author, with Jeremiah's prophecies before him, and with scanty knowledge of the period to check him, might easily suppose that the prophecies had been fulfilled. To this it is replied[2] that since his Old Testament included also the prophecies of deutero-Isaiah, with their clear references to Cyrus as the divinely anointed, and the prospective conqueror of Babylon, the alleged later author of Daniel ought to have been able to correct Jeremiah's predictions. Why should he have followed Jeremiah's alleged incorrect predictions, rather than the accurate predictions of deutero-Isaiah? But again the answer is clear, and it has been sufficiently elucidated above. He did not set these prophecies over against one another as mutually exclusive, and choose between them. He believed they were both fulfilled. And therefore he represents the Babylonian empire as going down before both Medes and Persians, and being divided between them.

Once again, therefore, we find that the author of the book of Daniel is working with confused memories of various

[1] Jer. li. 11, 28. Cf. also Isa. xiii. 17, xxi. 2.
[2] Cf. Pusey, op. cit., p. 124.

traditions, complicated here, doubtless, by these differing Scriptures. He knew there had been a Median empire before there was a Persian, knew that it had swept the Assyrian before it, and knew that it had been expected to sweep the Babylonian before it also. Yet he knew that Cyrus had established Persian supremacy over the Median empire, and knew that Cyrus had had some hand in the fall of Babylon. How better could he reconstruct history for his popular story from these scanty materials than by representing the establishment of Persian supremacy over the Medes as taking place a little later than the fall of Babylon, instead of a little earlier, with a brief period of Median control over Babylon preceding it? Into such a conception all the material the book of Daniel provides will fit harmoniously, and we are therefore confirmed in believing it belonged to the author.

It is claimed, however, that this view provides a less apt interpretation of the symbolism of vii. 5 f. than its rival can offer. On the Medo-Persian view of the second empire, the voracious bear with three ribs[1] in its mouth could be given some interpretation, while on the Median view, scholars are in a confessed difficulty to suggest anything suitable. So, too, on the Greek view of the third beast, its four heads could be given an interpretation in the closest harmony with the other visions. A slight examination shows, however, that as little weight can be given to these considerations as to the previous ones.

The symbolism of vii. 5 is extremely obscure. By holders of the Medo-Persian view the three ribs are generally held to be three countries conquered by the Medo-Persians, or the three nations that comprised the strength of the kingdom. Pusey says[2] 'the three ribs in its mouth *correspond accurately* to the three kingdoms which the Medo-Persian

---

[1] Many of the older commentators understood the reference to be to three rows of teeth, instead of three ribs. This idea goes back to the Vulgate rendering *tres ordines erant in ore ejus.*   [2] Op. cit., p. 72.

empire swallowed up'. It is strange, if the correspondence is accurate, that there is no agreement amongst holders of the Medo-Persian view of this empire as to which kingdoms they were. Some have held them to represent Media, Persia, and Babylonia[1], or Media, Lydia, and Babylonia[2], while Theodoret thought of Asia, Egypt, and Scythia[3], and Hippolytus of Media, Assyria, and Babylonia[4]. Others have held them to be Lydia, Babylonia, and Egypt[5], while Boutflower suggests Ararat, Minni, and Ashkenaz[6]. Wright contests this whole viewpoint, and says the ribs must be of one and the same animal[7]. By others the three ribs have

---

[1] So Jerome (on vii. 5, ed. Migne, col. 529), Petrus Comestor (*Hist. lib. Dan.*, ed. Migne, col. 1454), Nicolaus de Lyra (*Bib. Sacr.* iv, p. 309 b), Bullinger (*Dan. exp. hom. LXVI*, p. 75 b), Pintus (*In div. vat. Dan. comm.*, p. 138 a), Grotius (*Op. omn. theol.*, 1732 ed., i, p. 466), Cornelius a Lapide (*Comm. in quat. Proph. Maj.*, 1727 ed., p. 1324), Michaelis (*Adn. phil.-exeg. in Hag.* iii, p. 206), Calmet (*Comm. litt. sur Dan.*, p. 641), Rosenmüller (*Schol. in VT*, Part x, p. 222), and also Abravanel (see Hulsius רִיב יְהוָה עִם יְהוּדָה p. 530). Some who have identified the second empire with the Median, and not the Medo-Persian, have taken the same view. So Ephraem Syrus (*Op. omn.*, Syr. and Lat. ii, p. 214), Barhebraeus (*Schol. zum B. Dan.*, ed. Freimann, p. 9) and de Wette (*Lehrb. der Einl. in die Bib.* i, 1817, p. 277 n.). De Wette, however, later held the three ribs to be but 'emblems of frailty'— 'Bilder der Gefrässigkeit' (see *Lehrbuch*, 6th ed., p. 382, and ET ii, p. 487 n.).

[2] So Bertholdt (op. cit., p. 427), Hävernick (*Comm. über das B. Dan.*, p. 566) and Merx (*Cur in lib. Dan.*, p. 21). Cf. Fuller (*Speaker's Comm.* vi, p. 325), who holds that either the three is a round number, or the three ribs are Lydia, Bactria, and Babylonia. Chrysostom (*Op. omn.*, ed. Montfaucon, vi, 1724, p. 238), while holding them to be three places or kingdoms belonging to the Medo-Persian empire, does not specify which he believes them to be.

[3] The conquests of Cyrus, Cambyses, and Darius Hystaspis respectively. See his *Comm. in vis. Dan.*, on vii. 5 (ed. Schulze in Migne, PG lxxxi, col. 1416). And cf. Hertlein, op. cit., p. 34, where the identification is with Lydia, Egypt, and the Cimmerian north.

[4] Cf. Bonwetsch, *Hippolyt's Komm. zum B. Dan.*, p. 191, or ed. Migne, col. 681; ET in *Ante-Nic. Christ. Lib.* vi, p. 471.

[5] So Jahn (*Einl. in die göttl. Bücher des AB*, II. ii, p. 614, ET, p. 408), Hofmann (*Weiss. u. Erf.* i, p. 285), Caspari (*Zeitschr. f. d. ges. luth. Theol. u. Kirche*, ii, 1841, Heft 4, p. 148), Ebrard (*Die Off. Joh. erk.*, p. 47), Reichel (TSK xli, 1848, p. 950), Pusey (op. cit., p. 72), Keil (op. cit., ET, p. 226), Stokmann (op. cit., 104).

[6] Op. cit., pp. 18, 22 f. It may here be added that Van Hoonacker, who identifies the second kingdom with the reign of Belshazzar, suggests that the three provinces of his kingdom, viz., Sumer, Akkad, and Assyria, are intended (see *Le Muséon*, xliv, 1931, p. 175).

[7] *Dan. and his Proph.*, p. 151.

been held to be three Persian kings[1], or the three successors of Cyrus[2], while Kliefoth believed they symbolized the fact that the Persian empire would not attain universality, but would only spread in three directions, comparing viii. 4[3], an idea which is found in several older writers[4]. Hence Wright justly acknowledges that it is useless for Pusey to speak of the accurate correspondence of the symbolism, when there is no agreement, even amongst 'orthodox' commentators, as to what it corresponds with[5].

On the Median view of this kingdom no more agreement is possible, but here no support is claimed from this verse. It is only claimed that where the meaning is so obscure, the verse cannot rightly be used to embarrass or to support either view. Many attempts have been made, indeed, to attach some meaning to it, but they cannot be pronounced very successful. Hitzig[6], following Ibn Ezra[7], thought of three Assyrian cities conquered by the Medes, while Ewald[8] thought of Babylonia, Assyria, and Syria. Some have looked in the book of Daniel for the clue, and have found it in the

[1] So Rashi, who held that they were Cyrus, Ahasuerus, and Darius. See *Comm. heb. in Proph. maj.*, ed. Breithaupt, p. 761, or Gallé, *Dan. avec comm.*, p. 73. A similar view is found in Luther, who says they are 'die furnemesten Könige Cores, Darios und Xerxes welche das meiste yn diesem Königreich gethan' (*Der Proph. Dan. Deudsch*, p. c i a; cf. *Kurtze Erc.*, p. b i b). Cf., too, Osiander, *Bib. Sac., Proph. Omn.*, p. 73 b, and Gärtner, *Erk. des Proph. Dan. u. der Off. Joh.*, p. 103.

[2] This view is recorded *apud* Jerome, on vii. 5 (ed. Migne, col. 529), where, however, its propounder's name is not preserved. It is also found in pseudo-Saadia (cf. Gallé, op. cit., p. 72). [3] Op. cit., p. 195.

[4] Cf. Aphraates, Homily v. 14, ed. Wright, p. 93, German tr. by Bert, p. 81, ed. Parisot, PS I i, col. 217, ET by Gwynn, p. 358—the reference being v. 17 in Parisot and Gwynn; Jephet Ibn 'Ali, *Comm. on Bk. of Dan.*, ed. Margoliouth, p. 34; Piscator, *In proph. Dan. comm.*, p. 63; Polanus, *In Dan. proph. comm.* ii, p. 14, or in Poole's *Synopsis*, iii, col. 1472. Cf. also Hertlein op. cit., p. 34. It is to be observed that in viii. 4 the LXX adds πρὸς ἀνατολάς, making four directions, and Jahn (*Das B. Dan. nach der LXX herg.*, p. 76) and Charles (*Crit. Comm. on Dan.*, p. 200) allow that this may be original, but Bludau (*Die alex. Übers. des B. Dan.*, p. 49) regards it as an amplification.

[5] *Dan. and his Proph.*, p. 151.

[6] *Das B. Dan. erk.*, p. 106. Cf. Kamphausen, *Dan.* (in Bunsen's *Bibelwerk*), p. 660.

[7] Cf. Gallé, op. cit., p. 72. [8] *Proph. of OT*, ET v, p. 246.

three presidents appointed by Darius in vi. 3 (EV vi. 2)[1]. Others have claimed that the three is merely a symbol of plurality[2], and so have evaded the necessity for giving any further interpretation, while yet others[3] have confessed that whatever meaning it had for the author is irrecoverable[4], and with this view the present writer concurs.

But if this is the case with vii. 5, how stands it with vii. 6? For here it is claimed that the four heads of the third beast excellently set forth the fourfold division of the empire of Alexander that is elsewhere referred to in the book of Daniel[5]. In viii. 8 we are told that after the breaking of the Great Horn, which indisputably stands for Alexander, four horns came up towards the four winds of heaven. And again in xi. 4 we are told that Alexander's kingdom should be divided towards the four winds of heaven. Surely then,

---

[1] So Dereser (*Die Proph. Ezech. u. Dan.*, 2nd ed., by Scholz, p. 353), Maurer (*Comm. gramm. crit. in VT*, ii, p. 129) and Delitzsch (in PRE, 2nd ed., iii, p. 475). This view is an ancient one, and is referred to by Jerome (on vii. 5, ed. Migne, col. 529). Albertus Magnus (*Comm. in lib. Dan.*, in *Opera*, viii, p. 84) favours either this view or the identification with the Medes, the Persians, and the Chaldaeans, as above; so, too, pseudo-Aquinas (*In Dan. proph. exp.*, in *Opera Omn.*, Parma ed., xxiii, p. 162 b).

[2] So von Lengerke (*Das B. Dan. verd. u. ausg.*, p. 305) and Prince (*Crit. Comm. on Dan.*, p. 131). Similarly Calvin, who adopts the Medo-Persian view of this beast (see *Comm. on Bk. of Dan.*, ET ii, p. 16) and Briggs (*Mess. Proph.*, p. 418).

[3] Cf. Bevan, *Short Comm. on Dan.*, p. 121; von Gall, *Die Einheitl. des B. Dan.*, p. 94; Marti, *Das B. Dan. erk.*, p. 50. Similarly Driver (*Bk. of Dan.*, p. 82) says it is only a symbol of the voracious nature of the beast, and does not attempt to define the meaning of the number three, and is followed by Charles (*Crit. Comm. on Dan.*, p. 178).

[4] It may here be noted that Browne, who held the second empire to be the Macedonian, thought (*Ordo Saec.*, p. 677) that the three ribs referred to Antiochus Epiphanes, and paralleled the description of the Little Horn of chap. viii as one that waxed great toward the south, toward the east, and toward the glorious land.

[5] So Jerome (on vii. 6, ed. Migne, col. 530), Petrus Comestor (*Hist. Lib. Dan.*, ed. Migne, col. 1454), Luther (*Der Proph. Dan. Deudsch*, p. c i a, and *Kurtze Erc.*, p. b ii a), Calvin (*Comm. on Bk. of Dan.*, ET ii, p. 18), Oecolampadius (*Comm. in Dan. lib. duo*, p. 86), Hofmann (*Weiss. u. Erf.* i, p. 286), Caspari (*Zeitsch. f. d. ges. luth. Theol. u. Kirche*, ii, 1841, 4th Quartalheft, p. 144), Kliefoth (op. cit., p. 203), Keil (op. cit., ET, p. 228), Wright (*Dan. and his Proph.*, p. 154), and very many others. Merx, however, held the four heads to stand for the four parts of Alexander's empire, viz. Macedonia, Persia, Babylonia, and Egypt (*Cur in lib. Dan.*, p. 21).

it is claimed, we should interpret this verse by those, and find here a clear reference to the Greek kingdom. But against this it may be pointed out that both of the passages adduced make clear reference to Alexander himself, as well as to the fourfold division of his empire that followed his death. Yet vii. 6 would seem to allow no room for this. It might conceivably be argued that the four-headed leopard represented the divided kingdom of Alexander's successors. But it can hardly be supposed that it represented the single kingdom of Alexander which afterwards became divided. It is highly improbable that any one would think of the rise of the Greek kingdom without the person of Alexander dominating his thought, and it is certain that our author did not, if his mind be sought in these other passages, and he would have wished to set forth not alone the later division of the kingdom, but the person of him who founded it. The view which finds Alexander's kingdom in the fourth beast can find both its establishment and its climax symbolized in the character of the beast, but holds that as the fourfold division of the kingdom was irrelevant to the author's purpose here, he was not bound to note it in his symbolism. It can scarcely be argued similarly that he was not bound to note Alexander, if the third beast represents the Greek kingdom. For it is much more reasonable to suppose that the fourfold division was left unnoted than that the author's thought ignored Alexander.

But even though this Greek explanation of vii. 6 were wholly satisfactory, it would still remain to ask whether the Persian view of the third empire could show an interpretation of the four heads equally appropriate. And here, too, it is claimed that the book of Daniel itself supplies the key. For in xi. 2, in a vision which is dated in the reign of Cyrus, we read that 'there shall stand up yet three kings in Persia'. May it not be, therefore, that the four heads are the four kings of Persia, including Cyrus, that our author knew?[1]

[1] So von Lengerke (op. cit., pp. 307 f., 512), Maurer (op. cit., ii, pp. 130,

To this it is replied that the kings of Persia were more than four[1], and that we have no right to assume that our author was so ill-informed, especially if we place him later than the Persian era. There is some disagreement, indeed, as to whether the fourth king of xi. 2 is the fourth after Cyrus, or the fourth including Cyrus. By many the former view is held[2], the three kings who shall rise up being Cambyses, pseudo-Smerdis and Darius Hystaspis, and the fourth being Xerxes. By others[3] pseudo-Smerdis is omitted, and the three kings are held to be Cambyses, Darius Hystaspis, and Xerxes, the fourth king of the dynasty thus being Xerxes. These two views agree in holding the fourth king of verse 2,

---

176), Hitzig (op. cit., p. 108), Hilgenfeld (*Die Proph. Esra u. Dan.*, p. 81), Kamphausen (op. cit., pp. 660 f.), Ewald (op. cit., ET v, pp. 247, 294), Kuenen (*Prophets and Prophecy*, ET, p. 142 n.), Reuss (*Litt. pol. et pol.*, p. 254), Bevan (*Short Comm. on Dan.*, p. 122), Farrar (*Bk. of Dan.*, p. 61), Buhl (in PRE, 3rd ed., iv, p. 455), Prince (*Crit. Comm. on Dan.*, pp. 132, 170). Marti (*Das B. Dan. erk.*, p. 50, and HSAT, 4th ed., ii, pp. 476, note g, 485, note h), Charles (*Crit. Comm. on Dan.*, p. 178), Obbink (*Daniël*, p. 130). Delitzsch (in PRE, 2nd ed., iii, p. 475) takes as the four successors of Cyrus, and therefore does not share the idea that the author knew of but four Persian kings. Bousset (*Theol. Rundschau*, iii, 1900, p. 333) says there are parallels in later Persian tradition for the idea that there were but four Persian kings of the Achaemenid dynasty.

[1] Cf. Jerome (on vii. 5, ed. Migne, col. 529, and on xi. 2, col. 558), and Pusey (op. cit., p. 139).

[2] So Jerome (on xi. 2, ed. Migne, col. 558), Theodoret (on xi. 2, ed. Schulze in Migne, PG lxxxi, col. 1501), Ephraem Syrus (*Op. omn.*, Syr. and Lat., ii, p. 226), Grotius (*Op. omn. theol.*, 1732 ed., i, pp. 475 f.), Cornelius a Lapide (*Comm. in quat. Proph. maj.*, 1727 ed., p. 1372), More (*Exp. of Vis. of Dan.*, p. 159), Calmet (op. cit., pp. 700 f.), Bertholdt (op. cit., p. 715), Hävernick (*Comm. über das B. Dan.*, p. 449), Dereser (op. cit., p. 380), Auberlen (op. cit., ET, p. 63), Kliefoth (op. cit., p. 438), Keil (op. cit., ET, p. 430), Delitzsch (in PRE, 2nd ed., iii, p. 475), d'Envieu (*Le Livre du Proph. Dan.* ii, p. 1365), Knabenbauer (*Comm. in proph. Dan.*, p. 287), Goettsberger (*Das B. Dan. übers. u. erk.*, p. 81), Willet (in *Abingdon Comm.*, p. 757).

[3] So Nicolaus de Lyra (*Bib. Sacr.* iv, p. 322 b), Luther (*Der Proph. Dan. Deudsch*, p. d i b), Calvin (*Comm. on Bk. of Dan.*, ET ii, p. 169), Bullinger (*Dan. exp. hom. LXVI*, p. 116 b), Michaelis (*Adn. phil.-exeg. in Hag.* iii, p. 398), von Lengerke (op. cit., p. 308), Maurer (op. cit. ii, p. 176), Caspari (*Zur Einf. in das B. Dan.*, p. 159), Kamphausen, op. cit., p. 676), Deane (op. cit., p. 182), Meinhold (*Das B. Dan. ausg.*, p. 325), Bevan (*Short Comm. on Dan.*, pp. 171 ff.), Prince (op. cit., pp. 170 f.), Marti (*Das B. Dan. erk.*, p. 77), Driver (*Bk. of Dan.*, p. 163), Charles (*Crit. Comm. on Dan.*, p. 273), Obbink (*Daniël*, p. 130).

whether regarded as the fourth of the dynasty, or as the fourth after Cyrus, as being Xerxes. The leap from this point to Alexander in the following verse is justified, not by the author's ignorance of the intervening period, but by the fact that Alexander is said to have been stimulated to make his attack on Persia by the memory of the attack on the liberties of Greece that Xerxes had made[1]. If the reference in xi. 2 is to five kings of the Persian dynasty, the relevance of that passage to the four heads of vii. 6 immediately fails. But if, as many who have not shared the Persian view of the third empire have held, the reference is to four kings, that relevance is open to examination.

It is not agreed by all that the fourth king of xi. 2 is Xerxes[2]. Montgomery says it is absurd to suppose that Jewish tradition remembered Xerxes' attack on Greece, and he makes the four kings to be Cyrus, Xerxes, Artaxerxes, and Darius Codomannus[3]. Others have thought the fourth king is a conflation of Xerxes and Codomannus[4], and even a writer so orthodox as Fuller has declared the description of this king to be equally applicable to Xerxes and to Darius Codomannus, and has believed the latter to be intended[5]. Fuller, however, was of those who find five kings are referred to in the passage, and held them to be the most renowned Persian kings. He therefore identified them with Cyrus, Cambyses, Darius Hystaspis, Xerxes, and Darius Codomannus.

It has often been pointed out that in the Old Testament four names of Persian kings, and only four, are found, and that an author who rested perhaps largely on Old Testament

---

[1] So Wright (*Dan. and his Proph.*, p. 245); also Keil (op. cit., ET, p. 430), who quotes Arrian, *Anabasis*, II. xiv. 4 (ed. Dübner, p. 48). But Pusey (op. cit., p. 136 n.) declares this to be irrelevant, and not to refer to Xerxes at all.

[2] Ephraem Syrus (*Op. omn.*, Syr. and Lat., ii, p. 226) says of the fourth king 'this is Darius', without specifying which Darius, or how he arrived at him. If he intended Darius Hystaspis, then he found no reference at all to Xerxes in the passage, but found the prophecy to jump from Darius Hystaspis to Alexander. It is more likely, however, that he thought of Codomannus.

[3] *Comm. on Dan.*, p. 423.

[4] So von Lengerke (op. cit., p. 308), Delitzsch (in PRE, 2nd ed., iii, p. 475), and Farrar (*Bk. of Dan.*, pp. 61 f.). [5] In *Speaker's Bible*, vi, p. 372.

sources of information might easily suppose there were but four[1]. The four names that are found are Cyrus, Darius, Xerxes (Ahasuerus), and Artaxerxes. In what order our author may have conceived them as living is not agreed. Montgomery, as has been said, supposed them to be Cyrus, Xerxes, Artaxerxes, and Darius (Codomannus), while Ewald thought they were Cyrus, Darius, Xerxes, and Artaxerxes[2]. Others have thought rather of Cyrus, Darius (Hystaspis), Artaxerxes, and Xerxes[3]. To these the answer is presented that even in the Old Testament more than four kings are referred to[4], since two of the kings who bore the name of Darius are mentioned. Moreover, Artaxerxes reigned after Xerxes and not before, and if Xerxes is held to be the fourth king of xi. 2 there is no need to assume ignorance of history on the part of the author, when his words will agree with history so well. For even though he ignored pseudo-Smerdis, the inclusion of Cambyses, Darius and Xerxes would bring him to Xerxes as the fourth. And the most superficial reading of the Old Testament should have acquainted him with Artaxerxes as a fifth. Against this it has to be remembered that Cambyses is nowhere mentioned in the Old Testament, and we cannot rule out the possibility that he was unknown to our author. Further, in the haziness of his knowledge of the period, it is possible that he confused the order of Xerxes and Artaxerxes. And if more than four kings are referred to in the Old Testament, only

---

[1] So Hitzig (op. cit., p. 187), Hilgenfeld (*Die jüd. Apok.*, p. 26 n.), Bevan (*Short Comm. on Dan.*, p. 172), Kamphausen (*Das B. Dan. u. d. neu. Geschichtsf.*, p. 32), Marti (*Das B. Dan. erk.*, p. 77), Charles (*Crit. Comm. on Dan.*, p. 273), Obbink (*Daniël*, p. 130). [2] Op. cit., ET v, p. 294.

[3] So already Hippolytus (cf. Bonwetsch, *Hippolyt's Komm. zum B. Dan.*, p. 292. But cf. Migne, PG x, col. 359, where Hippolytus represents them as Cyrus, Darius, Artaxerxes, and Darius (sc. Codomannus)); so too, in recent years, Meinhold (*Das B. Dan. ausg.*, p. 325), Bevan (loc. cit.), Prince (op. cit., p. 171), Marti (loc. cit.), Charles (loc. cit.), Obbink (loc. cit.). Barhebraeus (cf. *Schol. zum B. Dan.*, ed. Freimann, p. 14) held them to be Artaxerxes Mnemon, Artaxerxes Ochus, Perseus (= Arses), and Darius the son of Arsaces, whom Alexander slew (= Codomannus).

[4] Cf. Pusey, op. cit., p. 139; Keil, op. cit., ET, p. 430; Wright, *Dan. and his Proph.*, p. 244; Hertlein, op. cit., p. 37.

four names are mentioned, and a writer who made so many confusions may well have failed to distinguish between the two Dariuses.

On all of these points, therefore, the argument is inconclusive. It may well be that our author knew of but four Persian kings, and that the four heads of vii. 6, and the four kings of xi. 2 alike point to them. But in that case, it seems to me that Montgomery's view is the only tenable one. For while if we had only xi. 2 to go by, we might suppose that the author jumped from Xerxes' attack on Greece to the Asiatic conquests of Alexander that were its sequel, we could not on that ground infer that he was ignorant of the succeeding kings. And it is hard to suppose that tradition had not preserved the name of Darius as the last Persian king. On the other hand, if the four heads of vii. 6 included Darius Codomannus as one of the only four kings of the Persian empire our author knew, then Codomannus must be one of the four kings of xi. 2. And in that case he must obviously be the last.

Attempts have been made to invalidate the connexion of the four heads with four Persian kings along other lines. Thus, it is said that the heads cannot be successive[1], and also that the heads cannot symbolize kings, since horns are used in the book of Daniel for kings[2]. So far as the first argument is concerned, its invalidity has already been noted in another connexion. For simultaneity of appearance in vision does not preclude succession in interpretation, and it may be remarked that those who maintain that the heads cannot be successive maintain that the three ribs of vii. 5 represent states that were successively annexed by the Medo-Persians. Of no more weight is the argument that heads must stand for kingdoms, since horns stand for kings.

[1] So Pusey (op. cit., p. 139), Kliefoth (op. cit., p. 202), Keil (op. cit., ET, pp. 228, 252), Behrmann (*Das B. Dan. übers. u. erk.*, p. 45), Wright (*Dan. and his Proph.*, p. 154).
[2] So Zöckler (op. cit., ET, p. 153 a), Meinhold (op. cit., p. 298) and Montgomery (op. cit., p. 290).

For again, those who present this argument themselves find
in viii. 3 that horns are used to represent, not individual
kings, but a Median and a Persian leadership in the Medo-
Persian empire, and in viii. 8 that horns are used to represent four divisions of the Macedonian empire, while in the
same chapter the Great Horn of viii. 8 represents Alexander,
and the Little Horn of viii. 9 another individual. If, then,
by common admission,[1] horns can stand for both individuals
and states, within a single vision, by what law of interpretation can it be claimed that individuals cannot be represented
by both horns and heads? Clearly there is no rigid uniformity of symbolism.

The view that the four heads are the only four Persian
kings known to our author, but perhaps confusedly arranged,
cannot be disproved therefore. But neither can it be proved.
And it must be allowed that it is possible that Kliefoth is
here right in holding[2] the four heads to be a symbol of
universality, showing that the power of this empire would
spread in all directions—a view which is also represented
amongst those who disagree with him in the identification
of the empire[3].

On neither of the two opposing views of the second and.
third kingdoms, then, can a really convincing explanation of the symbolism of vii. 5 f. be given. Their evidence
cannot fairly be used for or against either view, and we can
only say with confidence that in the mind of the author they
had some definite meaning, which is too obscure to be
recovered, in the absence of any assured clue in his work.
But that he believed that a Median empire stood between the
Babylonian and the Persian can be proved without the aid of
these verses, and this gives at once the simplest and most
satisfying solution of the problem of the four empires.

---

[1] Henry provides an isolated exception to this admission. For he claims
(op. cit., p. 99 n.) that a horn never stands for an individual king, but always
for a dynasty.   [2] Op. cit., pp. 199 ff.
   [3] So Bertholdt (op. cit., p. 427), Meinhold (op. cit., p. 298), Behrmann
(op. cit., p. 45), Driver (*Bk. of Dan.*, p. 83), Montgomery (op. cit., p. 290).

IV. THE INTERPRETATIONS THAT FIND FOUR KINGS, INSTEAD OF KINGDOMS, ARE UNSATISFACTORY.

OF the interpretations of the four empires, there remain to be examined some other schemes, which connect the visions neither with the Greek nor with the Roman empires. It has already been noted that a few interpreters have supposed that the first two of the kingdoms were to be understood as symbolizing individual reigns. The schemes which remain to be examined have carried this principle farther, and have claimed that all the four parts of the image of Nebuchadnezzar's dream represented individual reigns, though it is a feature of these schemes that the beasts of the vision of chapter vii are not usually interpreted in the same way.

(1) *The identification of the four kingdoms with the reigns of Nebuchadnezzar, Belshazzar, Cyrus, and Darius the Mede is unsuitable and improbable.*

Riessler propounded this view at the beginning of the present century,[1] and so far as I have been able to discover, he is without predecessors in it. He advanced many strange ideas about the book of Daniel, which are woven into this theory of the four kingdoms. In the first place he held that while the Nebuchadnezzar of chapter i is the son and successor of Nabopolassar, the Nebuchadnezzar of chapters ii–iv is really Nabonidus. Further, he identified Darius the Mede with Cambyses, as we have seen above. We have already noted that Cambyses was associated temporarily with his father on the throne, as king of Babylon, at the outset of the reign of Cyrus over the conquered Babylonian kingdom, and later he succeeded his father in the rule of the empire. In accordance with this, Riessler finds the references to Darius the Mede in the book of Daniel are

[1] *Das. B. Dan. erk.*, pp. 17 f., 68 ff.

M

to his temporary occupancy of the throne of Babylon, but his position in the visions of chapters ii and vii is that of his imperial rule after the death of Cyrus. The four reigns of Riessler's view, therefore, are to be equated with those of Nabonidus, Belshazzar, Cyrus, and Cambyses.

That Belshazzar did not really reign independently he admits, but thinks he exercised the regency for three years, and that these three years are the three ribs of vii. 5. The wide range of the kingdom of Cyrus well accords with the statement of ii. 39 that he 'shall bear rule over all the earth', and Riessler thinks the four wings of vii. 6 indicate the spread of his rule in all directions. The fourth beast, that destroyed and trampled down, he holds to be a fitting symbol for Cambyses, whom he identifies with the Artaxerxes of Ezra iv. 6–23. The veto of Cambyses on the building of the Temple is then held sufficiently to explain the attitude to him we find here. With the end of the beast, i.e. the death of Cambyses, Riessler believes the prophet looked for the resurgence of Israel, and with this he connects the prophecies of Haggai.

Some intractable elements remain, and with these Riessler deals surgically. The four heads of vii. 6 he believes to have come in from the hand of a glossator, who identified the third beast with the kingdom of Alexander. Similarly the ten horns will yield him no appropriate meaning, and they too must be eliminated as a gloss. This time they are attributed to one who identified the fourth beast with the Greek kingdom, and Riessler thinks the glossator meant by them Alexander and the Seleucids, down to Seleucus Philopator, with Heliodorus and the murdered son of Philopator to complete the number, and Antiochus Epiphanes as the Little Horn.

This view is distinguished only by its extreme improbability. The fact that Belshazzar is now known to have exercised authority in Babylon during his father's reign for a much longer period than three years does away with the proposed explanation of the three ribs, while the necessity to assume that chapter vii has been glossed is a weakness. Riessler assumes, indeed, that it has not only been glossed, but glossed at different times, and in the interest of mutually incompatible interpretations. For he believes the 'ten horns' passage was due to one who included Alexander in the fourth beast, while the 'four heads' gloss was due to one who thought of the successors of Alexander— Ptolemy, Seleucus, Lysimachus, and Cassander—as belonging to the third beast. The clear recognition that chapter vii, in the form in which we now have it, finds its climax in the reign of Antiochus Epiphanes lends no support, in the absence of any reasons for deleting any sections, to his view that its original climax was in the reign of Cambyses. For the mere fact that they do not harmonize with Riessler's theory is an insufficient reason for excising them. So completely subjective a view can carry no conviction, save to the mind in which it took its rise.

Further, it is difficult to see why Cambyses should be cast for the part. It is true that at the time of his death widespread revolt took place, and the Persian empire seemed broken into fragments, while Messianic hope broke out about that time amongst the Judaean community. But Cambyses does not appear to have been particularly severe on the Jews. Indeed, we learn on the authority of one of the Elephantine papyri that when the policy of Cambyses showed itself in the destruction of Egyptian temples, the temple of the Jewish colony in Yeb was untouched.[1] And the passage to which appeal is made to show that Cambyses vetoed the rebuilding of the Temple in Jerusalem says nothing whatever about the Temple, but deals exclusively with the city walls. Nor can Cambyses be equated with the Artaxerxes of that passage by more than the sheerest conjecture.[2]

[1] See Cowley, *Aram. Pap. of Fifth Cent. B.C.*, pp. 112 f. (30: 13 f.).

[2] See Batten, *Comm. on Ezra and Neh.*, pp. 160 ff. Cf. Bertholet, *Die Bücher Esra u. Neh. erk.*, p. 13, and Ryle, *Bks. of Ezra and Neh.*, pp. 64 ff. Note, too, that Keil held Ezr. iv. 6–23 to be an insertion, and disputed the

Nor does Riessler tell us what meaning we are to attach to the statement that when the fourth beast was destroyed the first three beasts continued to live for a time, though shorn of dominion. In what sense can Nabonidus, Belshazzar, and Cyrus be supposed to have outlived Cambyses, or to have been expected to outlive him?

Moreover, when Riessler asks us to believe that chapter vii was an actual vision of Daniel at the time noted in its heading,[1] when there were no indications that a special crisis should arise many years later, under a dynasty that had not yet annexed the Babylonian empire, and that the prophet's mind was then so clearly illumined that he saw the general break-up that would follow the death of Cambyses, we can only express surprise that the prophet should have falsely expected the unending kingdom to be set up at that time, and should not have known that the period of chaos after Cambyses' death would be but temporary, and that so far from the kingdoms being consumed and the sovereignty being left to no other people, in a very short time Darius Hystaspis would restore order and control throughout the empire. That a prophet should misread, in some measure, the signs of his own times is understandable; but that inaccuracy should mark his predictions, where the rational element is suspended and he writes of things wholly unrelated to his own contemporary conditions, is less understandable. Such a view of prophecy is only tolerable when it can show the strictest inerrancy.

Finally, Riessler shows so little confidence in his own theory that he presents us with another, and quite different, view, within the covers of the same book.[2] Nor does he attempt to relate them to one another, or to show which has his real preference. This alternative view is that the first kingdom is that of Nabonidus, the second that of the

identification of Cambyses with Artaxerxes (see *Bks. of Ezra, Neh. and Est.*, ET by S. Taylor, p. 74).

[1] *Das B. Dan. erk.*, p. xii. [2] Ibid., pp. viii, ix, 127.

Medes, the third the Persian, and the fourth that of the Umman-Manda. These were four contemporary states within the world of the Tigris-Euphrates region, that were expected, on this view, to acquire dominion successively. For the hostility of the fourth to the Jews, Riessler compares Ezekiel's reference to Gog. On this view he thinks the eleven horns of chapter vii may be original to the text. This is to confess that he knows of no reason, apart from his own other theory, for removing them from the text. It is also to confess that neither theory rests on any convincing grounds.

For this second view he is able to present such grounds no more than for the first. It is true that the Umman-Manda and the Medes were once distinct, but part, at any rate, of the Umman-Manda had become fused with the Medes by the time of Nabonidus, for the latter refers in one of his inscriptions to Astyages as king of the Umman-Manda.[1] It is therefore unlikely that a contemporary would look for an Umman-Manda empire distinct from a Median, and in succession to it. Nor is it explained why Daniel should look for a Median empire to precede the Persian at the time when he had the vision of chapter vii, for on Riessler's view of a three year's regency of Belshazzar, the Median empire had been already swallowed up by the Persian before Daniel had the vision,[2] and even though Belshazzar's authority be correctly carried back to the third year of Nabonidus' reign, it is hard to see how Daniel could have looked for a Median empire to follow Nabonidus, since the king's departure from Babylon, which led to the entrusting of authority to Belshazzar, appears to have been part of a concerted movement, the other side of which was Cyrus' revolt from the Medes.[3]

---

[1] See Langdon, *Neubab. Königsinsch.*, pp. 220 f. (Nabonidus No. 1, col. I, line 32).

[2] On p. viii, however, Riessler says that the years of Belshazzar are here reckoned from the first year of the reign of Nabonidus.

[3] Cf. Smith, *Bab. Hist. Texts*, p. 45, and Dougherty, *Nab. and Belsh.*, p. 144 f.

Where we are presented with two mutually exclusive theories by a single author, and where neither of them can present any antecedent probability, or any strong argument in its favour, we are certainly justified in decisively rejecting them both. As Riessler is without predecessors, so, it may be expected, will he be without successors, and the solitary original view on the four empires which the twentieth century has provided has little prospect of remaining in the field.

(2) *The identification of the four kingdoms with the reigns of Nebuchadnezzar, Evil-merodach, Neriglissar, and Nabonidus is equally improbable.*

Eerdmans has recently proposed this view for the interpretation of chapter ii.[1] The difficulty of applying the same interpretation to the vision of chapter vii is obvious, for that vision is represented as having been seen in the reign of Belshazzar, the son of the fourth of these monarchs. Hence for that chapter Eerdmans proposes the identification of the four beasts with Egypt, Media (including Assyria), Lydia, and Babylonia.

This is new in its interpretation of chapter vii, but in so far as it concerns chapter ii it is only a revival, with slight modifications, of a view which has been found in more than one writer. The oldest I have been able to trace is von der Hardt,[2] who thought the head of the image represented Nebuchadnezzar, the breast Evil-merodach, with Neriglissar and Laborosoarchad (Labashi-marduk) as the arms, the belly Belshazzar, and the legs Cyrus, with Cyrus as the iron and Darius as the clay of the feet. He held the horizon of the vision to be limited to the seventy years of Jeremiah's prophecy, and the stone cut without hands to symbolize the returning Jews.

---

[1] *Origin and Meaning of Aram. Part. of Dan.*, in *Actes du xviii^e congr. des orient.*, pp. 198–202; cf. id., *De Godsd. van Isr.* ii, pp. 49–55.

[2] *De quat. mon. Bab.*, pp. 15 ff. This view is criticized by Jan (*Diss. hist.-pol. de quat. mon.*, and *Ant. et perv. de quat. mon. sent. plen. ass.*, chap. vi).

Unlike all who have followed him in this type of interpretation of chapter ii, however, von der Hardt carried the same interpretation into chapter vii,[1] part of which therefore became retrospective. Again, he held the vision to be governed by the range of Jeremiah's prophecy, He wrote, *Non [est] longa quatuor in orbe Monarchiarum fabula, sed brevis historia captivitatis Babylonicae LXX annorum sub Nebucadnezare, Evilmerodacho, Belsazare et Cyro, quatuor Babyloniae regibus.*[2] He held the first beast to be Nebuchadnezzar, the second Evil-merodach, the three ribs being Evil-merodach, Neriglissar and Laborosoarchad, the third beast Belshazzar, and the fourth Cyrus. The ten horns he held to be either ten, or an indefinite number, of Median kings who preceded Cyrus, and Cyrus himself to be the Little Horn, with Cambyses, Astyages, and Cyaxares[3] as the three up-rooted horns.

When Harenberg[4] revived this interpretation, with some modifications, he found an immediate following.[5] The essential modification he made was in holding Cyrus to be the stone which fell upon the image. The image was therefore held to represent only the monarchs of the Babylonian empire, and in the absence of modern historical sources, Harenberg held these to be all related by blood or marriage to Nebuchadnezzar. The parts of the image he believed to represent Nebuchadnezzar, Evil-merodach his son (whom he identified with the Belshazzar of Daniel v), Neriglissar, the brother-in-law of the foregoing, Laborosoarchad (Labashi-marduk), the son of Neriglissar, and Nabonidus,

[1] *Dan. quat. Anim.*, pp. 18 ff.
[2] Ibid., p. 15.
[3] He identified Cyaxares with Darius Medus.
[4] *Aufk. des B. Dan.* ii, pp. 304 f.
[5] Dathe, *Proph. Maj.*, pp. 608 f.; Hezel, *Die Bib. mit vollst. erk. Anm.* vi, pp. 733 ff. Cf. also Scharfenberg, *Spec. animad.*, pp. 34 f. It is stated by Dathe (op. cit., p. 609) that Benzel anticipated Harenberg, and this has been repeated by others. I have been unable to find evidence of this. In his *Prob. hist. de quat. orb. mon.*, Benzel refers to the views of von der Hardt (pp. 31 ff.), but he himself holds that the climax of the prophecies belongs to the time of the Seleucids (pp. 36 ff.), and that what is said of the fourth beast fits Antiochus Epiphanes (pp. 41 ff.).

whom he identified with the son of Nebuchadnezzar by Nitocris.[1] It will thus be seen that he found five parts of the image, instead of the usual four, holding that the feet of iron and clay represented a fifth division of the image. It will also be observed that the only difference between this view and that of Eerdmans, apart from the unhistorical identifications of individuals, which do not, of course, stand in Eerdmans, is that the latter omits the reign of Labashi-marduk, and so reduces the kingdoms, or reigns, to the usual number. The reign of Labashi-marduk lasted for but nine months, and his name is therefore omitted from Ptolemy's Canon. To identify him with the iron kingdom, whose strength is so emphasized in the vision of chapter ii, was one of the major improbabilities of the view of Harenberg, and to this extent the theory is strengthened in the hands of Eerdmans.

For the interpretation of chapter vii, Harenberg and his followers adopted that form of the Greek view of the fourth kingdom which distinguishes between the kingdom of Alexander and his successors.[2] They held the first beast to represent the Chaldaean kingdom, the second to stand for the Medo-Persian kingdom, with the Medes, the Lydians and the Babylonians as the three ribs, the third beast to be Alexander's kingdom, with Greece, Egypt, Persia, and India as the four heads, and the fourth beast to be Alexander's successors, with Antiochus Epiphanes as the Little Horn. For the identification of the ten horns, Hezel adopts the views of Grotius, making Antiochus Epiphanes to be both the tenth and the Little Horn.[3] In all this there is nothing fresh, and it calls for no consideration here.

What does call for consideration, however, is the interpretation of chapter ii, and since this view appears in its strongest form as presented by Eerdmans, it will suffice to

---

[1] Dathe and Hezel identified Nabonidus with Belshazzar.
[2] See Dathe, op. cit., p. 629; Hezel, op. cit. vi, pp. 762 ff.
[3] Op. cit., p. 768. Hezel follows Grotius in including Ptolemy Eupator as the third in the list.

traverse his arguments. That he has freed it from one of the more glaring weaknesses of its earlier form has been observed. Nevertheless, he has been unable to present it in a convincing way. He holds that in the Aramaic part of Daniel no allusions to the Greek period are found, though chapters viii–xii he regards as Maccabean. Like Harenberg and his followers, he believes the image of chapter ii to represent a dynasty, each part being a *malkhu* or reign—not kingdom. The fourth was government by two kings, whom he is able, in the light of the authentic historical sources now open to us, to identify with Nabonidus and Belshazzar. These were related to one another by the seed of men (ii. 43), and were one of iron and one of clay. The Persian hordes, coming down from the mountains of Elam, are described as a huge piece of rock that destroyed the Babylonian dynasty, and became a great mountain that filled the earth.

It has already been noted that for the vision of chapter vii Eerdmans takes an original line. He maintains that the vision presents four beasts which existed simultaneously, and that they cannot stand for four successive world empires. He observes that the statement that when the fourth beast was destroyed the other three had their lives prolonged for a season cannot be given any explanation on either the Roman or the Seleucid view of the fourth beast. He therefore holds the four beasts to represent states that were conquered by Cyrus, the fourth being Babylon. The ten horns he maintains to be contemporaneous, since otherwise the eleventh could not come up between them and uproot three. These ten simultaneous kings in one kingdom he then takes to be local kings, adducing the title 'king of kings', borne by Babylonian monarchs. Finally he identifies Nabonidus with the eleventh horn, since he secured the throne by revolution and murder. That the eleventh horn tried to change times and the law is explained by Nabonidus' refusal to go to Babylon to celebrate the New Year, while his oppression of the saints is illustrated from deutero-Isaiah

(xlviii. 10, xlii. 7, li. 13 f). The saints who receive the kingdom are held to be the Jewish people, aided by the Persians,
and again Eerdmans refers to deutero-Isaiah for evidence of
the high appreciation of the Jews for Cyrus (xlv).

It thus appears that while Eerdmans interprets chapters ii
and vii quite differently from one another, he relates the
dénouement of the one to that of the other, and to this extent
again his view is a great improvement on that of Harenberg,
Dathe, and Hezel. It will also be observed that into his
interpretation of chapter vii he has brought an element of
von der Hardt's interpretation. For while he does not, with
von der Hardt, identify the stone of chapter ii with the
returning Jews, but with Cyrus and his Persian troops, he
does find that in chapter vii the Jewish people are to possess
the kingdom, but to be admitted to it by the power of Cyrus.

Finally, Eerdmans adds that the present text of these
visions cannot be older than the fourth century B.C., but
that probably the stories were orally transmitted by the
exiles long before they were written down. They were
later used, he thinks, in the time of Antiochus Epiphanes,
to encourage the people in their revolt.

Here we may observe that the claim that the four beasts
must be contemporaneous, and so also the ten horns, is
sufficiently answered by Eerdmans's own recognition that
the four parts of the image of chapter ii, though simultaneously seen, are successive in interpretation. Nor does he
explain why Babylon, which was the third of the four states
he names to be annexed by the Persians, should here be the
fourth, or why Egypt should figure among the conquests of
Cyrus.[1] No reason is apparent, save the exigencies of his
theory, which is clearly embarrassed by this necessity. We
also seek in vain for an explanation of the fact that Babylon,
the supposed fourth beast, is held to be described as one

[1] Xenophon, indeed, presents us with a wholly romantic account in the
Cyropaedia of Cyrus' conquest of Egypt. But in reality it was Cambyses who
conquered Egypt, and this conquest stood, not as the first of the Persian conquests, as Eerdmans puts it, but as the last of those he notes.

that devoured the whole earth, when three other independent empires were conceived as co-existing with it, within
the range of the same vision. His claim that no meaning can
be given to vii. 12 on the Greek or Roman view of the fourth
kingdom is not wholly correct, for it has been shown above
that a very appropriate meaning can be given on the view
which has been adopted there. On the other hand, Eerdmans himself fails to give an explanation of the verse. For
in what sense, that would not be equally true of Babylon,
could Egypt, Media, and Lydia, after their conquest by
Persia, be said to be alive?[1]

To these considerations others may be added. Eerdmans
recognizes chapters viii-xii to be Maccabean. The Little
Horn of viii. 9 is then Antiochus Epiphanes, and the 'time
and times and a half' of xii. 7 refers to his interference with
the Temple sacrifices in Jerusalem. But the Little Horn of
vii. 8 is taken to mean Nabonidus, and the 'time and times
and half a time' of vii. 25 is held to refer to his suspension
of the New Year Festival in Babylon. It is not natural to
interpret these similar expressions of different persons and
events, and particularly improbable that those in chapter vii
had any reference to Nabonidus. For what Jewish author
would be in the least concerned with Nabonidus' suspension of the Babylonian New Year Festival? And what
possible meaning can be given to the 'time and times and
half a time'? For Nabonidus suspended that Festival for
more than three and a half years.[2] Nor would an odd half
be appropriate in any case to that suspension.

[1] Eerdmans argues (*De Godsd. van Isr.* ii, p. 55) that the death of Antiochus
Epiphanes did not bring to an end the dynasty of the Seleucids, and that
hence the empire he represented cannot be said to have perished in his death.
But this in no way proves that a Maccabean author could not have anticipated
a greater disaster for the Seleucid empire than was actually realized. Nor does
it face the fact that the dynasty of Media and that of Lydia came to an end on
their conquest by Cyrus precisely as much as did that of Babylon, or explain
why their fall should be differentiated in this respect.

[2] The Nabonidus Chronicle tells us the Festival was omitted in the seventh,
ninth, tenth, and eleventh years of Nabonidus. There are gaps in the
Chronicle for the eighth and twelfth to sixteenth years, but when we come to

Nor is the interpretation of chapter ii free from difficulties. For while Nabonidus and Belshazzar were related, as father and son, they could scarcely be said to have mingled themselves together with the seed of men. Further, it is not clear how the reign of Nabonidus could be described in the terms of ii. 40, or how Cyrus could be said to have overthrown the rule of Nebuchadnezzar (ii. 44). On the view adopted above, that national empires are referred to, and that the fourth includes all the territories which comprised the first three, they could be conceived of as continuing to exist as nations within the fourth empire, though without dominion. And it has been shown that they could even be conceived of as surviving the fourth empire. But on the view that they were individual reigns, how can they be said to have been shattered together by the impact of the stone? Again, on this view ii. 40 describes the reign of Nabonidus, in contrast to those of his predecessors, while vii. 7, on the view of Eerdmans, describes in closely similar terms the character of the fourth beast (i.e. Babylon), before the Little Horn (i.e. Nabonidus) arose. How can the description be at once appropriate to Babylonian rule prior to Nabonidus, and to the rule of Nabonidus in contrast to that prior rule?

Yet again, Eerdmans holds that chapter vii recognized that Nabonidus was a usurper, who reached his throne by revolution. But chapter v represents Belshazzar, the son of Nabonidus, as the son of Nebuchadnezzar. It would seem that the fourth-century author, to whom Eerdmans attributes the Aramaic story-book, was unaware of any inconsistency here. He was therefore unaware of the meaning that Eerdmans finds in chapter vii, and must be supposed to have recounted old stories of whose meaning he was ignorant. No attempt is made to show any meaning they might have been given in his day, but it is said that they were invested with a new meaning in the Maccabean

the seventeenth year we learn that it was rightly celebrated. See Smith, *Bab. Hist. Texts*, pp. 112–17.

age. Is it really credible that an author would have composed stories whose original meaning was forgotten, and which had no meaning for his own day, but which were strangely destined to have much significance for a later day?

Furthermore, if the alleged fourth-century author had known this supposed original meaning, he could not but have disapproved of it. In the sixth century, as Eerdmans reminds us, high hopes of Cyrus were entertained. But by the fourth century every Jew would be disillusioned, and none would cherish hope of the possibility of a joint rule of Persians and Jews, and surely none would wish or expect the Persian empire to be eternal.[1]

Eerdmans asks us, therefore, to read into the visions a meaning which is unnatural and inappropriate to the terms of the visions, and which no fourth-century Jew would have approved, if he had understood; he suggests no rational motive for the composition of the stories in ignorance of their meaning, and makes no effort to explain the curious similarity between details of the visions and details of admittedly Maccabean compositions, or the strange chance that these visions should yield a clearer meaning to readers in the Maccabean age than to their supposed first readers in the fourth century B.C. We may therefore reject this view with confidence, and continue to find in the view above adopted the only satisfying solution of the problem of the four empires.

[1] In his *De Godsd. van Isr.* ii, p. 49, Eerdmans suggests that Dn ii–vii dates from the time of Nehemiah, i.e. from the fifth century B.C. One could understand high hopes of the Persians being entertained in that age, but not the telling of a story which events had plainly falsified by that time. For chap. vii connects the giving of the kingdom to the saints with the death of the fourth beast. Yet who in the age of Nehemiah could suppose that the Jewish saints had entered into the possession of 'the kingdom and the dominion and the greatness of the kingdoms under the whole heaven' on the death of Nabonidus and the collapse of the Babylonian empire?

CONCLUSION

OUR study has thus led us to reaffirm the views of what has been above called the critical orthodoxy of the beginning of the present century.

(*a*) So far as Darius the Mede is concerned, we have seen that there is no way of reconciling the book of Daniel with assured history, and all the efforts of the apologists, of whom the present century has seen a new and plentiful crop, definitely fail.

(*b*) So far as the four empires are concerned, the identification with the Babylonian, Median, Persian, and Macedonian empires, to the time of Antiochus Epiphanes, is the only one that can be found to accord with the data presented in the two chapters concerned.

Against the varied recent challenges, as against all their predecessors, these two positions stand unshakable. And from their acceptance certain consequences flow.

I. *The book of Daniel is not a work of the sixth century* B.C.

The case against the traditional date to which the composition of the book has been assigned rests on a variety of considerations, but the single one we have examined in the first part of our study would alone be sufficient to establish it. For a sixth-century person, who not only lived through the events of the period, but took a leading part in them, could not have made so gross an error as our author made in introducing Darius the Mede between Belshazzar and Cyrus. Nor could he have supposed that a Median empire stood between the Babylonian and the Persian.

II. *As certainly can we say that the book of Daniel is a work of the second century* B.C.

If the work is loosed from the sixth century by the inaccuracy of its knowledge of that age, it is anchored in the second century by the accuracy of the knowledge of that age which appears in its pages. Again, of course, the full case rests on more considerations than have arisen in the course of the present study. But the considerations we have examined are sufficient to warrant the conclusion. So long as the work was believed to be written in the sixth century B.C., the accuracy of its descriptions of the second century but served to establish the wonderful certainty of prophecy. But when the link with the sixth century is broken by the proved historical errors in the part of the book that relates to that age, the whole case is altered. It is impossible to believe that the mind of Daniel was illumined with accurate knowledge of future times, while, at the same time, thoroughly befogged as to the events in which he himself had played no mean part, and we can only find in the limited range of the accurate knowledge the indication of the author's period.

III. *The fact that a common error is spread throughout the whole book is an argument for its unity.*

Once more the whole case for the unity of the book does not rest on a single argument, but it finds definite support from the considerations we have examined. For a common error binds the two parts of our study. The first part presents us with the conception of a Median sovereign standing between the Neo-Babylonian dynasty and the Persian Cyrus, and the second part with the conception of a Median empire following the Neo-Babylonian and preceding the Persian. While community of error does not prove unity of authorship, since one author might derive the error from another, its testimony is on the side of unity of authorship. It can be overridden by sufficiently strong evidence against unity, but so far as it goes, its evidence of a common mentality and historical conception points towards unity of authorship.

For Darius the Mede is not localized in a single section of the book of Daniel. He is mentioned not alone in chapter vi, but also in ix. 1 and xi. 1. So, too, the conception of four successive empires, of which the second is the Median, stands in chapters ii and vii. In five of the separate compositions which go to make up the book of Daniel, therefore, we find this same error, which lies at the back of the fiction of Darius the Mede and of the scheme of the four empires.

It has been observed that a growing number of scholars believe the book of Daniel to be composite, but that while some divide the book at the end of chapter vii, others divide it at the end of chapter vi. Those who divide it at the end of chapter vi, and who therefore find chapter vii to be Maccabean, find no reason to doubt that that chapter is a unity. On the other hand, those who include chapter vii in the pre-Maccabean part of the book believe that the verses that relate to the ten horns and the Little Horn are unoriginal to the chapter. They acknowledge these verses to point definitely to the time of Antiochus Epiphanes, and therefore eliminate them from the original text as glosses. Similarly, most of the scholars who regard the book as composite find Maccabean glosses in chapter ii, though it has been noted that Torrey prefers to limit the reference in the verses which they remove.

It is a serious weakness of these division hypotheses that they are forced to reduce either chapter ii, or chapters ii and vii, to a colourless condition. For when they have removed the alleged glosses, these chapters merely indicate that four world empires should succeed one another, of which the fourth should be strong and should be the final empire that rests on human power. We are left without any means of detecting what were the four empires in the author's mind, and without any means of locating the time at which he expected the climax to be reached. The chapters might then have been written at almost any time, but would be scarcely worth writing. On these views, while the scheme of the four world-empires which has been above adopted is held to belong to the chapters as we now have them, we could not say what the original author meant by them. At no period could they have brought the slightest real hope to any one.

But it is relevant to our present study to observe that these division-hypotheses still leave the common error in both parts of the book. On any division chapter vi belongs to the first part of the book, and chapter vi introduces us to Darius the Mede. And on any division chapters ix and xi belong to the second part of the book. And here again there are references to Darius the Mede. Similarly, whether chapter vii is held to belong to the second part of the book or to belong to its first part, but to have been interpolated in the Maccabean age, we are left to find its present clear indications of a conception of four world empires, of which the second was the Median, in another mind than that of the original author of the first part of the book. And if, with some, this interpolator is held not to be the author of the second part of the book, but a third person, we but suppose that this common historical error was shared by a third writer.

Where it is admitted that the writer of the earliest section of the book held the mistaken view which figures also in the part which is alleged to be later, and in glosses which some have supposed to come from a third hand, and where this mistaken view is admittedly found to lie behind the present form of chapters ii and vii, and where the theory of division requires us to remove the indications of this mistaken view from those chapters, while leaving it elsewhere in the first part of the book, and in so removing it from chapters ii and vii to rob them of all point and purpose, we are entitled to say that so far as this consideration is concerned, the probability is strongly against the theory of composite authorship.

IV. *The religious value of the book is not weakened but strengthened.*

The apologists for the traditional view of the book of Daniel have often written as though they are the defenders of the Christian faith against a godless attack. They have implied that the whole structure of the Christian faith rests on the case for the sixth-century origin of this book, and that belief in God and in the possibility of divine revelation would be destroyed by the acceptance of the views which have been argued for in the present work. In truth their fears are groundless. The view which has been adopted does not destroy faith but strengthens it, in that it provides a reasonable ground for it.

The conclusions we have reached have not been born of *a priori* disbelief in accurate prophecy, but of *a posteriori* demonstration that we have not accurate prophecy. On the traditional view, there should have been the most exact accordance with history. If the rational factor were entirely eliminated, and the prophet were given a wholly divine revelation of things unrelated to the conditions of his own day, then, since it were all of God and none of man, it should be utterly inerrant. Yet so inexact is the accordance with history that the interpretations of the orthodox, as we have seen above, are innumerable, and there is absolutely no agreement as to what are the historical events that the inspiring God intended accurately to set forth in the visions. How then can the divine power to inspire exact prophecy be held to be demonstrated here?

Further, of what use would be a book which somehow set forth unidentifiable events? It could not demonstrate Divine power, nor could it help us. A God who buried His meaning so securely that the pious of all ages, including many of the most honoured and consecrated, as well as the most learned, men of all Christian history, have failed to find it, and have differed by two thousand years and more in their identifications of the climax of the visions, would but rob His revelation of all worth. Instead of unfolding future events, He would be but veiling them, and that is not revelation, but its antithesis.

The recognition that there are historical errors in the

book of Daniel, and that the author's imperfect knowledge of past history and exaggerated hopes for the future find a place in these visions involves a different view, not of the reality of revelation, but of its character. It means that the book cannot be held to be exclusively of God, for in Him is no error. There is something of man in it, and to this fact is due all that is mistaken in it. But that does not involve the further conclusion that it is all of man, and that there is nothing of God in it.

The author whose mind and outlook we have found in our study was not a man who transmitted a puzzle which it should baffle the ingenuity of saint and scholar to solve. He was a man who lived in critical days when a great battle of faith was in progress. Of his contemporaries some had forsaken the faith of their fathers and slipped into an easy worldliness, while others were casting away their lives rather than disobey the God they knew and loved. And his soul burned with the passionate certainty that these had chosen the worthy path, and he wished to hearten them for their struggle, and to assure them that the God they had not failed would not fail them. This was a greater and more divine mission than the supplying of a cryptic outline of future events that should prove a snare to eighty generations of curious folk who should try in vain to pry into the future. Here was a man whose soul was afire with love for God, and who wished to set the souls of others on fire. He was a man who was bringing a divine word of cheer to men, and performing a living service, a man who rendered the richest service to succeeding generations through the service of his own.

The minute unfolding of future events would be supernatural, but not in itself religious; but this was an essentially spiritual service that he performed. An inspiration whose content was completely unrelated to a man's own personality would be a very wonderful thing indeed; but it could not compare with the yet greater wonder that God can use the organ of the prophet's fallible personality. The author of our book had in his mind sundry confused historical traditions, and God was able to use these in His service. He is able to take the best that His servants can offer Him, in all its imperfection, and to use it. For He is God. Had our author been writing a scientific work of history in Maccabean days, he would have needed to give much patient research to it. And it is highly improbable that he had access to adequate sources for that task. But there is no evidence that he was interested in history as such. He was but interested in it as the vehicle of a divine message. That it was a message of God is not to be doubted, but the form in which he presented it was his own.

To destroy the belief in the historical value of these stories and visions is but to release their richer power, by teaching men to read them for what they are, and not for what they are not. The religious value of the parables of Jesus does not depend on the historical accuracy of the details of the stories. Nor does the religious value of the story of Darius the Mede. It depends rather on whether the message enshrined is true to the heart of God.

When, therefore, we read the book of Daniel no longer as a Chart of the Ages, but as the work of a man who saw the world in the light of what he had seen of God, and whose interest was essentially and wholly religious, we are free to feel its religious power, and to understand its message. To the heroes of the Maccabean days it gave encouragement and hope. And beyond that it enshrined abiding principles which are as valid in our day as in those. It tells us that every force which elevates itself against God shall be broken, and that they who are humbly loyal to Him, and who find in His fellowship their strength, shall be able to laugh at the lions, for theirs shall be the Kingdom.

And deeper than this lies another abiding message, also of rich spiritual import. It is that God is great enough to take us, with all our imperfect thoughts and false expectations, and to make us the instruments of His service. Had there been naught of error in the book, it could not have said this to us. But its very historical mistakes add to the fullness of its religious message to our hearts, for the God Who maketh the wrath of men to praise Him can also convert the mistakes of His servants, whose hearts are consecrated to His service, to rich use.

TABLE OF VARIETIES OF INTERPRETATION OF THE FOUR KINGDOMS

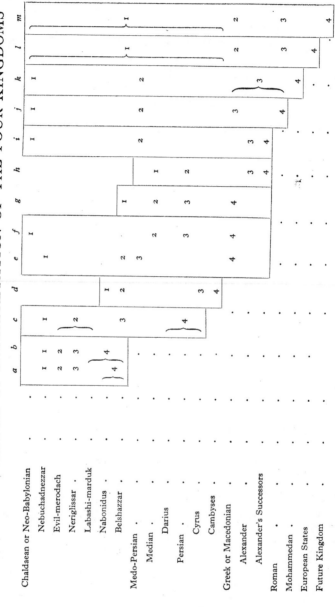

NOTES TO PRECEDING TABLE

(a) Eerdmans—for chap. ii only. (For chap. vii, Egypt, Media, Lydia, and Babylonia.)

(b) Harenberg, Dathe, Hezel—for chap. ii only.

(c) Von der Hardt.

(d) Riessler.

(e) Van Hoonacker, Goettsberger; also Conring, Hitzig, Redepenning for chap. ii only.

(f) Peshiṭta MSS., Ephraem Syrus, Cosmas Indicopleustes, Anonymous in Mai, Barhebraeus, Venema, Eichhorn, de Wette, Bleek, Dereser, von Lengerke, Maurer, Bade, Hilgenfeld, Westcott, Davidson, Kamphausen, Kranichfeld, Graf, Delitzsch, Kuenen, Reuss, Vatke, Schürer, Bevan, Behrmann, von Gall, Curtis, Buhl, Prince, Driver, Marti, Bertholet, Steuernagel, Andrews, Bewer, Haller, Baumgartner, Montgomery, Charles, H. L. Willet, Obbink, Eissfeldt; also J. Jahn, Merx, and Meinhold—for chap. ii only—and Polychronius—for chap. vii only.

(g) Hitzig, Redepenning—for chap. vii only.

(h) Conring, Merx—for chap. vii only.

(i) Porphyry, Grotius, Junius, Broughton, Rollock, Polanus, A. Willet, Piscator, l'Empereur, the Westminster Assembly's Annotators, Lightfoot, Becmann, Calmet, Amner, Bertholdt, Rosenmüller, Herzfeld, Stuart, Desprez, Cowles, Zöckler, Turmel, Lagrange, Buzy; also Polychronius—for chap. ii only—and Harenberg, Dathe, Hezel, J. Jahn, Meinhold—for chap. vii only.

(j) 4 Ezra, Josephus, Ep. Barnabas, Irenaeus, Hippolytus, Origen, Lactantius, Eusebius, Rabbi Joḥanan, Aphraates, Cyril of Jerusalem, Sulpicius Severus, Chrysostom, Jerome, Augustine, Theodoret, Isidore of Pelusium, Rabbi Tanḥuma, Jephet Ibn 'Ali, Rupert of Deutz, Petrus Comestor, Hugo of St. Chère, pseudo-Aquinas, Nicolaus de Lyra, Ibn Yaḥya, Luther, Oecolampadius, Joye, Calvin, Bullinger, Pererius, Bellarmine, Abbot, Maldonatus, Osiander, Graserus, Cornelius a Lapide, Parker, Alcazar, Huit, Poole, Mede, Calovius, Cocceius, Prideaux, Newton, Wintle, Mencken, Hengstenberg, Tyso, Auberlen, Hofmann, Birks, Lee, Pusey, Gärtner, Kliefoth, Caspari, Rule, Keil, Rohling, Trochon, d'Envieu, Düsterwald, Knabenbauer, Lagarde, Vigouroux, Wright, Hertlein, Stokmann, Boutflower, Möller, and many others. The agreement here is only superficial, however, and the vast differences that exist amongst these writers as to the duration of the Roman kingdom have been dealt with in the text of the foregoing work. Some terminate that kingdom at the birth of Christ, some at the Crucifixion, some later in the first cent. A.D., some continue it in various selections of European states, some in the Holy Roman Empire, some in the Mohammedan power, some in the Papacy.

(k) Ibn Ezra.

(l) Lacunza—for chap. ii only. For chap. vii he held the reference to be to false religions—idolatry, Islam, false Christianity, anti-Christianity. With this latter, cf. pseudo-Aquinas—Jews, Pagans, Arians, Saracens.

(m) Maitland, Todd, Browne.

INDEXES

I. SUBJECT

Alexander, identified with third kingdom, 64 n., 139 ff., 142, 168; held to be one of ten horns, 106 f.; eliminated from chap. xi, 130 n.

Alexander's empire, divisions of, 95, 98 f., 107, 124 n., 154 f., 163, 168; identified with second kingdom, 84.

Antichrist, found in Little Horn, 88, 128 n., 130 n.; in chap. xi. 130 f.; typified by Antiochus Epiphanes, 136 f., 137 n.

Antiochus Epiphanes, identified with Little Horn, 25 n., 91 f., 101 ff., 120 ff., 124 n., 162, 168; persecution of Jews, 93, 97; its causes traced, 97 n., exercised effective Macedonian power, 104 f., 122 f.; in *Sib. Or.*, 118 f., 122; in chap. xi, 128 ff.; held to be type of Antichrist, 136 f., 137 n.

Antiochus Magnus, held to be one of uprooted horns, 109.

Antiochus, son of Seleucus Philopator, held to be one of uprooted horns, 110 n., 111, 114, 162.

Artaxerxes, spelling of name, 49 f.; significance of Biblical spellings, 50 n.; I or II contemporary of Ezra and Nehemiah? 49 f.

Artaxias, held to be one of uprooted horns, 108.

Asia Minor, identified with third kingdom of chap. vii, 124 n.

Assyrian view of first kingdom, 68 f.

Astyages, traditions of, 30 f., 34; identified with Darius the Mede, 6, 30 ff.; view contested, on grounds of paternity, 33, name, 33 f., irreconcilability with Greek sources, 34 f., with cuneiform sources, 35 f.

Babylonian view of first kingdom, 64 n., 67 ff., 168; of fourth kingdom, 64 n., 166 ff.

Belshazzar, supposed identifications of, 10; death held to be recorded, 20; identified with second kingdom, 64 n., 67, 142 ff., 152 n., 162 f.; with first kingdom of chap. vii, 67,

142; with third kingdom, 166 ff.; his feast read into vii. 5, 143 f.

Britain, identified with enduring kingdom, 84 n.

Cambyses, identified with Darius the Mede, 5, 12 ff., 161 f.; view contested, on grounds of age, 13 ff., name, 15 f., race, 16 f., paternity, 17; associated on throne, 12; nowhere mentioned in OT, 158; identified with fourth kingdom, 162 f.; attitude to Jews, 162 f.

Chaldaean, *see* Babylonian.

Chaldaeo-Medo-Persian view of first kingdom, 64 n., 84.

Clay and Iron, *see* Iron.

Constantine the Great, found in chap. xi, 131.

Cyaxares II, Xenophon's account of, 16, 37 f., 40; a fiction, 41 ff.; identified with Darius the Mede, 5, 37 ff.; view contested, on grounds of name, 39 f., inconsistency with Dan., 40 f., with inscriptions, 41 f.; name identified with Ahasuerus, 18 n., 39.

Cyropaedia, a romance, 34, 41 ff., 170 n.

Cyrus, Greek traditions of, 16, 30 f., 38; age and reign, 55 f.; race, 42 n., 57; identified with third kingdom, 64 n., 162; identified with fourth kingdom, 166 ff.

Daniel, Book of, its unity denied, 2 ff., 65, 91 n.; affirmed, 176 f.; alleged interpolations, 2 n., 4, 18 n., 54 n., 65, 91, 102 n., 132 f., 162; held to be in part post-Christian, 3 n., 5, 7, 78, 84, 87; this view contested, 84 n., 85 n., 87 f.

Darics, origin and name of, 44 ff.

Darius Codomannus, place in xi. 2, 157.

Darius the Mede, Biblical data, 9; alleged significance of age, 14 f.; supposed length of reign, 24 n., 25, 36; held to be not really king, 26 f., authority held to be delegated, 51 ff.; spelling of name,

Darius the Mede (*cont*.).
47 ff.; not free creation, 5 n.; un-historical, 44 ff.; fictitious confla-tion of traditions, 54 ff.; not mere transposition of Darius Hystaspis, 54 f.; supposed different from Darius, son of Ahasuerus, 56 n.; identified with second kingdom, 64 n.; with Cambyses and fourth kingdom, 161 ff.
Demetrius, held to be one of uprooted horns, 108 f., 112, 114; objections, 111, 114.

Egypt, identified with first kingdom, 64 n., 67, 166 ff.; Ptolemaic Egypt identified with first kingdom of chap. vii, 124 n.
Empires, four, *see* Four Empires.
European states, identified with fourth kingdom, 64 n., 77, 88.
Evil-merodach, identified with Belshazzar, 10; with father of Belshazzar, 10 n.; with second kingdom, 64 n., 166 ff.
Ezra, date of, 49 f.
4 *Ezra* (2 *Esdras*) witness of, 70, 73.

Four beasts, fate of, 87, 88 n., 122 f., 124 n., 141 f., 147, 164, 169, 171.
Four Empires, identical, 64 f.; dis-puted by a few, 64; original signi-ficance alleged disguised, 68; number held to be taken from older tradition, 69; identified with re-ligions, 64 n., 83 n.
Four heads, 141, 154 f., 162, 164, 168; simultaneous or successive in interpretation? 159.
Four horns, *see* Horns, four.
Futurist views, 82 f., 88, 125 n., 128, 129, 136; criticized, 88 f., 130.

Gaps in prophecies alleged, 82, 84 n., 88 n., 125 n., 127 n., 128 n., 129 ff., 136.
Geographical argument, 90, 147.
German empire, identified with en-during kingdom, 86 n.
Gobryas, records and traditions of, 19 ff., 23; identified with Darius the Mede, 5, 19 ff.; view contested, on grounds of name, 21 f., paren-tage, 22 f., race, 23, rank, 24 ff.
Graeco-Roman view of third king-dom, 80.
Greek view of fourth kingdom, 64 n., 68, 70 ff., 142; varieties of, 72 f.,

91 f.; oldest view, 70; does not rest on disbelief in prophecy, 71; alleged fulfilment in birth of Christ, 72, 92; criticized, 92 f.; alleged to be in Josephus, 74 n.; supported by other visions, 124 ff.; Greek view of second kingdom, 64 n., 154 n.; of third kingdom, 81, 138, 154 f.

Heads, four, *see* Four heads.
Heliodorus, held to be one of uprooted horns, 110 ff.; view contested, 111, 113, 162.
Holy Roman Empire, 78, 89.
Horn, Little, identified with Antio-chus Epiphanes, 75 n., 91, 101 ff., 120 ff.; with Papacy, 79 f., 84 n., 128 n.; with Khalifate, 81, 84 n.; with Julius Caesar, 82; with Caesars, 82 n.; with Vespasian, 85; with future Antichrist, 88, 128 n., 130 n.; with Seleucus Nicator, 99, 120 n.; with Cyrus, 167; with Nabonidus, 169; identi-cal in chaps. vii. and viii, 124 ff.
Horns, four, 95, 107, 124 ff., 140; varieties of identification, 96 n.—
Horns, ten, held to be drawn from Babylonian legend, 69 n.; future kings, 74 n.; Greek kings, 75 n.; states formed out of Roman, 77 f.; first ten Caesars, 78, 85; successive or contemporaneous? 78, 100, 169 f.; number indefinite, 78 f., 100, 109 n.; future states, 79, 82, 89; Arab kingdoms, 80 n.; Senate of Rome, 82; Hasmonaeans, 85; divisions of Alexander's empire, 98 ff.; Seleucids and Lagids, 101 f.; Seleucids, 105 ff.; Alex-ander and Seleucids, 106 f., 162; Median kings, 167; local Baby-lonian kings, 169; supposed key in chap. xi, 102 f., 109; in *Sib. Or.*, 115 ff.
Horns, three uprooted, anti-papal view, 80 n.; Egypt, Libya, Ethio-pia, 74 n.; Asia, Greece, Syria, 81 n.; Galba, Otho, Vitellius, 85; varied Greek views, 108 ff.; Anti-gonus, Demetrius, Lysimachus, 99 n.; Egypt, Armenia, Palestine, 110 n.; Persians, Egyptians, Jews, 110 n.; Persia, Egypt, Asia Minor, 110 n.; Cambyses, Astyages, Cy-axares, 167; found outside the ten horns, 101, 106 n., 108, 109 n., 112 n.

Inspiration, character of, 86 n. 93, 164, 179 ff.
Iron and Clay, alleged significance, 64 n., 76 f., 166; Seleucids and Lagids, 94.

Jewish interest of author, 96, 98, 104 f.

Kingdoms, four, see Four Empires.
Kings of xi. 2, 155 ff.; four or five? 156.
Labashi-marduk, identified with Darius the Mede, 10; with fourth kingdom, 167 f.
Legs of image, alleged significance of, 76, 94.
Lydia, identified with third kingdom, 64 n., 166 ff.

Maccabean revolt, identified with stone cut without hands, 97.
Macedonia, identified with second kingdom of chap. vii, 124 n.
Macedonian view of fourth kingdom, see Greek view.
Medes, alleged undistinguished from Persians in Dan., 148 f.
Median view of first kingdom, 64 n. 67, 139 n., 142; of second kingdom, 64 n., 138, 140 n., 142, 144 ff., 152 n., 153 f., 165, 166 ff.; objections met, 147 ff.
Medo-Persian view of second kingdom, 64 n., 139 ff., 148 f., 151 f., 168; of third kingdom, 68, 142 ff.; of first kingdom, 138 n.
Memphis inscription, 50.
Mohammedan empire found in visions, 73, 76, 80 f., 84 n.

Nabonidus, identified with Darius the Mede, 9, 37 n.; with Belshazzar, 10; with Cyaxares, 37 n.; with Astyages, 37 n.; with first kingdom, 162, 164; with fourth kingdom, 64 n., 166 ff.; with Little Horn, 169; view criticized, 171.
Nebuchadnezzar, identified with first kingdom, 64 n., 67, 142 ff., 166 ff.; identified with Nabonidus and first kingdom, 161; madness found in vii. 4, 67 f.; disputed, 68.
Nebuchadnezzar's successors, identified with second kingdom, 64 n., 142.
Nehemiah, date of, 49 f.

Neriglissar, identified with Darius the Mede, 10; identified with third kingdom, 64 n., 166 ff.
Numerals, use of letters for, 13 f.

Papacy, found in visions, 73, 79 ff., 128 n.; view criticized, 89 f.
Papyri, Elephantine, 47 f., 84 n., 163.
Period of persecution, 121, 127, 128 f., 134 f., 171; see also Year-day theory.
Persian royal names, supposed identifications, 17 f., 39; Biblical spellings, 47 ff.; four only found in OT, 157 f.; held only four kings known to author, 59, 155 f.
Persian view of third kingdom, 64 n., 140 n., 142, 144 ff., 155, 165; objections answered, 159 f.; of second kingdom, 64 n., 139 n.; of first kingdom, 81.
Peshitta glosses, 70, 144 n.
Praeterist view, 81 ff.; criticized, 86 f.
Prophecy, influence on author of Dan., 57 f., 150 f.
Ptolemy Euergetes, identified with an uprooted horn, 106 n.
Ptolemy Eupator, 101 n., 168 n.
Ptolemy Philometor, one of uprooted horns, 108 f., 112; objections met, 112 f., 114.
Ptolemy Philopator, held to be one of uprooted horns, 106 n., 108 f.
Ptolemy Physcon, held to be one of uprooted horns, 108.

Ribs of third beast, interpretations of, 151 ff., 162 f., 167, 168.
Roman view of fourth kingdom, not oldest, 70; disagreement with visions, 73, 85 ff.; profusion of varieties, 73 ff.; dictated by a priori considerations, 73 ff.; of third kingdom, 64 n., 83; of fifth and enduring kingdom, 78 n., 86 n., 142; of second kingdom, 81.

Sardis bilingual inscription, 49.
Seed, mingling of, alleged significance, 77; intermarriages between Seleucids and Lagids, 94 f., 96 f.; Torrey's view, 94, 96; criticized, 97.
Seleucus Nicator, identified with Little Horn, 99, 120 n.
Seleucus Philopator, held to be one of uprooted horns, 108 ff., 162.

Sibylline Oracles, testimony to meaning of ten horns, 70, 103, 115 ff.; date of passage, 119.
Son of man, identifications of, 62 n.
Stone cut without hands, identified with Virgin Birth, 61 n., 76, 86 n.; with Maccabean revolt, 97; with Roman empire, 86 n., 142; with Jews, 166; with Cyrus, 167, 169.
Syria, identified with fourth kingdom of chap. vii, 124 n.

Theodotion and pre-Theodotionic readings, 62 n., 85 n., 87 n.

Umman-Manda, identified with fourth kingdom, 165.

Virgin Birth, found in stone cut without hands, 61 n., 76, 86 n.

Weeks, seventy, varieties of interpretation, 135.

Xerxes, spelling of name, 50; relationship to Darius, 56 f.; place in xi. 2, 130 n., 156 ff.

Year-day theory, 80 n.

II. AUTHORS

Abbot, 79 n.
Abravanel, 131, 152 n.
Abydenus, 33 n.
Albertus Magnus, 154 n.
Albright, 19, 24 n., 49 n., 50 n.
Alcazar, 82.
Alexandre, 115 n., 116 n., 118, 119 n.
Alfrink, 2, 11, 12 n., 19 n., 21 n., 25 n., 30, 32 f., 35 f., 44, 46 f.
Amner, 86 n., 102, 111, 139.
Andrews, 63 n., 107, 110, 146.
Annotators of Westminster Assembly, 10 n., 14, 68 n., 71, 72, 109 n., 139.
Anonymous, in Mai, 71, 106 n., 145.
Aphraates, 68, 75, 153 n.
Appian, 113 n.
pseudo-Aquinas, 83 n., 154 n.
Aristophanes, Scholiast on, 44.
Arrian, 157 n.
Athenaeus, 16 n.
Auberlen, 63 n., 77 n., 147 n., 156 n.
Auchincloss, 5, 38 f., 82 n., 138 n.
Augusti, 2 n., 6.
Augustine, 78.
Ausonius, 41.

Babelon, 19, 45 n.
Bade, 90, 106, 112, 145.
Barhebraeus, 71, 110 n., 145, 152 n., 158 n.
Barnes, 49 n., 63 n.
Barton, 2.
Bate, 116 n., 117 n.
Batten, 49 n., 163 n.
Baumgartner, 4, 63 n., 84 n., 146.
Beausobre, 3.
Becmann, 71, 72, 90, 101, 139.
Behrmann, 62 n., 100 n., 122 n., 146, 159 n., 160 n.
Bellarmine, 79 n.
Bengel, 55 n.

Bensly, 52 n.
Benveniste, 46 n.
Benzel, 77 n., 167 n.
Bernfeld, 85 n.
Bernstein, 51 n.
Berossus, 46 n.
Bertholdt, 2, 6, 95 n., 106, 112, 140, 141, 152 n., 156 n., 160 n.
Bertholet, 50 n., 63 n., 68, 85 n., 146, 163 n.
Bevan, A. A., 51, 57, 58, 63 n., 81 n., 105 n., 107, 111, 113 f., 146, 154 n., 156 n., 158 n.
Bevan, E. R., 94 n., 95 n., 101 n., 104 n., 106 n., 107 n., 108 n., 111, 113 n., 114, 117 n., 119 n., 120, 124 n.
Bewer, 107, 110.
Birks, 80 n., 131.
Bleek, 98, 120 n., 121 n., 145.
Bludau, 87 n., 153 n.
Boeckh, 52 n.
Böhmer, 62 n.
Bosanquet, 2 n., 55 n., 102 n., 132 n.
Bouché-Leclercq, 94 n., 95 n., 101 n., 111 n., 113 n., 115 n., 117 n., 119 n.
Bousset, 5 n., 63 n., 118, 156 n.
Boutflower, 2, 5, 11, 12 f., 15 ff., 18 n., 20 n., 47 n., 51 n., 62 n., 63 n., 78 n., 80 n., 125 n., 133 n., 148 n., 152.
Box, 63 n., 70 n.
Briggs, 62 n., 69 n., 79 n., 154 n.
Broughton, 71, 102, 108 n., 139.
Browne, H., 83, 84 n., 154 n.
Browne, L. E., 49 n.
Buhl, 110, 146, 156 n.
Bullinger, 61 n., 76, 79 n., 152 n., 156 n.
Bunsen, 69.
Buttenwieser, 63 n.
Buzy, 6, 63 n., 140.

Calmet, 71, 72, 106, 110, 135 n., 139, 152 n., 156 n.
Calovius, 77 n.
Calvin, 79 n., 81, 86 f., 131, 154 n., 156 n.
Cary, 119 n., 123 n.
Caspari, 76 n., 152 n., 154 n., 156 n.
Cedrenus, 30.
Ceriani, 70 n., 144 n.
Charles, 51, 52 n., 54 n., 57, 62 n., 74 n., 85 n., 87 n., 107, 110, 118, 146, 153 n., 154 n., 156 n., 158 n.
Cheyne, 63 n.
von Christ, 42 n.
Chrysostom, 61 n., 75, 152 n.
Cicero, 41, 46, 55 f.
Clay, 20 n., 48 n., 56 n.
Clemens Alexandrinus, 135 n.
Cocceius, 76 n.
Conring, 7, 64, 67, 78 n., 86 n., 139, 142, 149 n.
Cook, 49.
Cooke, 50 n.
Cornill, 62 n.
Cosmas Indicopleustes, 61 n., 71, 72, 86 n., 100, 145, 149.
Cowles, 80 n., 90, 102 f., 104 n., 109 f., 130 n., 132 n., 140.
Cowley, 47, 49 n., 50 n., 163 n.
Ctesias, 16, 31, 32 f., 37, 55 n.
Curtis, 146.
Cyril of Jerusalem, 75.

Dalman, 3.
Dathe, 7, 10 n., 64, 167 n., 168 n., 170.
Davidson, 99, 145.
Deane, 19, 44 n., 125 n., 127 n., 156 n.
Delitzsch, 19, 20 n., 106, 112, 145, 154 n., 156 n., 157 n.
Dereser, 10 n., 37, 106, 112, 145, 154 n., 156 n.
Desprez, 102 n., 109 n., 133 n., 140.
Des-Vignoles, 19 n., 55 n.
Dinon, 16, 55 n.
Diogenes Laertius, 41.
Dougherty, 2, 20 n., 24 n., 37 n., 58 n., 165 n.
Driver, G. R., 48.
Driver, S. R., 20 n., 42 n., 63 n., 78 n., 85, 118, 137 n., 146, 154 n., 160 n.
Drummond, 63 n.
Düsterwald, 131.

Ebrard, 9, 10 n., 152 n.
Eerdmans, 4, 7, 64, 166, 168 ff.
Eichhorn, 3, 106, 112, 145.

Eisenmenger, 75 n.
Eissfeldt, 3, 50 n., 146.
l'Empereur, 71, 109, 139.
d'Envieu, 10, 62 n., 72, 79 n., 80 n., 132, 156 n.
Ephraem Syrus, 6, 62 n., 70 n., 71, 144 f., 149, 152 n., 156 n., 157 n.
Eusebius, 33 n., 44, 46, 52, 55 n., 56 n., 58 n., 75.
Ewald, 62 n., 68 f., 106, 112, 116 n., 118, 119, 153, 156 n.

Farrar, 106, 112, 156 n., 157 n.
Fischer, 75 n.
Fruin, 58.
Füller, 10 n., 37, 131.
Fuller, 152 n., 157.

Gadd, 33 n.
Gaebelein, 77 n., 88 n., 131 n.
von Gall, 63 n., 69, 107, 110, 146, 149 n., 154 n.
Gardner, 45 n.
Gärtner, 77 n., 80 n., 131.
Geffcken, 115 n., 116 n., 117.
Geier, 131.
Génébrard, 55 n.
Goettsberger, 7, 63 n., 68, 142 f., 156 n.
Graf, 145.
Graserus, 76 n., 131.
Gray, 43 n., 56 n.
Gressmann, 63 n.
Grotius, 9, 10 n., 71, 86 n., 101 f., 108 f., 139, 152 n., 156 n., 168.
Gunkel, 63 n., 102 n.
von Gutschmid, 10 n., 111.
Gwynn, 62 n.

Hagen, 20 n.
Halévy, 20 n.
Hall, 43 n., 56 n.
Haller, 4, 65 n., 146.
von der Hardt, 7, 166 f., 170.
Harenberg, 7, 10, 64 n., 167 ff.
Harpocration, 44.
Haupt, 54 n.
Hävernick, 10 n., 37, 152 n., 156 n.
Havet, 3 n., 64, 84 f.
Hawkins, 84 n.
Head, 45 n.
Hengstenberg, 10 n., 37, 39, 44, 71 n., 79, 82 n., 114 n., 140 n., 141 n., 148 n.
Henry, 75 n., 88 n., 118 n., 160 n.
Herntrich, 1.
Herodotus, 16, 21, 23, 30, 31 n., 37, 42, 47, 52 n., 55 n., 58 n.
Hertlein, 5, 7, 68, 77 n., 78, 84 f., 87,

Hertlein (cont.).
125 n., 148 n., 152 n., 153 n., 158 n.
Herzfeld, 140.
Hezel, 7, 10 n., 64, 167 n., 168, 170.
Hilgenfeld, 111, 118, 120 n., 145, 156 n., 158 n.
Hill, 45 n., 46 n.
Hippolytus, 68, 74, 130, 152, 158 n.
Hirsch, 63 n.
Hitzig, 7, 63 n., 64, 67, 68, 107, 110, 112 n., 140 n., 141 n., 142, 153, 156 n., 158 n.
Hoffmann, G., 45.
Hoffmann, J. F., 130 n.
Hoffmann, J. G. E., 51 n.
Hofmann, 77 n., 82 n., 152 n., 154 n.
Holleaux, 95 n.
Hölscher, 1, 3 f., 65 n.
Holtzmann, 69.
Holzinger, 63 n.
Hommel, 19, 20 n., 22, 63 n., 69.
Van Hoonacker, 7, 49 n., 142 f., 152 n.
Horner, 11 n.
Huet, 76 n., 77 n.
Hugo of St. Chère, 61 n., 76 n., 130 n.
Huit, 76 n., 81 n., 131.
Hulsius, 131 n., 152 n.
Hultsch, 45 n.

Ibn Ezra, 62 n., 80 n., 89, 131, 135 n., 153.
Ibn Yaḥya, 10 n., 80 n., 131.
Imbert, 50 n.
Irenaeus, 74, 82 n.
Isidore of Pelusium, 75.

Jahn, G., 65 n., 69, 87 n., 148 n., 152 n.
Jahn, J., 64, 71, 139, 152 n.
Jan, 74 n., 78 n., 166 n.
Jelf, 118 n.
Jephet Ibn 'Ali, 14, 68, 77 n., 153 n.
Jeremias, 63 n.
Jerome, 6, 30 n., 52, 68, 74 n., 75, 82 n., 96 n., 101 n., 108 n., 112, 113 n., 130, 136, 139 n., 152 n., 153 n., 154 n., 156 n.
John of Antioch, 111.
Josephus, 3 n., 10 n., 15, 17, 18, 37, 40, 46 n., 52 n., 74, 114, 121 n.
Joye, 79 n.
Julianus Africanus, 135.
Junius, 71, 106 n., 109 n., 139.
Junker, 63 n., 65 n., 69, 104 n., 144.
Justin, 31 n., 55 n.
Justin Martyr, 87 n.

Kahrstedt, 121 n.
Kamphausen, 54 n., 107, 110, 145, 153 n., 156 n., 158 n.
Keil, 10 n., 25, 37, 39, 44 n., 51 n., 63 n., 68, 82 n., 99 n., 100 n., 125 n., 127, 139 n., 147 n., 148 n., 152 n., 154 n., 156 n., 157 n., 159 n., 163 n.
Kelly, 131.
Kennedy, 45 n.
Kennett, 1.
King, 20 n.
King and Thompson, 21 n., 22 n., 43 n., 55 n.
Kittel, 49 n., 63 n.
Kliefoth, 10 n., 37, 51, 54 n., 68, 76 n., 77 n., 79 n., 89 n., 99 n., 125 n., 131, 140 n., 153, 154 n., 156 n., 159 n., 160.
Knabenbauer, 5, 37, 38 n., 62 n., 77 n., 156 n.
Köhler, 79 n.
Kolbe, 119 n.
König, 63 n., 69 n.
Kosters, 50 n.
Kraeling, 63 n.
Kranichfeld, 10 n., 37, 145.
Kuenen, 145, 156 n.
Kühner, 118 n.
Küper, 2 n., 132 n.

Lactantius, 82 n.
Lacunza, 64, 83.
Lagarde, 3 n., 75 n., 78, 84 f., 87.
Lagrange, 6, 55 n., 63 n., 106, 112, 140.
Lanchester, 116 f., 118, 122 n.
Langdon, 20 n., 32 n., 58 n., 165 n.
Lange, 2 n., 132 n.
a Lapide, 10 n., 61 n., 76 n., 79 n., 152 n., 156 n.
Larocque, 120 n.
Lee, 70 n.
Lehmann-Haupt, 19 n., 20 n.
von Lengerke, 106, 112, 145, 154 n., 155 n., 156 n., 157 n.
Lenormant, 2 n., 4 n., 19 n., 33, 54 n.
Lidzbarski, 49.
Lightfoot, J., 30, 71, 139.
Lightfoot, J. B., 70 n.
Littmann, 49 n.
Lofthouse, 49 n.
Löhr, 65 n.
Lowth, 10 n.
Luther, 61 n., 81 n., 131, 153 n., 154 n., 156 n.
de Lyra, 61 n., 68, 76 n., 78 n., 137 n., 152 n., 156 n.

Madden, 45 n.
Mahaffy, 101 n., 114.
Mai, 71 n.
Maitland, C., 128 n.
Maitland, S. R., 83, 84 n.
Maldonatus, 79 n., 82 n.
Malter, 14 n.
Manchester, Duke of, 56 n.
Margoliouth, J. P., 52.
Marsham, 30, 44 n.
Marti, 63 n., 85 n., 107, 110, 146,
    154 n., 156 n., 158 n.
Mathews, 14 n.
Maurer, 6, 106, 112, 145, 154 n.,
    155 n., 156 n.
Mede, 77 n., 80 n., 135 n.
Meillet, 46 n.
Meinhold, 2, 4, 63 n., 64, 68, 106,
    112, 146, 156 n., 158 n., 159 n.,
    160 n.
Mencken, 76 n., 78 n.
Merx, 64, 67, 106, 140, 154 n.
Meyer, 42 n., 45 n., 46 n., 63 n., 69.
Michaelis, 152 n., 156 n.
Möller, 19, 50 n., 76 n.
Montgomery, 3, 15, 21 n., 52, 54 n.,
    65 n., 68, 100 n., 134, 146, 157 f.,
    159, 160 n.
de Moor, 19, 26 n., 45 n.
Moore, 97 n.
More, 61 n., 68, 76 n., 79 n., 131,
    156 n.

Nestle, 124 n.
Newton, 3, 80 n., 125 n., 135 n.
Nicolaus of Damascus, 31.
Nicolaus de Lyra, see Lyra.
Niebuhr, 10 n., 30.
Niese, 74 n., 105 n., 111.
Nikel, 30 n.
Nöldeke, 56 n.
Noth, 65 n.

Obbink, 63 n., 102 f., 111, 146,
    156 n., 158 n.
Oecolampadius, 61 n., 79 n., 80,
    131, 154 n.
Oehler, 10 n.
Oesterley, 49 n., 50 n., 56 n., 70 n.,
    104, 119 n.
Oesterley and Robinson, 49 n., 98 n.
Oestreicher, 1.
Orelli, 62 n.
Origen, 75.
Osiander, 68, 76 n., 80 n., 81 n.,
    131, 153 n.
Otto, 111 n.

Parker, 76 n., 79 n., 80 n., 140 n.

Paton, 54 n.
Peake, 63 n.
Peiser, 12 n., 55 n.
Pererius, 76 n.
Petrus Archidiaconus, 75, 82 n.
Petrus Comestor, 30 n., 68, 74 n.,
    75, 152 n., 154 n.
Photius, 31.
Pinches, 19, 20 n., 55 n.
Pintus, 10 n., 61 n., 76 n., 108 n.,
    131, 152 n.
Piscator, 71, 106 n., 109 n., 139,
    153 n.
Plato, 41.
Polanus, 71, 72, 90, 106 n., 135 n.,
    139, 153 n.
Polyaenus, 16.
Polybius, 114.
Polychronius, 6, 71, 110 n., 139.
Polyhistor, 33 n.
Poole, 76 n., 132 n.
Porges, 14 n.
Porphyry, 6, 70, 101, 108, 113, 139,
    144, 149.
Prášek, 20 n., 45 n., 46 n.
Preiswerk, 3.
Prideaux, 37, 44, 76 n., 82, 135 n.
Prince, 46 n., 54 n., 63 n., 68, 107,
    110, 146, 154 n., 156 n., 158 n.
Pusey, 44 n., 51 n., 68, 72, 76 n.,
    78 n., 98, 99 n., 101 n., 108 n.,
    112, 118 n., 125 n., 130 n., 131,
    140 n., 147 n., 148 n., 150 n.,
    151, 152 n., 153, 156 n., 157 n.,
    158 n., 159 n.

Quatremère, 10 n., 44 n.

Rapoport, 14 n.
Rashi, 12 n., 14, 131, 135 n., 153 n.
Redepenning, 7, 142.
Reichel, 79, 152 n.
Reuss, 63 n., 145, 149 n., 156 n.
Révillout, 45, 46 n.
Ricciotti, 49 n.
Riehm, 62 n.
Riessler, 7, 8, 12, 63 n., 161 ff.
Rigaux, 100 n., 109 n., 132 n., 133 n.
Rogers, 32 n., 42 n., 56 n.
Rohling, 19 n., 131.
Rollock, 10 n., 71, 106 n., 139.
Rosenmüller, 10 n., 37, 71, 101, 108,
    140, 152 n.
Rowley, 2 n., 54, 70 n., 85 n., 117,
    119 n.
Rule, 80 n.
Rupert of Deutz, 61 n., 75, 76 n.
Ryle, 163 n.
Rzach, 115 n., 116 n.

194   INDEXES

pseudo-Saadia, 14, 153 n.
Sayce, 43 n.
Scaliger, 9, 10 n., 39.
Schaeder, 49 n.
Scharfenberg, 167 n.
Scheil, 20 n.
Schmidt, 63 n.
Schrader, 20 n.
Schürer, 63 n., 118, 146.
Schwenzner, 19 n., 20 n., 21 n.
Scott, 65 n.
Sellin, 4, 49 n., 65 n.
Smith, J., 1.
Smith, S., 20 n., 32 n., 58 n., 165 n., 172 n.
Spiegel, 14 n.
Spinoza, 4.
Staerk, 1.
Steuernagel, 107, 110, 146.
Stevens, 77 n., 131 n.
Stier, 63 n.
Stokmann, 2, 10 n., 18 n., 19, 21 f., 25, 63 n., 78 n., 140 n., 152 n.
Strack, 3 n.
Strong, 106, 112.
Stuart, 72, 90, 106, 112, 140.
Suidas, 45, 47.
Sulpicius Severus, 25 n., 55 n., 77 n.
Swete, 6 n., 62 n., 85 n., 87 n.
Syncellus, 9, 30, 33 n., 37 n., 55 n.

Tanḥuma, 75 n.
Tarn, 94 n.
Tattam, 81 n.
Theodoret, 6 n., 61 n., 75, 152, 156 n.
Thilo, 19, 65 n.
Tiele, 20 n.
Tillmann, 62 n.
Tisdall, 47.
Todd, 83, 84 n., 128 n., 129 n.
Torrey, 1, 3, 14 f., 49, 50 n., 94, 96 f.
Tregelles, 78 n., 80 n., 82 n., 125 n., 129 n.
Trochon, 19, 79 n., 132 n.
Turmel, 106 n., 112 n., 140.
Tyso, 77, 80 n., 125 n., 129 n., 135 n.

Unger, 30.

Vatke, 106, 112, 145.
Venema, 10 n., 37 n., 51 n., 71, 78 n., 99, 145.
Vernes, 49 n.
Victor of Antioch, 61 n.
Vigouroux, 19, 61 n., 76 n., 132 n.
Violet, 70 n.
de Vogüé, 49, 50 n.
Volck, 125 n.
Völter, 63 n.
Volz, 62 n.

Walton, 52 n.
Watson, 37.
Weissbach, 21 n., 22 n., 42 n., 56 n.
Welch, 1, 4, 5, 63 n.
Westcott, 30, 71, 130, 145.
de Wette, 145, 152 n.
Whiston, 74 n.
Whitla, 80 n.
Wilcken, 113 n.
Willet, A., 10 n., 18 n., 71, 72, 88 n., 106 n., 109 n., 139, 141.
Willet, H. L., 63 n., 146, 156 n.
Wilson, J. D., 2, 19.
Wilson, R. D., 2, 5, 17 n., 19, 20 n., 21 n., 22 n., 24 n., 26 ff., 39 n., 51 n., 54 n., 138 n.
Winckler, 10 n., 12, 14, 18 n., 57 n.
Winer, 30.
Winter and Wünsche, 80 n.
Wintle, 80 n., 130 n.
Wright, C. H. H., 2, 12 n., 19, 51 n., 62 n., 68 n., 71, 77 n., 78, 79 n., 80 n., 88 n., 89, 99 n., 100 n., 114 f., 125 n., 130, 131 f., 136, 137 n., 148 n., 149, 153, 154 n., 157 n., 158 n., 159 n.

Xenophon, 16, 19 f., 23, 31 f., 34 f., 37 f., 40 ff., 45, 55 n., 170 n.

Zimmern, 63 n.
Zöckler, 2 n., 10 n., 37, 39 n., 63 n., 71, 79 n., 90, 100 n., 106 n., 112 n., 132 n., 140, 159 n.
Zündel, 10 n., 37 n., 99 n.

III. TEXTS

1 Chron.

xxix. 7 . . 45 n.

2 Chron.

xii. 22 . . . 48.

Ezra

i. 1 . . . 25.
i. 69 . . . 45.
iv. 5, 6, 7, 24 . 39.
iv. 6 . . 11 n.
iv. 6-23 . 162 f.
vi. 14 f. . . 39.

Neh.

xii. 22 . . . 48.

Esther

i. 1 . . . 54.

Isa.

xiii. 17 . 57 n., 150 n.
xxi. 2 . 58 n., 150 n.
xli. 2, 25 ff. . 58 n.
xlii. 7. . 170.
xlv . 170.
xlv. 1 ff. . 58 n.
xlvi. 1 f. . 58 n.
xlvii. 1 ff. . 58 n.
xlviii. 10 . 170.
xlviii. 14 . 58 n.
li. 13 f. . 170.

Jer.

l. 9, 41 . . 57 n.
li. 11, 28 57 n., 150 n.

Dan.

ii. 37 f. . . 143.
ii. 38 . . 67, 69 n.
ii. 39 . . 162.
ii. 40 . . 97, 172.
ii. 43 . . 77, 169.
ii. 44 . . 172.
iii. 2 f. . . . 27.
iii. 27 . . . 27.
iii. 31 . . 53 n.
iv. 13 . . 68 n.
iv. 31 . . 68 n.
v. 28 . . 148.
vi. 1 9 n., 15 n., 51.
vi. 2 . 9 n., 40 f., 53 n., 54 n.
vi. 2-4 . . . 28.
vi. 3 . . 154.

vi. 8 . . . 27.
vi. 26 . . 53 n.
vi. 29 . . 9 n., 58.
vii. 4 . . 67 n.
vii. 5 . 144, 162.
vii. 5 f. . 151, 154.
vii. 6 144 n., 155 ff., 162.
vii. 7 70 n., 119, 172.
vii. 8 110, 125, 171.
vii. 11 . . 92 n.
vii. 11 f. . 122 n.
vii. 12 . 124 n., 144, 171.
vii. 14 . . 63 n.
vii. 18 . . . 51.
vii. 21 . . 63 n.
vii. 21 f. . 92 n.
vii. 22 . . . 83.
vii. 24 . . 110.
vii. 25 . . 171.
vii. 25 ff. . 92 n.
vii. 26 f. . . 83.
viii. 3 . . 160.
viii. 4 . . 153.
viii. 8 . 95, 125 n. 154, 160.
viii. 9 . 110 n., 125, 160, 171.
viii. 13 . . 125.
viii. 21 . . 140.
viii. 22 . . 125 n.
ix. 1 9 n., 24, 25 n., 51 f., 177.
ix. 26 . . . 14.
ix. 27 . . 125.
xi. 1 . 13, 25 n., 29 n., 177.
xi. 2 . 59 n., 155 ff.
xi. 2 f. . . 130 n.
xi. 4 154, 128 n., 129.
xi. 5-9 . . 102 n.
xi. 6 . . . 95.
xi. 10 . . 103.
xi. 11, 13 . 102 n.
xi. 14 . 102 n., 103.
xi. 15 . . 102 n.
xi. 17 . . . 95.
xi. 19 . . 109.
xi. 20 . 102 n., 109.
xi. 21 . 128, 130.
xi. 22 . . 102 n.
xi. 25 . 102 n., 109.
xi. 26 . . 130.
xi. 31 125, 130, 134.

xi. 36 . . 130.
xi. 36-40 . 131.
xi. 39 . . 132.
xi. 40 . 102 n., 132.
xi. 45 . . 132.
xii. 7 . . 171.
xii. 11 80 n., 125, 134.

4 Ezra (2 Esdras)

xi. . . 73 n.
xii. 10 ff. 70 n., 73 n.

Tobit

xiv. 15 . 17, 33, 39.

Bel and Dragon

1 . . . 52.

1 Macc.

i. 16-39 . 122.
i. 24 . 120 n.
i. 41 ff. . . 121 n.
i. 59 . . 121 n.
iv. 52 . . 121 n.
xi. 13 . . 114.

2 Macc.

iv. 7 . . . 52.

4 Macc.

iv. 15 . . . 52.

1 Enoch

xlvi. 2 ff. . 62 n.
xlviii. 2 . . 62 n.

2 Baruch

xxxix . . 73 n.

Sib. Or.

iii. 388-400 . 115 ff.
iii. 397 . . 70 n.
iii. 613 . . 122.
xii. 48, 56, 100 116 n.
xi. 250 ff. . 116 n.

St. Luke

xv. 8-10 . 64 n.

Heb.

xii. 28 . . . 51.

Rev.

xiii . . 73 n.